Hallmar

2·99

Hallmarks of Pentecost

Discerning the True Spiritual Gifts

by

George Canty

Foreword by Reinhard Bonnke
(Christ for all Nations)

Marshall Pickering

Marshall Morgan and Scott
Marshall Pickering
34–42 Cleveland Street, London, W1P 5FB. UK

Copyright © 1989 George Canty
First published in 1989 by Marshall Morgan and Scott
Publications Ltd
Part of the Marshall Pickering Holdings Group

British Library Cataloguing in Publication Data
Canty, George
  The hallmarks of Pentecost.
  1. Pentecost
  I. Title
  263'.97

  ISBN 0–551–01843–7

Text set in Linotron Times by Input Typesetting Ltd, London
Printed in Great Britain by
Cox & Wyman Ltd, Reading, Berks.

to
My wife Rietta
who was left alone so long while this book
was being written that she learned to play
the saxophone

Contents

Foreword

By the Rev. REINHARD BONNKE
Evangelist-Founder, Christ for All Nations

The words of Jesus are being fulfilled today, because not only is the Spirit of the Lord being outpoured but there are false signs and wonders which if possible could deceive the very elect. Where there is the real, the devil will produce the counterfeit. Because God is moving in power Satan has to copy Him.

The danger is that the devil's tricks might seem the same as the Lord's wonders. The expedients of imitators to produce signs and wonders might be copied by believers. But there is no need. God will give us the real thing, in His way, if we strictly follow His words only.

We see it in Africa and everywhere else on a tremendous scale. The devil can't compete, though he tries to rival God. But there is a vast increase in lying signs and wonders and believers need help and discernment. This book is therefore coming at the right time, as a gift from the Lord.

I read all the writings of George Canty I can, as he is on my wavelength. He is an original and independent author. No doubt he shakes common opinions, but he is hard to disagree with, and always leads readers further along the road of faith. He has life-long experience of Pentecost, and is a signs and wonders evangelist himself.

We must contend earnestly for the faith once delivered to the saints in these last days of opportunity. Moses' rod will swallow up the serpent-rods of the Egyptians.

New things are happening today. We must know what lies behind them especially when they imitate the Holy Spirit. This book is an important contribution to understanding it all, and makes many things clear which previously were not clear.

I highly recommend this book.

Introduction

What We Are Getting At In This Book
'The Good Old Days' . . . ?

The Neath Valley under water. Ships driven ashore at Swansea with ninety-mile-an-hour winds. Cold rain drilling the murky night like sharpened lances. A catastrophe fund opened.

Outside the Swansea Central Hall the crowds queued, poor, ill-clad, wetter by the minute, undeterred by discomfort, and being Welsh, singing: *'Just the same, just the same, God is just the same today'*. George Jeffreys was conducting one of his early historic crusades, having arrived little known and much abused from pulpit and press. But for the first time the city was hearing about a Christianity like it used to be in Bible days, power-preaching confirmed by signs and wonders. In a couple of weeks over a thousand people came to Christ, more than in any chapel during the Welsh revival twenty-four years before.

The excitement was not an isolated instance. Other evangelists, in fact including other members of the Jeffreys family were at work. One saw the day of Pentecost repeated both afternoon and evening with 3,000 receiving salvation. A lorry took the discarded medical appliances to a hired storehouse, for it was not evangelists but God at work. It all went on until war loomed on the world horizon.

Could anybody be blamed if they measured religious events by such great days in the past? Is that the test of what is real?

In my case, as with many people, first impressions became the standard. When my family were converted, the chapel had all the joy of a first home, away from the streets where there were fights, domestic rows and where the highlight of life was a win on the horses. Everybody in the congregation here was to us an angel, known to us only by nicknames – Mr Shoe (because his wife, thwarted when her husband didn't take her to the pub anymore, waited outside the church to hit him with a shoe); Mrs Dripping (too poor to buy butter); and Happy Jack, who even greeted the cat with 'Good Morning' since he was converted.

A seraph in black, unknown by face because her hat was so big, magicked heavenly strains from the harmonium right through an hour of the most relaxed worship I've ever known, as spontaneous as the winds. People seemed lost in God; there were tears of joy. That included me, a mere boy, as I listened awed to young men whose eloquence in prayer seemed inspired. I've honestly heard nothing better to this day – the acme had been reached for me.

If the past were the hallmark – any past, I would not need to write this book. Everybody remembers 'the real thing' in days gone by, just as I always think of going to school when it wasn't raining. But I know the question is unanswered – where is perfection found – the real thing, Pentecost with hallmarks?

What in fact ARE the hallmarks of Pentecost? Qualities? Results? Or What? And who's to say? Will freedom, joy, exuberance, holiness, love, establish what is genuine? Or evangelism, or worship, or wonders? How do we decide? And isn't it very important?

Important, yes – if only because people are always judging. One yardstick or another is applied. But nostalgia is no test, and anyway, what mighty things are taking place today!

Early Church Saints?

What about the past in the early Church itself? Everybody looks back to those pristine times when Christianity began its conquering course – halcyon days in all our minds.

Could those churches be our standard? I think we should look at them as they are mirrored in the epistles. What extraordinary exhortations the apostles had to make! I've always been amused that Wesley should write to his early preachers to keep themselves clean from lice – not easy in those days, but that's nothing to what Paul felt it necessary to write.

Imagine if any good pastor, Baptist, Anglican or Pentecostal, appealed in his church newsletter today like the apostle did to Christians in Colossae, to give up fornicating, uncleanness, passion, evil desires, and stop being idolatrous covetors, angry and wrathful, blasphemers, and not to use obscene abuse. How would suburban congregations react, even in our permissive society?

In fact we owe the existence of the New Testament epistles mainly to the fact that the original churches *were* so flawed and needed correction. How many would have been written if the church members of those days had all been first grade hall-marked Christians?

What about the Corinthians sick and dying for their wickedness at the very table of the Lord? Or the Ephesians told to stop getting drunk, or the Galatians given that infamous list of sins of the flesh, or prominent Philippians told off publicly for being at loggerheads, and everybody needing reminding about the need to avoid the grossest sins? That is what they meant by holiness and sanctification in those days. James thought fit to warn pastors about class distinction and Christian rich men about oppressing and defrauding their employed labourers.

However, my commission was to write a book to show what is real Pentecost. I agreed to do it thinking it would be fairly undemanding after a lifetime of activity in the Pentecostal scene, but I've never had to put in such countless hours of mental labour. Maybe others should have given closer thought to these matters long ago.

God's Best

Coming right to the core of the question, I saw that 'hallmarks' meant nothing less than God's genuine best. Now many think God's best is revival. Of course, God doesn't have two bests, a best for Pentecost and a best for everything else. So the first hallmark of Pentecost is revival. True Pentecost is revival and true revival is Pentecost.

That deduction seems logical enough to me, however startling. However, I could not leave it at that. I had to look thoroughly at such a suggestion. Part Three of this book is the result. Nothing is so frequently written about than revival. I needed a pretty good excuse to add to the volume. My excuse is that I write as a Pentecostal, not merely as an orthodox evangelical, so what I have said is bound to be new. The result is a total revision of the subject in five radical chapters.

Some original thought on revival was long overdue anyway. There has been fog on that road from the start. To write fulsome and repeated accounts of revivals long ago is pretty common, and also to repeat the traditional definitions. To analyse matters was however another thing – it almost took courage. But having done so I could then talk about revival as the hallmark of Pentecost – which it certainly is.

Revivalism

So I launched into my task by reading again every book in reach on the subject. Most of them simply assume this is God's best and retell the stories again, without attempting to make harmony out of the various opinions about revival. They left me confused. Revival is a marvellous thing – that's what we want, but what about all the questions it raises?

Six years earlier, I had ventured a letter to Dr J. Edwin Orr, expert and writer on revival, and founder of the Oxford Revival Fellowship. I explained the problems every book on revival presented to me. I hoped this respected authority could help clarify some of my questions, but unfortunately no reply ever reached me. Perhaps my letter, correctly addressed, never reached him, I don't know. But now I knew I must turn to the Holy Spirit for instruction. I trust it looks as if I did by what follows.

Revival, the *sine qua non* of spiritual possibility. First, where was it actually, this idyllic manifestation of God as He most truly is? In Brazil? Korea? Or always in the past? Pondering, writing and erasing, fleeting days worried me. Still fog hung around. Where was that central fact and essence of revival by which to judge true Pentecost? Then, a chance sentence appeared, and precipitated order. Things came together. And I began to see what the hallmarks were. I had gone a long way round, but labour had accumulated many good things on the road – serendipities, which will find their place in due course in this book.

When we see the varieties, innovations, practices and phases of the mass of life in the Charismatic-Pentecostal world today, there has to be some kind of pole star, some way to identify what is right and valid. By what criteria should we make our judgements?

Radicalism . . . Or The Word?

What would one of the first Pentecostals, Paul, spokesman on all such matters, say? There were enough varieties of religion in his day, and the whole question troubled him constantly. He himself never spoke ambiguously, but always with positive and vigorous certainty. There was no dialogue for him. Writing to one of his appointed pastors who was also faced with a hundred religious speculations, he laid down where authority alone could be found.

> All Scripture is given by inspiration of God, and is profitable for doctrine, for reproof, for correction, for INSTRUCTION IN RIGHTEOUSNESS, THAT THE MAN OF GOD MAY BE PERFECT, thoroughly furnished unto all good works. (2 Tim. 3:16–17) (my emphasis)

Whatever we think is gold or silver must be submitted for assayal to the institute of the Word of God, 'the only rule of faith and practice'; *and that includes revival itself*.

That is the Pentecostal court of appeal, and always has been. But the Charismatics are not always Bible-bound. That happens to be an important fact which accounts for some ideas and practices among them. Not all had held previously conservative views of the Bible, and maybe still do not.

It means their charismatic experience began differently. Unlike the 'classic' Pentecostals, they did not seek tongues inspired by what they read about the gift in Scripture. They knew it was there, but critical scholarship had dealt with that. Their interest arose because they heard of other people's experience, perhaps Pentecostals, and began the search for the same 'renewal'. I ministered to a convent full of eager seekers for the gifts of the Spirit and not one brought a Bible.

One told his story and had to face the question, whether

Charismatics should revise their scholastic interpretations and become fundamentalists.

One British Charismatic has written books 'to make people think', aiming to be provocative, with obviously no high opinion about those who went before him. Sitting down for a whole day with his book and a notepad, I noted many passages where it seemed to me the Scriptures had not been called in, but should have been. Whether he accepts the evangelical view of Scripture as the infallible Word of God or not I could not tell.

It seems to me that such writings as his contain an awful lot of words, but not much 'Word'. Some of my colleagues will accuse me of speaking far too mildly about books that quote Scripture no more than Shakespeare, as if evangelicals were so different. But that might be the raven calling the crow black, for I have found the same thing occasionally in the most fundamentalist circles. For example, Albert Barnes' Calvinistic work *The Atonement*, has 358 pages with scarcely a Bible quotation anywhere except in one chapter, and I cannot imagine a less profitable volume.

Perhaps some are different. Not all are written either simply to shock people and 'make them think'. It might be a 'courageous' book – even nonsense takes courage sometimes. But making people think is not necessarily the greatest aim in religion. In fact the usefulness of thinking could be a matter of thought itself. The Christian church is not a philosophic society. Thought has proved to be a misguided guide in the past in the things of the spirit. Some better authority is wanted for Christian stability than mental considerations. That way we would have as many opinions as people.

There is no other direction we can look for truth and rightness about these things, except the Word itself.

There is another aspect also. The Bible must come first. To think up our own beliefs and practices first and then look in the Bible afterwards to see if it happens to support us, is a sure way to go wrong. 'Can I quote it? Let me see what it might say.' I tripped up that way when I first went forth to dazzle the world from my pulpit. Each week I got together a wonderful speech out of my head and out of the library, and then looked for a text to fit it. *No amount of charisma, no display of gifts, will make up for a WORD-less ministry.*

But, of course, the Bible is recognised, for that is where the idea of miracles originates. Can't we just go ahead once we've got the general thought about God working wonders without too many niceties from the Bible? Well, we shall see. But I wouldn't like to set up my own hallmarking establishment, so the succeeding chapters will be as I have outlined here, a referral of all things to the Word of God. We will start with that, the Word, and then many other things.

In the course of this book I shall refer to many deviations, great and small. In 1906, in the original Pentecostal meetings at Azusa Street in Los Angeles, a prophecy was made and recorded. Having now completed labours on this book of mine, it does seem to me that what the Spirit said to churches over eighty years ago has an alarming percipience for our times and a powerful relevance for what I have written. It runs as follows:

IN THE LAST DAYS JUST BEFORE THE RETURN OF JESUS CHRIST:
1   IN PENTECOSTAL CIRCLES, THERE WILL BE AN OVER-EMPHASIS ON *POWER* RATHER THAN RIGHTEOUSNESS.
2   THERE WILL BE AN EMPHASIS ON *PRAISE* TO A GOD THEY NO LONGER PRAY TO
3   THERE WOULD BE AN EMPHASIS ON *GIFTS* RATHER THAN THE LORDSHIP OF JESUS CHRIST.

1 Confident Religion

How To Doubt Doubts

Doubt, they say, bridges no rivers, tunnels no mountains. It is successful in not doing a number of things. One of its achievements, for example, was that I never became a world-famous water skier.

I attained to that complete inability like this. My brother helped to found a water-ski club. He took me along to the chilly lake with flattering enthusiasm about my potential. 'You're just the right build and balance'. I watched first. Hapless volunteers were swooshed across the cold and menacing waters at the mercy of the towing-craft driver, twisting and turning at his sovereign whim. In sympathy I identified with them, anticipating this luxury trip, especially re-arrival back on shore, a process as vague and apprehensive to me as amusing to observers.

The fact of my physical suitability loomed before me as a tragic misfortune of birth. I made my great resolve. I would sacrifice the thrill of skiing and just enjoy the pleasure of giving somebody else the privilege. I wouldn't be selfish. Or . . . was it my doubts?

A lady onlooker spoke to me. She also was indulging in the virtuous sense of yielding opportunity to others. At any rate both of us can contemplate the striking absence of our names from the sports pages today, thinking how we gave preference to other people. It is amazing what doubt can do.

The lady had other doubts, however. Discovering I was a man of the cloth, she aired her piety. She 'absolutely adored' the Anglican Church. In her village they had a gem of a church, the sermons were short and Evensong was really beautifully rendered. In fact she had even been once or twice. I was suitably impressed, but modestly she added 'Not fanatically often, mind you'. She particularly remembered one bad patch. A visiting preacher had been a proper Bible thumper, bawling and yelling 'Jesus is alive! Jesus is alive!' There was no need to get so excited just about that. Nor so positive.

'What we need is dialogue, isn't it? Something open-ended you know. A talking point.' Christians should not be dogmatic, as 'they didn't have a monopoly of the truth. Christians are seekers for truth – aren't they?'

Actually no, Christians are not seekers for truth; they are 'of the truth' as John put it. They have found Christ, and Christ said, '*I am the Way, the Truth, and the Life*' (John 14:6). To look for the Truth after finding Christ the Truth would hardly be brilliantly consistent. Looking *into* Truth can only begin when you have discovered it.

David Frost interviewed Billy Graham on British television and asked him, 'What do you do with your doubts?' Billy didn't understand. 'Doubts? What doubts?'. David's face registered the reactions of being asked, 'The moon? What moon?' Off-guard, he stammered, 'Well, we – we all have our doubts, don't we?'. Billy smiled, 'No, we don't all have doubts. When you are born-again and know Christ, there's nothing left to doubt. There are many things you don't know, but you're certain of Christ and that's all that matters'.

Several years ago, four leaders of free church denominations talked on BBC national radio about preaching. They agreed that the sermon was an opportunity 'to share one's doubts with the people'. Congregations uncertain could be offered this comfort that their leaders were also uncertain. O glad message! Nobody need have a bad conscience if they didn't know where they were going, as their shepherds didn't know either.

That prize champion of the ridiculous, Spike Milligan, gave us a marvellous parable. The stage, in featureless white. He appeared on it, looked round and said, 'Help, I'm lost'. A second man came to show him the way, but also professed to be lost, then another and another until a number of would-be rescuers bunched together shouting, 'Help, somebody show us the way!'.

By modern preaching standards if nobody knows the way it doesn't matter. Everybody will be fine as they are all lost together. Then they can laugh at people all on their own who stride along with assurance of the road.

Christ's parable (Matthew 15:14) reads 'If the blind lead the blind, both shall fall into the ditch'. A letter recently came from one of Britain's distinguished ecclesiastics. Having been challenged about a joint service with Buddhists, Hindus and others, he replied that he accepted the uniqueness of the Christian faith but that dialogue with other religions could only benefit our own faith. A Pentecostal editor described 'dialogue' as 'a code word for surrender of the truth'. Every faith is unique anyway, and to consult what others believe means we are not so sure about what we believe ourselves. Pentecostals don't dialogue with unbelief.

Somebody said, 'Well, we don't know we are right, do we?' That is absurd. If you think and say you might be wrong you have no convictions. We haven't found Christ the Truth. We are joining Spike Milligan's lost crowd in the middle of the stage, befogged and bewildered.

If you are right, then the others are wrong. It is a schizophrenic attitude to talk about everybody being right. Somebody is bound to be wrong. The popular fallacy is that as 'all roads up the mountain lead to the top, so all roads lead to God'. This isn't possible. For one thing all roads up a mountain don't lead to the top. They drop over many a precipice. But in any case how can a road lead to God when it is not even made to get there? How can Buddhism or Karma lead to God when it doesn't have a God to discover?

The GCSE examinations for school children in 1988 included the following: 'Discuss the truth of the statement that "It is better to travel hopefully than to arrive" '. The 'truth' of this statement? Have we really put the rising generation into the hands of educationalists who consider it a 'truth' that travelling hopefully is better than getting somewhere?

Maybe that is the modern lunacy. Our scientific and technological age based on super-accuracy is careless about the basic meanings of life. 'Fog, fog, fog', as Dickens described things outside and inside the Court of Chancery. It describes things

in many a pulpit and theological seminary today, and outside
in the street also.

'Travelling hopefully', but hopeful of what? Not knowing
whether the road leads anywhere, for instance? The end may
be pretty awful, so enjoy the travel! It sounds too risky to
travel at all. We seek the Truth, but don't know what it is and
may not recognise if we stumble on it. Jesus said, 'Seek and
ye shall find', but that is what we are afraid of, in case the
truth turns out to be God.

Inconfidence

Some years ago the *British Weekly* published a photograph
stretching across the entire page. A long, wide beach was
packed with people crowding right to the water's edge at a
Pentecostal baptismal service for tens of thousands of Third
World nationals. This illustrated an article entitled 'Do people
like confident religion?'.

I fancy they do like confident religion. I fancy also that they
like confident surgery, confident aeroplane flying, and confident
medicine. When it comes to religion it is hardly surprising that
they look for assurance. It is a matter of eternal destiny. I
wouldn't care to launch my soul on its everlasting course
through a trackless heaven on a raft cobbled together out of
surmises and guesswork. That is what is being offered us in
many a new theology.

There is simply no correspondence between uncertainty and
the Bible. Churchmen parley with Buddhists, Moslems,
Hindus, and Sikhs, saying, 'They have much to teach us'. One
thing they do teach is what Christian churchmen are not learning, namely dogmatic belief. Some people will believe anything
providing it is not in the Bible. What passes for religious faith
today is often no more than 'secular philosophy dressed up in
vestments' as an Anglican bishop said of some of his fellow
churchmen's piety.

But We Know

The early church filled the world with a ringing Gospel note of glorious, unequivocal, unqualified confidence. True apostolic succession is to say with Peter:

Blessed be the God and Father of our Lord Jesus Christ, which according to his abundant mercy hath begotten us again unto a lively (living) hope by the resurrection of Jesus Christ from the dead, to an inheritance incorruptible, and undefiled, and that fadeth not away, reserved in heaven for you, who are kept by the power of God through faith unto salvation ready to be revealed in the last time, wherein ye greatly rejoice. (1 Pet. 1:3)

Even before the Light of Christ shone, the Old Testament was found to be 'A light to my path'. It is a book of assurance. Its most characteristic phrase is 'thus saith the Lord'. The word 'truth' occurs about fifty times in the Psalms and Proverbs. God is *'the God of truth'*, that is He gives us the truth, just as being the God of salvation He gives us salvation.

The New Testament bursts upon us with a far more brilliant blaze. Jesus offered no ambiguities or suggestions. He never said, 'I think', or 'Perhaps', or 'We may presume'. His most common expression was 'Verily, verily'. (literally truly, truly!) He described His words as the rock for the foundation of our lives.

What His style was we may judge from the reactions He created. *'The people were astonished at his doctrine: for he taught them as one having authority, and not as the scribes'*. The scribes relied upon other Biblical interpreters. Their authority was other people's authority. Today's erudition similarly consists of heaping together the subjective interpretations of previous academics. Authority is a row of books all leaning on one another.

The disciples had exactly the same certitude, so that when the Jewish leaders saw their boldness, *'and perceived that they were unlearned and ignorant men'* (i.e. had not been to the Rabbinical schools), *'they took note that they had been with*

Jesus.' Travelling hopefully without ever reaching finality, does not carry the faintest echo of the Christian Gospel of 'a living hope'.

Butcher Birds

The false teachers would not be outside but inside the church Jesus indicated, like the birds lodging in the mustard tree branches (Matthew 13:31–32). As Paul said to Timothy (1 Tim. 6:5), they *'consent not to wholesome words, even the words of our Lord Jesus Christ, and to the doctrine which is according to godliness, perverse disputings'*.

In the nature of the case, we need to go beyond human philosophy to attain to certainty. Human thinking is always pro tem but in the urgent death-or-life issues of sin, righteousness and judgement we cannot afford to wait. We must KNOW, now. Wouldn't God want us to know?

The world dies gasping for the Gospel while the learned always find something more to discuss'. Ever learning and never able to come to a knowledge of the truth. Israel hath not obtained that which he seeketh for; but the elect hath obtained it, and the rest were blinded'(2 Tim. 3:7; Rom. 11:7). Jesus said *'Seek and ye shall find . . . and he that seeketh findeth'* (Matt. 7:8). One can open the Bible almost at random and its trumpet never quavers with an uncertain note.

Take for instance Proverbs, 4:18: *'The path of the just is as the shining light, that shineth more and more unto the perfect day. The way of the wicked is as darkness: they know not at what they stumble'*. The picture is a man on the shore at dawn, with the streak of light glittering across the tops of the rippling water right to his feet as he walks. The path always ends where he is. If he followed it across the water over the horizon it would bring him to the full light of day. The man of faith always has the path at his feet as he takes the Word of God. *'Thy Word is a lamp unto my feet, and a light unto my path. THY LAW IS THE TRUTH'* (Ps. 119:105, 142).

God takes no pleasure in our gropings after truth. Christ emphasised over and over that the truth was with us. He could not understand gropers. *'Ye shall know the truth and the truth*

shall set you free' (John 8:32). The word 'truth' is used positively
in John's Gospel twenty times, by Christ, and only once cyn-
ically, and that by Pontius Pilate.

The age in which we live ought to look again at Psalm 1.6:
*'The Lord knoweth the way of the righteous: but the way of the
ungodly shall perish'*. *It is the road itself, not the traveller of
which he speaks*. *'THE WAY of the ungodly shall perish'*, not
the ungodly themselves (though the ungodly do perish as we
know from other references).

The feature of the way of the ungodly is that it gets worse
and worse, a maze of crossroads, a thousand diversions without
a signpost. It 'peters out' as Dr G. Campbell Morgan translates
it. That is a perfect photograph of modern philosophy and
speculative theology, our only substitutes for the Word of God.

Something similar may be read in Matthew 7:13: *'Wide is the
gate, and broad is the way, that leadeth to destruction. Straight
is the gate and narrow is the way which leadeth to life'*. Liberalism is broad, accommodating every kind of traveller, but it
leads to a state where destruction is at work, getting so narrow
that it vanishes as a road and leaves everybody wandering. On
the other hand, the narrow way broadens to carry travellers
into the fullness of day. Proverbs 14:12 says:*'There is a way
that seemeth right to a man, but the end thereof are the ways of
death'*.

It is the hallmark of a man of the Spirit that he has received
the Spirit of truth, as Christ promised. *'When he, the Spirit of
truth is come he shall guide you into all truth'* (John 16:13). The
first epistle of John underlines this as a feature of all who are
born-again. *'We know that we are of the truth. Ye have an
unction from the Holy One and ye know all things'* (1 Jn. 3:19,
2:20). This does not make anybody a learned theologian.

Theology is not the aim. Truth is greater than any definition.
The vitality of truth is not words, but a Person. It is Christ the
Lord. *We don't know everything but we know the truth about
everything – Jesus*. So John said, *'Ye know all things'*, So he
uses the word 'know' thirty-six times in that short letter.

The man who begins to protest that unlearned people cannot
claim to have found and to know the truth, is saying a dangerous thing. He is saying only a few mortals were designed to

know the truth. He is also saying that God cannot be bothered to show us the truth – we must always be kept guessing. The brain is the wrong instrument. Truth is not a laboratory subject, any more than love. God makes us all capable of knowing the truth, just as all can know love, joy, beauty and goodness.

Behind everything is a God of truth, who wants His children to walk in the truth. Instinct carries us back to God, where we came from, like the salmon crossing oceans to the rivers where they began.

In Understanding Be Men

Knowing the truth is not a matter of education. Peter was unlearned but Jesus said he had been taught by the Father. He declared who Jesus was. He had found the truth, and Jesus said, *'I thank thee Father that thou hast hid these things from the wise and prudent and hast revealed them unto babes'*. One of those babes was Peter.

John never uses the word 'knowledge' but frequently uses 'knowing'. In John 'knowing' is not carrying facts around in one's head, but personally trusting Jesus. People who lived in His street will say they knew Him, but it was not 'knowing' as John meant it Jesus declared He would say to them, 'I never knew you'.

The only proper knowing is trust. John never mentions the word faith, but uses the verb 'believe'. You know the truth when you are believing actively in Jesus.

Where there is doubt there can be no knowledge of the truth. The mathematician and philosopher René Descartes (1596–1650) influenced intellectual thought in an entirely opposite direction to the revelation of the Word of God. The Cartesian argument was that the beginning of all knowledge is reason working from doubt to knowledge demonstrated with mathematical accuracy.

He missed the point. Nobody knows anybody by logic, but only by trust. Faith is faith in a person, not information of concrete facts. The astronomer Kepler attempted to work out logically what made the best marriage. The wife he chose as a

result was somewhat of a martyr to him and to his theory –
and so was he.

Truth is God – personal. No man will make much of the
Bible unless the Spirit of God is in him. As Paul said:

> The natural man receiveth not the things of the Spirit of God
> for they are foolishness unto him: neither can he know them,
> because they are spiritually discerned. But God hath revealed
> them unto us by His Spirit: for the Spirit searcheth all, things,
> yea, the deep things of God. For who hath known the mind
> of the Lord, that he may instruct him? But we have the mind
> of Christ.

The God of the Pentecostals we identify as the very God the
Bible describes. 'We see Jesus', and we 'know in whom we
have believed'. He is the God of Pentecost, the God of Scripture. The likeness is unmistakeable.

A fine Anglican preacher spoke from a Methodist pulpit and
one hearty old Yorkshire worthy met him at the end with the
remark, 'Why, you're nothing but just a good old Methodie,
one of us'.

Listening again to Paul and Peter in the Word, with their
positive ringing witness, I feel the same affinity, and would
like to say to them 'Why, you're nothing but just good old
Pentecostals, one of us'.

Confident religion, the hallmark of Pentecost – and of
Christianity.

2 Gifts or Giver?

Near our home a double-fronted shop with windows painted bottle green bore a large poster which to us children rendered the place spooky. It announced 'MEETINGS FOR THE DEEPENING OF SPIRITUAL LIFE'.

Outstanding ignorance about all religion led us to suppose that here was an emporium of spirits, Spiritualism, and seances. If we had known, it denoted the accession of the Pentecostals into our city. Unrealised by most passers-by, and most did pass by, that poster was almost an historic document. It summed up the basic aim of the Pentecostal movement, namely, a deeper religious life. Already, however, it was dubbed 'the tongues movement' by those who knew it only by popular report, vastly mistaking its character.

The last decades before 1900 had been marked in many countries by greatly awakened Christian interest in the book of Acts and true New Testament Divine fullness. Believers saw there a further reality beyond salvation received by faith, and they hungered for it. It was not merely gifts or power they wanted, but a new richness of Divine blessing, richness of a quality that would manifest itself in the miraculous conditions of Acts.

Jesus Only

When people began to speak with tongues, that was not their primary interest. Their position was that of Paul, *'That I might know Him . . .'* That desire created another desire, holiness, to be 'a vessel fit for the Master's service'. There were searchings of heart, the shunning of everything tainted by 'the world and the flesh'. Puritanical rules about dress, hair, cosmetics and relationships were simply to be sure that there was *'Nothing between lord, nothing between'*, as they sang in E. H. Hopkin's hymn.

It might be true that this 'separationism' did become an

end in itself unfortunately, a new form of legalism or spiritual eugenics. But otherwise the intention was a genuine longing for righteousness and the enjoyment of God's presence. When the twentieth century dawned these strong urges were felt powerfully everywhere within the evangelical churches.

When the first believers were baptised in the Spirit, in Britain from 1906 onwards, it fulfilled a heart cry for God. That was the notable feature of the experience. I remember hymn-writer E. C. W. Boulton. He had been baptised in the Spirit around 1914 or 1915, a mere seven or eight years after the fire first fell at Sunderland. 'Pa', as we affectionately called him, told me about that notable lady Mrs Crisp, the first Principal of the Women's Bible School in Hackney from 1910. She complained that the baptisms in the Spirit then (about 1915) were not the same as at the beginning. There was a release and new reality in the lives of the earliest Pentecostals which those coming into the blessing a few years later did not seem to enjoy to the same degree.

I can believe that. The explanation is that for many years before they heard of the Pentecostal outpouring of the Spirit, those first Pentecostals had caught the vision of what the New Testament clearly indicated – 'rivers of living water', the fullness of God. Their quest turned into endeavour for the highest reaches of spirituality. They wanted to be high-calibre people of God. There were 'giants in those days', such as Mrs Crisp herself. When after so much searching they found what they wanted, their satisfaction was deep indeed.

Today, a couple of generations later, I wonder what Mrs Crisp would say? Pentecostal rivers have overflowed across the denominations and brought an incredible variety of views and teachings. Varying creeds or creeds forgotten have brought affirmations of neo-Pentecostalism. While this has been a marvellously helpful development, maybe there are elements within it which Mrs Crisp and other Pentecostals would feel sometimes lacked the glory of the original experience. While claiming to be an advance, knowledge may show it to be a step backwards.

Charismata Or Pneuma?

The first Charismatic I met did not give me an initially favourable impression of this second wave 'forward move' I had been delighted to hear about. He was an Anglican vicar introduced to me in a college room. He said he wanted to be filled with the Holy Spirit. Cautiously I delved into things, and eventually explained about the initial evidence of speaking with tongues. His response left me bewildered. 'Oh, I've spoken with tongues, but now I want the Spirit'. But . . . tongues, without the essential, the baptism in the Spirit. How?

However, one thing pleased me, he still felt his need of the Spirit, and was not prepared to be content because somehow he had been induced to speak with tongues. In recent years speaking with tongues seems to have come to many people so easily, casually, almost prematurely. I dare not make general judgements but we might ask whether baptisms in the Spirit are so frequently preceded by a deep longing for God's fullness as was certainly once the case?

When Jesus spoke of the Spirit he associated it with importunate asking, seeking, knocking (Luke 11.9–11). 'Waiting meetings' became a popular object of attack some years ago; another supposed fault of the 'classic' Pentecostals. The term 'receiving meetings' was insisted upon. The objection never rang quite clear in my mind. What is wrong with 'waiting meetings'? Surely it is a healthy and Scriptural state to wait upon God? Jesus clearly indicated it might be necessary to importune God for the Holy Spirit, asking, seeking and knocking persistently. He also said, *'Blessed are they which do hunger and thirst after righteousness: for they shall be filled'* (Matt 5:6).

We need the Holy Spirit urgently, that is true. But that need has to be recognised and become clamorous. *People who are to bring others to God should themselves begin with a craving for God*, if only for the power to witness. The objective should not consist of inducing people to speak with tongues, making charismatics, but of bringing people to the Cross. They speak of 'getting people through to the baptism'. It sounds to me like pot-holing, and is sometimes accompanied by as much labour and heavy breathing on the part of the person 'getting them through' as that curious subterranean activity of caving involves. Can we baptise people in the Spirit, or isn't it Christ's prerogative?

That world-famous little Irish nun, Briege McKenna, was remarkably healed of acute arthritis on 10th December 1970 without asking, just while seeking God. Constantly she had it brought to her that she was called to heal the sick, but she rejected it for a long time as all she wanted was to know God and love Jesus. She said she 'prayed' 'Jesus, I'm going to find you whatever it takes'. My soul was thirsting for the living God'. Even when she was in acute pain she said, 'Physical healing was not on my list'. When her instant healing took place her only thought was, 'My Lord and my God! You're right here!'

I think they have written her book as a piece of propaganda for the whole Roman Catholic scenario, and I cannot go along with very much in her book *Miracles Do Happen*. But her attitude of desire for God before gifts is an example perhaps greatly needed.

One still hears of those who 'teach' speaking with tongues, and of those who are 'picking it up'! There are techniques such as 'Say the word in your mind'. But it is a very doubtful process. The cerebral generation of speech is not the actual mechanics by which the Spirit operates. Others give subjects phrases 'to start them off', or to keep on repeating the same praise words (which leads to babbling). Excessive personal attention, shouting in tongues into people's ears, handling and shaking people physically, or prolonged and exhausting concentration, perhaps accompanied by commands to 'breathe in the Spirit' with much hissing and blowing rendering people light-headed, these and ever-new methods have led to disenchantment.

God has the real thing to give and emotional incoherence is anything but real. It is unbelief. In large meetings when there is 'singing in the Spirit' and many sing in tongues, sometimes a leader will encourage all to do the same. Carried along unselfconsciously people will mouth a few unEnglish syllables on the dominant or key note along with all the rest. The sounds are in fact meaningless, not the *glossalalia*. But some mistakenly suppose they are then 'charismatic'. In fact their heart experience is no deeper than their original desire. They had only passing interest or even only shallow curiosity. It is not the baptism in the Spirit. And that should not be forfeited for or confused with speaking gibberish. Pentecostal leaders should make that plain.

What The Anointing Is

1   *In the Old Testament there were two kinds of anointing – the symbolic and the real.* The real anointing was the presence of God Himself. Everything connected with the priestly Jewish order was oil-anointed with a special sacred preparation (Exodus 30). Nothing was anointed a second time, as it was assumed that once anointed it had became sacred for ever 'unto the Lord.' Priests and kings were also permanently anointed similarly with a sacred composition of anointing oil (Ex. 28, 2 Sam. 2:4), but never a prophet as prophets were moved by the reality of anointing. Elijah was told to anoint Elisha (1 Kings 19:16) but he never did so, and God Himself gave him a double portion of Elijah's spirit (2 Kings 2:9–10).

2   *The great antetype appears, with the real anointing.* The Scripture, Isaiah 61, was fulfilled in Christ who quoted it of Himself: *'The Spirit of the Lord is upon me because He has anointed me . . .'* Peter confirmed that *'God anointed Jesus of Nazareth with the Holy Ghost and power'*. To know what that means, the first thing is that He didn't speak with tongues, but manifested the anointing by *'going about doing good and healing all who were oppressed by the devil FOR GOD WAS WITH HIM'*.

Luke 4 describes what His anointing meant. Verse 1 describes Christ as *'FULL of the Holy Ghost and was LED by the Spirit'*. Verse 14: *'Jesus returned IN THE POWER OF SPIRIT'*. Verse 18: Jesus said *'The spirit of the Lord is UPON me'*. Verse 36: *'With authority and power he commandeth the unclean spirits and they came out'*. Luke 5 verse 17: *'the power of the Lord was present to heal them'*. His ministry was beyond gifts. He was full of power wherever He went, and insisted that the Father was with Him doing the works. *The anointing upon*

Jesus meant total union and the presence of the Spirit, not merely endowments, which is why He did not speak with tongues.

3 In Acts we find the same thing said of believers. *The entire emphasis throughout is that they were God-filled.* 'Peter, filled with the Holy Ghost, said . . . (4.8). 'They were all filled with the Holy Ghost' (4:31). 'the Holy Ghost whom God hath given to them that obey him' (5:32). 'Seven men, full of the Holy Ghost' (6:3). 'Stephen, a man full of faith and of the Holy Ghost . . . and power' (6:5.8). 'They laid hands on them and they received the Holy Ghost' (8:18), and so on.

4 *The New Testament epistles express the same idea.* Paul speaks about a deep involvement with the Spirit. In his peak chapter, Romans 8, 'the Spirit' is named fourteen times in the first seventeen verses. He speaks of: *'living according to the Spirit', 'their minds set on what the Spirit desires', 'controlled by the Spirit', 'quickening by the Spirit', 'led by the Spirit', 'the Spirit testifies with our spirit that we are God's children'*, and so on. Here is something more than a *'charisma'* experience, that is of being gifted; it is a *'pneuma'* experience, being in the Spirit. A true Pentecostal is not merely charismatic but 'pneumatised', to use my own word.

The Ultimate Resource

THE HOLY SPIRIT IS THE GREAT GIFT OF GOD AND THERE IS NOTHING GREATER AND NO GREATER POWER. When the Pentecostals first presented their message to the church they had already reached the ultimate resource, the power of the Spirit. It was not a halfway stage, or first wave. It was all there was or ever could be no matter how people judged and spoke of new 'waves'. There is only one Holy Spirit, and He is the fullness that fills all things. No doubt knowledge and experience would increase, and so would light, but that is normal in Christian life.

In an earlier book I testified to the inexplicable goodness of God to myself. After I was baptised in the Spirit and 'learned the hard way' by drifting into theological studies and to the application of logic to spiritual problems, and much praying for power, God led me afresh to His Word and a revolutionised ministry. I also showed in that personal account that I received nothing new at that time but simply as Paul said found my *'eyes enlightened that I may see what is the exceeding greatness of his power toward us that believe'* (Eph. 1:18,19). *There was no new anointing, but a realisation of the old ever-new one.*

From that burst of Divine illumination upon my mind and spirit I broke into the entire field of the gifts of the Spirit, at a time in the early 1950s when I knew of almost no other Pentecostal operating in this country similarly and regularly. (If there was I shall be pleased to hear of them.) There is nothing in the new charismatic 'wave' different from what God has been pleased to give before and which was not familiar to us before any 'second or third wave'. What has happened is that the river has become wider, world-wide and deeper, with more use of the gifts, as was always anticipated.

Though at the time it brought me criticism, it was not long before things changed to approval, and that happened before the charismatics of the 1960s appeared. Our 'classic' Pentecost was the filling of the Spirit, which came upon us *as we sought God, not merely charismata*. No further endowments, enduments, anointings, fillings, new waves, new things, new Penecots, new baptisms were ever needed. God called me (for example) of all people, to evangelism, and there has never been any lack of signs and power-ministry, and what God was pleased to do is not exceeded by any 'new thing' I have seen to this moment. WHAT GOD HAD GIVEN WAS ALREADY HIS BEST AND EVERLASTING, THE HOLY SPIRIT, AND THE MOST POTENT, MOST PERMANENT, ETERNAL POWER IN THE UNIVERSE.

Perhaps I should mention that there has been (perhaps still is) a trendy emphasis upon the Kingdom, and 'kingdom power', as if some previously secret Divine oil-field had been located. So far as 'Kingdom' teaching is concerned we shall look at it briefly later. The suggestion that there was an extra something which had been neglected in 'kingdom power' is nonsense.

If the term helps anybody, I for one don't object, but I must insist that there is no special endowment floating around us in the Kingdom because we have suddenly discovered we are in a Kingdom. (Didn't we always know?) The 'promise of the Father' is complete.

Gifts Without The Baptism?

There is a new suggestion, that to wait for the baptism in the Spirit and speaking with tongues is no longer needed. One can have a power-signs ministry without the Pentecostal baptism. The Pentecostals are thrust aside as being outmoded. The signs-following baptism (tongues) was only an early stage and God is doing a new thing, they say.

There is rather disturbing confusion here. First, *if we seek the other gifts of the Spirit without the baptism in the Spirit and tongues, that is no new concept.* We always knew that was possible. That's mere history. It was exactly the position before the Pentecostals came on the scene. To go directly for gifts without seeking the baptism simply turns the clock back a hundred years. It is retrograde, not an advance in the progressive revelation of the Spirit. In fact it makes the entire Pentecostal movement of the past eighty years a mere parenthesis, almost a side track, and perhaps reverses it.

The new teaching brings us again to a confused period when believers healed the sick, cast out devils, and even knew speaking with tongues, but did not understand the baptism with the Spirit.

Progress in true Pentecostal revival world-wide only broke out when the Baptism with the Spirit attested by tongues became the standard basis of thousands of new churches. We shall lose the secret of the global revival if we adopt again the unclear theology of the 1890s, and bypass what happened in 1901.

Certainly it is not new that gifts may be exercised without the baptism in the Spirit. It happened throughout the Old Testament. Pentecostals never taught otherwise. A non-Pentecostal, R. A. Torrey, was probably the first to lay it down that one needed the baptism in the Spirit to enjoy use of the gifts. But as many had operated the gifts of the Spirit (Smith Wigglesworth is one, out of many examples), and then entered into the experience of the baptism later, they could hardly teach that the baptism was needed before they could heal the sick.

These early people knew that the baptism was an unique anointing which transformed even the most God-blessed healers and exorcisers. The baptism in the Spirit is a mighty thing FOR ALL, even for the most silent person in the pew. It can never be substituted for by charismatic endowments or abilities. Of what use would the gift of discernment or of miracles be to the average church member, however far the 'body-ministry' is allowed? *It is not gifts most of us need so much as the fullness of God in the Spirit.*

It seems to me impractical to encourage congregations of 5,000 people to exercise all the gifts. How and where will they do it? Further, such teaching misunderstands a great deal, particularly 1 Corinthians 12–14. I have already found people with a sense of frustration because they believe, or have been told, they have this or that gift, but complain their circumstances give them no room to operate. They blame their church, or their circumstances, rather than their misunderstanding of the entire subject of the gifts. Ambitious to do great things they become a worry to their pastors who have to watch them running around to find where there are great things to be done.

A common scene today is of meetings which consist of Christians with everlasting needs and problems to be met by words of knowledge or miracle deliverances, as if this was the main object of coming together. If church-goers were once mere sermon-tasters they are now wonder-seekers. The expounding of the Word itself is often no longer an event, as it should be, but merely psychological preparation for deliverances of some sort. If they haven't a problem, then one can be found for them so they will crowd to the platform. A Yorkshire friend sat with me while the preacher put forward various needs and reasons why they should come forward to him for help. After ten minutes he remarked to me *sotto voce*, 'He'll be offering them Green Shield stamps soon.' Too often people come away only with a deeper impression of their need of help than they had before.

The 'classic' Pentecostal believes God does deliver, but the stress is not on Christian hang-ups, habits, failures, ailments, but on winning the lost, bringing men to Christ. If it is only Christians' needs to be met, why, the gifts of the Spirit will do, perhaps. But if it is a case of obedience to the Lord's commands to disciple all nations, that is another thing, and that is where the baptism in the Spirit is essential.

A Charismatic editor recently invited chosen writers to discuss the question: 'Why has the Charismatic movement made so little impact?' Maybe the question is premature, as the effects of the Charismatic development are still being processed through the training colleges in Britain. But otherwise, it was fairly unanimous that the acceptance of the charismata had not been accompanied by evangelism.

Indeed sometimes a mere 'charismatic' stance had worked in reverse, discouraging evangelism, refusing to support evangelists, concentrating on 'the work of the Spirit' doing something 'in our church', relying upon good meetings and the drift from the churches into house groups and Charismatic centres. Even community-style living had been set up which is a direct handicap upon witness, since it may isolate Christians from the world and may take them out from among the ungodly where their light should shine and place it 'under a bushel'.

Witnesses Of What They Never Saw

When Peter addressed the multitude on the day of Pentecost he said, *'This Jesus hath God raised up, whereof we all are witnesses'* (Acts 2:32). In fact they did not see Him raised up. Nobody did. And when they subsequently saw Him alive they were doubtful, and scared anybody should attack them. How then were they witnesses?

The resurrection of Christ alone, and His appearances to them left them worried and confused. But when Christ sent upon them the Holy Spirit, all doubts turned to irrepressible certainty. There was no doubt now as to who Jesus was and what He had done. He had conquered death.

They became witnesses not merely to SAY they had seen Jesus alive, for in fact Peter did not mention it, but because 'he hath shed forth this, which YE NOW SEE and hear'. They were not mere witnesses, but concrete evidence in themselves of all they said. And it was not merely tongues or prophecy, but something beyond that – these men were full of God.

Peter announced Christ, the Messiah, the Anointed one. That is what Christ means. A Christian is one who accepts the Anointed One as the Anointer.

If the reality is to be made known, we must go forth to the world with more than healing powers, which the sorcerers of the devil will try to imitate, but as men conscious of the glory of God in their souls. The world will respond to men and women of God, people who know God, people of the Spirit, anointed ones, rather than to signs and wonders.

There is a mistaken presumption that the miraculous will win the day. I have seen thousands or miracles and healings in my own itineraries, but it was always the Word which proved to be the effective weapon to bring salvation, plus the sense and reality of the presence of God among us.

Whether called Pentecostal or Charismatic, there must never be any release from this discipline, to know Him, and grow in knowledge.

3   Gifts – Real and Unreal

When Rebekah met Isaac, her husband-to-be, she was adorned in rich raiment, and silver and gold sent by the father of Isaac for his son's bride. Maybe it is not too fanciful to see in that twenty-fourth chapter of Genesis a delightful suggestion of greater gifts from a greater Father for the greater Bride of a greater Son.

Clothed in His righteousness the Bride of Christ should be adorned with the Father's gifts brought by the Holy Spirit – the Servant sent to find a Bride. The Church should have this glittering attire.

God had many gifts to bestow. Among them 'silver and gold', or if it is not straining the allegory too much, the silver non-miracle and the golden miracle gifts, that is, gifts of grace (charismata) and gifts of the Spirit (pneumatika).

Some call both the supernatural gifts and the natural gifts by the same name, spiritual gifts, but this takes no account of Scriptural distinctions. All gifts are of grace (charismata), but not all are of the Spirit. If we call grace-gifts 'spiritual-gifts' there is a blurring of Biblical terms. Professor Peter Wagner limits gifts to twenty-seven or so and calls them all spiritual gifts. There are countless grace gifts, but in Scripture only nine grace-gifts are also named spiritual gifts (pneumatika).

They are so attractive that they can and certainly will be imitated. Cheap jewellery can be charming but false. *The gifts are one thing. More important is from where they come*. Are they from the Father? Or substitutes? Their value lies far more in their origin than in their decoration. Old master paintings can be forgeries, identical or even better, but not by the hand of the masters they claim to be.

Turning to the famous chapter of 1 Corinthians 12, verse 7 says *'the manifestation of the Spirit is given to every man to profit withal'*. That is the vital reality – the manifestation of the

Spirit. That is what gifts are, and what is not of the Spirit is worthless. *It is the Spirit we want far more than the gifts.*

The Scripture warns us about this, insisting it is *'by that one and the selfsame Spirit'* (v. 11) not by any other means, certainly not by any other spirit, that the true gifts operate. Let us look at them.

The Word Of Wisdom

Paul says no more than that. He does not explain it. We have only the context of all the gifts and their general purpose.

Wisdom is one of the major blessings of God constantly extolled. Here, however, is not a general gift of wisdom such as Solomon was granted. Wisdom is available to us all. (James 1:5). This Corinthian mention is a manifestation of the power of the Holy Spirit – a miracle moment of insight. If the gifts might be falsified, this one particularly may be.

1 *Its primary object is the edification of the church*, either to be received by all or by individuals needing particular help from God. It may also be wisdom God gives to a believer quite privately. *Wisdom is not information nor instruction. It is UNDERSTANDING, a grasp of what is the true situation.* It is not a Divine command or directive. Wisdom in Scripture is never simply an order. No action is laid down. That is most important to grasp.

2 *Wisdom gives enlightenment on a situation, but more likely on the principle behind it*. What action to take is then left to our responsibility and discretion. Not one of the gifts of the Holy Spirit can be used to give orders. Neither this gift, nor prophecy, nor discernment lays obligations upon anybody. It is up to us, once we have received the word of wisdom, and we see the Divine principle involved to take our own decision. God doesn't give orders to the sons and daughters of His house.

It is most likely that if we are given such a word, illuminating a situation which otherwise might be shadowed, we will do something about it, but nobody should get up and tell a congregation to do this or that.

The same rule applies to prophetic words. This is not the Old Testament day. The word of the Lord was given then only to one man for all, but under the New Covenant, the Spirit is being outpoured not upon one prophet but upon all flesh, and that function of the prophet is heard of no more. God can speak to us Himself without third parties. Even the relationship itself has changed, for we are not servants serving under strict orders and laws but we carry all the authority of sons.

3 *The Word of wisdom may certainly be imitated*. With enough ego, or arrogance, some are always wise and dominating. Nevertheless the Spirit of wisdom dwells also among God's people. If 'the word' offered does not strike a note of sympathetic agreement, it should be rejected. God does not suddenly pounce upon us with some odd or erratic idea out of the blue.

In meetings held by good men but men still novices in matters of the Holy Spirit, simply going by other men's experience and ideas, one has seen a degree of naïvety hard to believe. It reflects too great an openness and too great subservience. *No prophet was implicitly obeyed after the day of Pentecost*. Their words were taken as no more than a help.

4 *There are 'words of wisdom' from a non-Divine source*. It is not likely that a Christian would listen to an astrologer, or a spiritualist, or a necromancer, if they knew who they were. But the word of wisdom is offered us daily in newspapers through horoscopes, and many Christians are foolish enough to read these prognostications.

But right through the New Testament we are warned about false prophets, whose wisdom is earthly sensual, or inspired by what Paul calls *'another spirit which ye have not received'*. John says, 'Believe not every spirit, but try the spirits whether they be of God; because many false prophets are gone out into the world.' (1 John 4:1). Do not believe horoscopes in other words, or words by spiritualists or crystal-gazers. Their words could well come to pass since demon forces will engineer the very circumstances predicted, especially predictions of accidents and sickness.

When a medium tells a Christian that they have healing hands, or a gift of healing, one should beware. A trap is being laid to lead to spiritist or occult forms of healing practice.

5 *Particular peril lurks in blank-mind waiting*. When we wait passively we are using a dangerous method, exactly that

of systems which are non-Christian, such as TM., Yoga, and the mystics. It is in fact a form of mysticism, and there has never been a truly orthodox mystic in the Church. I have a recording of a well-known charismatic leader speaking to a large congregation urging everyone to wait upon God and listen in quietness each day for the voice that Samuel and many more heard. It sounds quite good Christian advice, and harmless. In fact is is neither good nor harmless. The gift of discernment operated in me as I listened.

The only person in the Bible who waited in silence for God to speak was the prophet Habakkuk, and that was not for instruction but because he was in a unique prophetic dialogue with the Lord. God speaks when He chooses. Samuel and all the others He addressed were never waiting for instructions. The idea that we can get God to speak when we chose to listen is presumption. It is also rather arrogant to suppose He must always have special instruction for us, as if God's Word itself is inadequate for our daily direction. The expression 'quiet time' came from MRA and means the same thing as the 'quietism' of eastern paganism. Paul is never described as waiting for this Voice.

People talk of 'meditating' – thinking of nothing particularly except what God might put in their mind. No such suggestion is found in the Word of God. Psalm 1.2 tells us to *'meditate IN HIS LAW day and night'*. Prayer is not normally a conversation and there is simply nothing in Scripture to encourage the idea.

The Psalm prayers are not dialogue. God may speak to us as we pray, but He may speak to us when we are eating our dinner, and why not? Isn't he just as much present after prayer as during prayer? Of course we should always be alert to hear His voice; *'my sheep hear my voice'*, but sheep don't tell their Shepherd to say something. *'Whatsoever things are true, honest, just, pure, lovely, of good report, any virtue, any praise think on these things'* (Phil 4:8).

Dr John White (a medical psychologist) whose book of Guidance is the best I have read, explains in another excellent study that *if we wait upon God long enough to say something, sooner or later we shall conclude He has said what we wanted Him to say*. For example, many leading British charismatics constantly wrote about the need to wait upon God for a new direction, or a new structure in the church. Apparently the rest of us were going in the wrong direction after all our sincere prayer and dedication to God's will.

But how did they know God HAD a new direction for the Church? That was pure presumption. If God said He had, he wouldn't have been furtive about it and kept it to Himself for us to wheedle out of Him. 'I want you to go in a new direction or I can't give you my full blessing. But I'm only telling you if you pressurise me with fasting and prayers for a long time, otherwise you'll never know, and I'm not telling everybody.' Would we go on like that, much less the Lord? In fact He would tell us all, not a select super-heavenly-minded coterie. That is what the Word of wisdom is for.

If we assume a new direction is needed, and spend long enough meditating, we shall get one. Something will drop into our thoughts, usually what we've considered ought to be, but it will be our own mental state. The devil too could drop in a suggestion or two. If we get a pleasant idea in our heads first and then pray about it long enough it will assume Divine importance. We shall do exactly what we wished! *We cannot coerce God into saying yes or no on demand.* He leaves so much to our own wisdom and responsibility that He may not wish to influence us either way. He will remain silent. He likes us to please ourselves in most practical matters.

5   *That the Word is wisdom is for that very reason remarkable.* Wisdom is given us anyway, and the method of God is to make us wise through His Word so that we can make up our own minds on most issues in life. That accords with human sovereignty granted us by God. A Word of wisdom will apply where we cannot be wise because the situation is unique, or human sagacity inadequate. There is no question of God answering us when we pray, for He promised to do so. *'Call upon me and I will answer you and show you great and mighty things which thou knowest not of'* (Jer. 33.3). His answers however are not mystic voices and mental promptings, but all the ways He answers a prayer. His answers are objective not subjective.

The Word Of Knowledge

1 *'Knowledge' was the one area which gave the apostles most anxiety, reading from their letters.* Every New Testament epistle writer makes reference to 'gnosis' teachings. They had in mind knowledge acquired outside the faith, as in the mystery religions; initiation in esoteric things, mystical knowledge.

2 *The gift is open to misuse.* The Word of knowledge was not prophecy, though obviously it overlapped and might be regarded as prophecy in certain manifestations. But there is a difference or it would not be named differently.

3 *It is sometimes information given by the Holy Spirit.* Peter knew of the deceptions of Ananias and Sapphira, and Elisha knew the war plans of the Syrians. It is not fortune telling, for it always has a Divine purpose for the Church or the salvation of the lost. It can also operate for the care of God's children, and that remarkably often, and in miraculous ways. Volumes could be filled with stories. I'll give one example.

My son was trapped under a car which had fallen on him while he was underneath carrying out a repair. He was alone in my garage, and confident we would arrive to find him dead. Suddenly he found he could quite miraculously lift the vehicle sufficiently to squirm from underneath, without harm except bad bruising. Two days later, giving thanks in a local Bible college, one of the students, astonished, told us he had actually had a powerful dream about that very thing and felt an urge to pray for the safety of the person being crushed to death.

4 *The main function in the beginning of the Church was spiritual knowledge or understanding of the Word of God.* Scriptures were few and the Word was a matter of verbal teaching. A Word of Knowledge would be immensely valuable. Insight into truths only partially known would particularly invest teachers and pastors. There is always a place for this gift, and constantly seeking to understand the Word one must testify to it. It comes with all the force of a revelation, inspiring and exhilarating.

5 *The false Word of Knowledge is not the true word of God.* This was illustrated only too powerfully I recall on an itinerary abroad. The national head of a Pentecostal body allowed me

to see a document submitted by leaders of a large church and asked what I thought of its theology. I didn't need to probe it deeply. One of the several divergences from the Word of God laid down that the leadership should have the right to determine new truth, but the senior pastor would have final authority. This gave him papal infallibility, outside the Word of God. This constitution made a man, not the Word of God the final authority.

In fact some are paying scant respect to Scripture where they believe their ideas are good or fit their experience.

6   *But the essence of the Word of Knowledge is that it is about the Word, or else in accord with it. The Holy Ghost . . . shall teach you all things, and bring all things to your remembrance, whatsoever I have said unto you'.* It is the safeguard against the subtleties of false doctrines of which birds there are always a flock or two flying around, perching in the branches. It is His Word brought into remembrance in a vivid way. The need for this gift, especially for the less doctrinally instructed, is obvious, and so is the danger of its counterfeit. But we shall have to refer again to this presently.

Faith

In my previous book *The Practice of Pentecost*, I showed that the Gift of Faith relates to special service where special faith is required. George Muller was called to the work of the Bristol orphanage and is often quoted as an example of faith. He is an example – if we also are called to a particular task requiring that kind of trust. All Christians have faith, or they would not be saved. Also, if they have fruits of the Spirit in their lives, one of them also is faith (Gal 5:22).

1   *The Gift of faith relates to particular situations outside normal life*, and cannot be produced to order. It is HIS faith, given us, not worked up by us.

2   *It is faith for specific situations according to God's will*. If he calls us to move mountains we shall have faith to move mountains, but not otherwise. If the Lord calls us to be an evangelist, we shall have faith for an evangelist, or of a pastor,

a missionary, and for every situation which arises in a particular calling.

3 *Faith has however become a province of novel notions*. One of these is Positive Confession or 'authority' already referred to. this is a pseudo-faith formula. Because it has a faith stance and even Scripture behind it, its appeal is the greater, and its error. It is a technique to make faith work, and that means to make God work.

The error does not consist of disbelieving Scripture but of selecting Scriptures for their purpose and believing them rather than trusting God. It is faith in word-power, similar to the Coue system repeating constantly 'Every day in every way I am getting better and better'. There is something akin to pagan superstition in word-power ideas of a miracle in your mouth, linked with casting spells and even witchcraft and the use of incantations.

When people 'confess' to get a miracle, do they suppose their words are magic? Or haven't they realised only God can work miracles? We cannot use a formula to get Him to work, as if it were an incantation or spell. God cannot be pushed into activity by words and formulas.

'Confession' (Gr *homologeo* and *exomologio*) is found nearly forty times in the New Testament alone. It frequently occurs in confession of sin, also a few times as admitting a belief, and especially of confessing Christ, or confessing in Christ. The best known texts are 1 John 1:9: *'If we confess our sins . . .'*; Romans 10:9 *'If thou shalt confess with thy mouth the Lord Jesus, and shalt believe in thine heart that God raised him from the dead, thou shalt be saved'*. These tests give us the main use of the word.

The Positive Confession doctrine uses it differently. The teaching is to confess positively answers to prayer, or confess that certain things should happen and they will happen. *It is a faith technique, but not faith in God primarily but in the power of our own words*. One exponent actually calls it 'The miracle in your mouth'. He finds many Scriptures showing that men confessed victories or miracles beforehand, and makes the assumption that that is why the victories or miracles came. But it was not the reason. There is no shortage of that kind of material. Men of faith would naturally talk faith. What is lacking is proof that it was by speaking faith words that anything took place.

One example offered is David's confrontation with Goliath. David positively declared all he would do to the giant in the name of the Lord. David didn't kill Goliath by confession, however, but with a sword. David had faith and went ahead. His positive confession was not the essential part in any way. He could have killed Goliath without saying a word to him, for Hebrews 11:32–34, declares that it was by faith IN ACTION not mere talk. *Goliath did not die by a miracle in David's mouth*. It is completely overlooked that Goliath himself also gave a powerful speech of positive confession (1 Sam. 17:44), in the same threatening strain as David, but it didn't work. Faith and fighting was the formula for David's victory, not talk.

Positive confession has its varieties. The thought behind it is that we must never confess negatives, but only positives. That will bring us success, blessing, prosperity and good health. Believers have a simple formula in their hands, speak in the right way, and keep on confessing all good things, and the good life follows. Never confess negatives, such as I am sick, or I'm short of money, or my business is going bankrupt, but the reverse. The answer to all problems is confession. Of course positive talk is good but . . .

It is of course too simplistic, and takes no note of the negatives confessed in Scripture before God worked mightily. The disciples confessed negatively they could not feed the multitude before they actually did (Luke 9:12,13). Before they had a great fish catch they confessed they had caught nothing (John 21:3–6). Paul confesses his thorn in the flesh and Trophimus' sickness, and long lists of his own problems, but he enjoyed the signal blessing of God and knew God far beyond any of us.

There is more to it than what is positive and what is negative. It is a matter of what is TRUE. Truth may be either positive or negative. Truth consists of the Word of God, and all the teaching therein regarding faith, the promises, and the will of God. It cannot be reduced to a simple matter of 'confess and possess'. Indeed where then is the place of prayer? Why the teaching of Jesus and others on how to pray? And why the exhortations by Christ and the apostles to pray?

Faith does not mean a life without difficulty or shortages or even suffering. Faith is shown as most truly displayed in the extremities of life, when all things seem against us. *The Gift of faith may be given exactly for such times, as for example, faith to die, to suffer, be hungry, be poor for Christ, just as Hebrews 11:35 tells us.*

Having just listened to a confess-possess sermon, sent me on tape from America, I wondered if I was listening to the Gospel at all, or a new religion using Christ's name. The preacher manipulated the audience making them repeat statements over and over, in a kind of brain-washing act. Faith must be linked with all the truth of redemption and the Cross of Christ. Unless it is anchored there it is no more than *faith in faith*, only-believism.

There are other gifts of the Holy Spirit, which are considered in other chapters, where we study the hallmarks of tongues, discernment, prophecy and healing. As this book tackles a vast subject I had to abbreviate and omit much I would have liked to say.

4   The Holy Spirit

Amazing Grace was printed in the Olney Hymns and published in 1779 by William Cowper and John Newton. I first heard it about thirty years ago when an American preacher assumed we would all join him in singing it from memory, but none of us knew of it. Newton's song had become part of the spiritual folk music of America.

Grace was a dominant theme in 'the old-time religion'. The eighteenth-century evangelicals, Whitfield, Edwards and others, who laid the real foundations of American life, preached a Gospel of grace. The heavenly force sweeping thousands into the kingdom of God in their theology was 'Grace'. British life was also affected by the same 'grace' revivals, 'SAVED BY GRACE ALONE'.

Old-time conversions were thought to be wrought by grace as a supernatural power. Grace was regarded as a Divine element or 'thing' even from the ancient days of Christian tradition. Church doctrine was built as a system around grace by Augustine (fourth century) and remains in that state today. The Reformation theology followed suit, and also the evangelicals of the eighteenth century emphasised grace in their Gospel.

Grace was a liberating message from the old legalism. From the days of Wesley they rejoiced in its power, filling their songs with it. Grace was the dynamic truth of the evangelical awakening. Hymns of sovereign grace are characteristic of that period. Hearing them now one gets the impression of grace as a kind of impersonal energy from heaven working out the purposes of God. It was a theology of grace as a potent force. To many grace was both discriminating and irresistible. Grace determined whether people would be saved or not according

as to whether grace touched them. It was Divine in itself.
Newton's famous hymn is really an anthem to grace. Hymn-
book versions now mention God only once and that incidentally

> T'was grace that taught my soul to pray,
> And grace my fears relieved;
> How precious did that grace appear
> The hour I first believed,
> Thro' many dangers, toils and snares
> I have already come;
> 'Tis grace hath brought me safe thus far,
> And grace will lead me home.

What Is Grace? A Simple Explanation Of Its Theology

The doctrine of grace was a tradition coming down from Catholic and sacramentalist church belief. For many centuries the
Church thought of grace as a Divine element that could be
accumulated – a quantifiable asset, a Divine currency, to save
one's soul. That explains the expression 'the means of grace',
'the means' being religious acts which banked grace to one's
salvation account. Some had a surplus – a person became a
saint when they had acquired more grace than they needed
for themselves, and the surplus became a grace mountain for
distribution to those less well off in that commodity.

The idea of grace as a 'thing' can be found right from the
second century with Ignatius who was marytred *c*. AD 110,
and in the Epistle of Clement, *c*. AD 100. The great Augustine
(354–430) and his opponent Pelagius (355–425), John Calvin
and his opponent Jacob Armenius in the sixteenth century,
wrapped their teachings around grace. They all saw it as an
active force.

The word grace is found 150 times in the New Testament,
mostly in Paul's writings. Jesus never used the term. Generally
Pentecostal thought and Pentecostal evangelism does not pivot
on grace, though it is important in our minds. Pentecostal
revival has a new base different from the old revival theology
of grace.

Pentecostals don't think of grace as a spiritual substance, something which can be gathered like manna, but simply as God's attitude, Grace is God's smile, or His disposition. It means He turns His face towards us. Ezra described it as 'the hand of the Lord my God upon me' (7:28)

Grace In Scripture

There is no separate power from God called grace. The word is often used in Scripture as a figure of speech. It sums up all the blessings Christ bestows. Grace stands for what is in God's heart. Also it stands for everything God gives us because of His grace. In the same way, we say 'charity', that is, human kindliness, when we mean money given in charity. Paul often says 'grace', which is God's kindness, when he means God's gifts given in kindness. Grace should be interpreted that way.

GRACE IN NOT ANOTHER CREATED GIFT OR NEW POWER. It is a word describing all grace-gifts, the '*charismata*', the idea behind the charismatic movement. One of God's grace-gifts is the Holy Spirit, and another is salvation.

In the New Testament the power of God drawing us to Christ is the Holy Spirit. 'Ye shall receive power after that the Holy Ghost is come upon you' (Acts 1:8). This is what Jesus taught in those three great chapters of John, 14, 15 and 16. All the typical effects of revival are produced by the Holy Spirit. '*And when he is come, he will reprove the world of sin, and of righteousness, and of judgment.*' We do not read of the 'power of grace', but only the power of the Spirit.

The revival which the old evangelicals thought of as the power of grace in action (an impersonal power) we think of as the Holy Spirit. Grace describes the disposition of God who sends the power of the Spirit. John Wesley in his famous Sermon number nine, makes grace synonymous with the Holy Spirit. In a sense it is. But grace describes the MOTIVE and the Spirit is the OPERATING POWER.

The Oxford Dictionary of the Christian Church takes the old line and speaks of grace as some kind of force emanating from Christ. '*In Christian theology (grace) is the supernatural assistance of God bestowed upon a rational being with a view*

to sanctification'. It also speaks of '*the necessity of this aid*', as
if it were an independent thing.

Unmerited Favour

Grace is '*the unmerited favour of God*'. Sometimes grace has
a non-theological meaning, patience. Commenting on Wesley,
Rupert E. Davies says, '*The grace of God is not a thing at
all. We should do better, perhaps, if we spoke of God who is
gracious . . . grace is really "love in action"* '. An article by F.
Baudraz in Allmen's *Vocabulary of the New Testament* also
says: '*Grace is not a thing, but its essential significance is simply
God Himself, in His goodwill towards men. The grace of
God . . . is a personal relationship which God establishes
between Himself and men. He regards them with favour and
kindness*'. John Oman's *Grace and Personality* also makes this
a strong point, describing grace as '*a gracious personal
relationship*'.

Christ saves us, that is perfectly well understood. We don't
mind expressing it poetically singing 'Saved by grace alone'.
We can 'abound in grace', that is in all the favours God bestows
upon us.

Some think of the power of grace and the power of the Spirit
as the same thing (see 1 Corinthians 15:10, 2 Corinthians 12:9,
Acts 6:8(5)), but others do not agree. Dr J. K. Mozley says
'Close as is the connection between grace and the Holy Spirit,
I do not think the New Testament allows for an absolute identi-
fication'. Dr Mozley may mean the grace at work and the Holy
Spirit at work are two different things, but Pentecostals don't
think that way.

Holy Spirit Evangelism

This brief venture into theology is important. I want to make
something very clear. It is this: *Pentecostal evangelism represents a new era in tradition. If you like, it is a revolution. We
can now clearly understand that this age is the age of the Holy
Spirit*. It has brought a different outlook on revival, on grace
and on evangelism.

It is rather more vital than a matter of a name or term. Classical revival had a grace theology. But the subject of grace held many problems. Such matters as the 'election of grace', whether it was irresistible, or persevering, or selective and so on. Wesley and Whitfield clashed on this issue. This affected evangelism. When revivals burst forth, these questions were involved. Was it 'sovereign grace' at work, selecting and choosing where and who to save? This fitted in well with Calvinistic and similar thought. Revival appeared to be a pure act of God making up the number of the elect. Any other effort was often considered presumptuous, and not of God.

This explains why some have described evangelistic campaigns as 'man doing the work instead of God'. It looked as if man by his own will and choice was trying to make up the number of the elect by organised effort, which God alone had the right to do. Revival was the proper way, and the answer was not evangelism but revival. Planned efforts were often considered as human, fleshly, and indeed still are thought to be so in some circles.

So the theology of grace with all its graceless controversy was imported straight into the whole question of evangelism and revival. When, however, the Pentecostals began to study Scripture regarding the power of God, they saw that it was the Holy Spirit which was described as the power behind salvation, and that was by the unmerited favour of God. In New Testament teaching of the Holy Spirit election did not come into it.

When Christians Turned To The Acts Of The Apostles

The study of grace was confined to Paul's epistles. Grace was Paul's word. But by the end of the nineteenth century attention had turned to the Gospel of John (the Holy Spirit Gospel) and the book of Acts. A new picture emerged. The Acts of the Apostles portrayed the Church and Apostles in free-ranging expeditions preaching to all and sundry. The apostles and early church never showed the slightest sign or qualms about God's election. They did not depend upon spontaneous revival outbursts. They preached to everybody, and went everywhere to everybody. It was evangelism to everyone without any complicated questions of grace. *They did not ever or even wait for guidance as to whom they should preach to or where they should go. He had already told them – go everywhere and to everybody.*

When evangelism is seen as a work of the Holy Spirit we are talking the same language as the early church. It related evangelism to all the promises of the Spirit. His gifts, fire, conviction, healing, unction, power, receiving the Spirit of Christ, and so on are all involved. The Welsh revival was the last of the old and the beginning of the new. Until then revival was understood to come from the mysterious unpredictable movings of sovereign grace. But the Holy Spirit was recognised as the true secret of what happened in 1904. Before it took place there had been development in understanding the Spirit.

Actually, it was from the seminal mind of John Wesley that the seed-truth of the baptism in the Spirit originated. It came in the form of his new teaching of perfect love as a post-conversion experience. This thought of a 'second blessing' produced the Holiness movement with its idea of the need of a cleansing baptism of fire. The 'baptism' concept led to power and finally it was seen as the baptism in the Spirit for service.

1904

At this point, in 1904, Evan Roberts was baptised in the Spirit, speaking with tongues either then or later. From the moment of his great experience the shaking of Wales by the Holy Spirit began. *That event also stimulated the infant Pentecostal movement and prepared thousands for the fullness of the Spirit, as I have described elsewhere.* Whether it was realised or not, *the reality behind grace had been identified, namely the Holy Spirit.* The power of grace in revival was in fact the power of the Holy Spirit – the truth had been opened up.

Something that would profoundly affect Christian work and outreach had become clear:

The HOLY SPIRIT, THE SPIRIT OF REVIVAL WAS PROMISED TO EVERY INDIVIDUAL BELIEVER WHO CALLED ON THE LORD.

REVIVAL NO LONGER WAITED FOR AN UNCER-
TAIN POWER, SOVEREIGN GRACE.

REVIVAL POWER WAS THE HOLY SPIRIT GIVEN
TO ALL WHO ASKED.

REVIVAL RESTED WITH THE CHURCH AND ITS
FAITH AND ANOINTING

The way was now open for every believer to enjoy the experience Charles Wesley longed for, expressed in his great hymn:

> O Thou who camest from above
>   The pure celestial fire to impart,
> Kindle a flame of sacred love,
>   On the mean altar of my heart!
> There let it for Thy glory burn
>   With inextinguishable blaze;
> And trembling to its source return
>   In humble prayer and fervent praise.

World Conversion

This put a new face on the entire possibilities for world conversion through evangelism. There had been much evangelism,
but many waited for the mysterious uncertainties of revival.
Because of prevailing doctrines of grace missions both abroad
and at home were affected.

The first English foreign missionary organisation was established by Act of Parliament in 1649, to reach Indians in Massa-
chusetts, America, but William Carey, the 'father of modern
missions', was slapped down when he proposed among senior
ministers missions to convert the heathen. He was told that
God could do it Himself if He wanted it done. It wasn't for
Carey to anticipate who should be offered salvation. Evangelism could be presumption, man stepping into to do what only
God could do, and did do in revivals. Carey's answer in 1792
was his 'Enquiry into the Obligations of Christians to use means
for the Conversion of the Heathens'.

For Pentecostals – and others – there was now no hesitation. The Spirit bade them go. *Depending on God to reach souls in revival turned out to be the reverse of what God intended*. God intended man to reach souls, and not spend time praying for God to do it Himself.

> It pleased God by the foolishness of preaching to save them that believe. How shall they call on him in whom they have not believed? and how shall they believe in him of whom they have not heard? and how shall they hear without a preacher? and how shall they preach except they be sent? Go into all the world and preach the Gospel to every creature (1 Cor 1:21. Rom. 10:14–15, Mark 16:15.)

This is the explicit command, 'even unto the end of the world' (Matt. 28:20). Evangelism was no longer a despised organised and human effort, scorned as 'not revival'. That is what it had been and still is to some unperceiving minds. But the Pentecostal recovery of a Holy Ghost ministry put revival power in our hearts and lives to scatter fire across the face of the earth. That was the New Testament plan.

But what about the undoubted truth of the sovereign will of God? It had previously been thought of as demonstrated in the spasmodic outbreaks of revival. Was God really spasmodic in soul-saving? The answer was simple. God had already exercised His sovereign will in sending the Holy Spirit into the world, not in sudden wild bursts, but '*He shall abide with you for ever*'. His will was in His Word, and not to be discerned from will o' the wisp appearances. *His will was revealed for the entire Christian age. He sent forth his servants to preach the Gospel and He would go with them everywhere*. He had acted already in sovereign grace, giving them the Great Commission and the Holy Spirit to fulfil it. His sovereign will is constant revival. It had been spasmodic because men were spasmodic.

The Pentecostals felt the strivings of the Spirit and read their marching orders. Their feet are now heard around the whole globe. By the Spirit world-wide revival was possible through evangelism, evangelists knowing their own possession of the Spirit of revival in the baptism in the Spirit.

The influence of Calvinism and its teaching of election was strong (and still is) in revival teaching, seeing revival as an act of God outside human planning. Dr J. Packer has written an evangelistic encouragement to all who accept Calvinistic theology, on the grounds that we must do it because Christ commanded it. Charles Finney clashed with much church opinion because he spoke of using means to bring revival, but he still thought in terms of God's grace. By his contemporaries he was accused of Armenianism especially when he began inviting people into the enquiry room to find the Lord. But soon he was not alone.

Evangelistic Theology

Pentecostals have a new evangelistic theology, the Holy Spirit in demonstration. The outpouring of the Holy Spirit, and indeed the whole doctrine of the Spirit carries no questions of election. Human effort it may be, *but it should be*. I will qualify that. It is the Holy Spirit's work, who has come forth from the Father to convict and convert. We are only co-workers, called in to enjoy the privilege of fellowship-sharing with the Holy Spirit. Any effort we make is supplementary to His ceaseless activity, but by invitation.

Prayer? Why certainly and urgently. '*I would that ye pray for all men everywhere,*' *says Paul*. BUT WHAT SHALL WE PRAY? For God to enter the field and lift the burden from our shoulders in a mighty harvest of souls which He brings about Himself? That is precisely the very task He has laid upon us! He reminded in John 4:35 that the fields '*are white already to harvest*'. Pray? For Him to enter the field? Jesus said '*The harvest truly is plenteous, but the labourers are few; pray ye therefore the Lord of the harvest, that he will send forth labourers into his harvest*'.

We cannot ask God to do what He has told US to do, 'by all means save some'. God is not the evangelist. The Church is. God has given us power, the Gospel is power and the baptism in the Spirit brings power.

Power From On High

That brings us to another important point, power from on high. How does it come, and when?

I have collated and analysed every reference to prayer in the entire New Testament. What does the Word say? I can discern no suggestion anywhere that would encourage us to pray 'Lord send the power, the old-time power'. There is no evidence that any such praying took place in apostolic times as is common today for power. Prayer was certainly important to people then but they did not seem to be anxious about being spiritually impotent. They didn't believe they were, for they certainly showed no signs of such worries.

Paul asked people to pray for him. But for what? Certainly not for him to have power. It was that he would have utterance, be preserved from enemies, and similar practical requests. He in turn prayed for his friends for their enlightenment in the truth, for grace and peace, for their wellbeing and spiritual growth and so on. But when it came to the question of having power he declared it was already there *'working mightily'* within him.

If this is not popular teaching, I am not concerned, as it is not my teaching but a simple New Testament fact. We can make what we like of it, but it presents clearly to me a picture of a church harvesting, not waiting four months, as Jesus described in John, Chapter 4.

Prayer cannot be neglected. The New Testament is full of praying and references to prayer. It is 'the Christians' native breath'. We die without it. We should pray for our friends and OUR ENEMIES, their safety, their health, their prosperity, sharing their worries and burdens in prayer. We should pray especially for the nations and their rulers, and for all God's servants, and for evangelistic and missionary success.

We should pray for the 'best gifts', and in prayer 'wait on our ministry'. We should pray for our eyes to be opened to understand the Scriptures – our daily bread, and for God's will to be done on earth when so often it is not. We should remember those who suffer for Christ, for those in difficult circumstances, for the bereaved, the aged, and the young; for ourselves and others not to fall into temptation and besetting sins. For those sinning and endangering their souls. For our pastors. For a hundred other things. But when it comes to power – you ask and receive the Holy Spirit and He abides with you. *'I will pour out of my Spirit upon all flesh'*. *'The Spirit and the Bride say "Come", and whosoever will let him take the water of life freely'* (Joel 2:28, Revelation 22:17).

Preaching is not a defence lawyer's logical presentation of the case for Christ demanding a clinical decision, to be followed by a signing-up process. It is a Holy Ghost and the Cross business, the only word the Holy Ghost will acknowledge and use is the Gospel of Christ and His redemption. They cannot be converted to a Kingdom, but only to a Saviour. This age is Joel's 'the last days' (i.e. later days). The New Testament is the charter of the Spirit, the manifesto of the Christian economy. It is a day of renewal, revival, evangelism.

> 'The arms of love which compass me
> Would all mankind embrace'.

5 Anointed

For a long time I 'tried' to have anointing for my preaching. This I judged by such criteria as my warmth of heart, flow of words, fertility of thought, or how much I prayed. Sometimes I felt God was not the slightest bit interested in my pulpit labours, and left me struggling on alone. Maybe He wasn't. He's only promised to bless His own Word, not our philosophising – that's a non-conducting element for His power.

What Is It Like?

If we are to have a continued experience of the Pentecostal indwelling, WHAT IS IT LIKE? Human feelings are so many and varied. How does one identify the presence of the Holy Spirit? The experience of the indwelling Spirit should not be hard to recognise. It is like nothing else, in fact.

We should give a preliminary warning. *God is bigger than a feeling*. He is all things to us, the fullness of life. We live, move and exist in Him. But I am talking about one aspect of His presence, the anointing of the Spirit. What is that like?

There are various reactions to God's presence depending on why He comes to us. Adam was guilt-stricken in the garden, Abraham in a trance saw a 'horror of darkness', Jacob was in awe at Bethel, Moses stood barefooted on wilderness ground at the bush, Joshua conquered by the sheer presence of the Man with the drawn sword, Peter was overcome by his sinfulness on first meeting Jesus, and the presence of Christ blinded Paul and converted him on the Damascus Road. Vivid experiences are recorded by Isaiah, Ezekiel and Daniel. Jeremiah said that the word of God was in him like a fire burning in his bones.

All these were passing moments, and obviously did not continue night and day. But THE ANOINTING IS PERMANENT. Can you always 'feel' it however. Or does it come and go? For instance, I remember my first trip to the USA on an old Britannia prop plane starting at midnight and landing thirteen hours later with several more hours travelling to keep my preaching appointment. I had not slept for thirty-six hours. The church was carpeted, acoustically dead, and also too hot. At the close the pastor said 'Do you think you got liberty tonight?' Maybe he thought I wasn't anointed, but could I have been, although I was staggering with weariness.

It must be SEEN AND BELIEVED FROM THE WORD that the baptism in the Spirit is a continuing experience. It is an obvious tactic of the devil to destroy our faith in God's promised peace. The devil would like us to believe that the anointing depends on so many things that we will never be sure of it.

Let it be thoroughly realised that we are IMMERSED in the Spirit, not merely dipped. 'Waters to swim in,' as Ezekiel says. The idea of a river which we visit for a plunge from time to time is not how Scripture speaks. 'By one Spirit we are all baptised into one body and have been all made to drink into one Spirit' (1 Cor. 12:13). Such a verse is obviously not about something that is only a matter of memory, past and gone. We ARE baptised and we DO drink, now. The Holy Spirit cannot be static, for His essential nature is that of a moving Spirit – wind blowing and rivers flowing.

It is also the Spirit taking up residence; 'Ye are the temple of the living God; as God hath said, "I will dwell with them, and walk in them; and I will be their God, and they shall be my people" '. God does not flit in and out of His temples along with worshippers going in and out of the church on Sundays.

The Old Testament revelation of the presence of the Spirit was that of a fleeting experience, but the New Covenant promised a new thing, God walking and dwelling with men. He comes to abide. The baptism in the Spirit is not for repetition. Christ described the future Christian experience as 'rivers of living water'. Rivers do not flow on and off by repeats, but by an uninterrupted flow. To speak of 'another Pentecost', or 'Lord do it again', 'O for a new anointing', or of new baptisms, misses the whole genius of New Testament truth. The familiar phrases really belong to pre-Pentecostal times and are a traditional hangover from nineteenth-century 'holiness' language. Jesus' promise of 'rivers' presents a quite difference picture of unending renewal, not renewal from time to time like a sea tide.

It is staggering that with all we know of the grace and of the faithfulness of God that most Christians are everlastingly in doubt about whether they have done enough to ensure God is with them. As I said, this is the devil's strategy.

Some preaching compares the eternal Spirit to a natural power, like electricity in a battery which deteriorates as time passes and has to be renewed. Any use of such figures of speech for the Holy Spirit is unscriptural. Begin to realise that the baptism sets up a personal relationship with the everlasting and faithful God. That is not something one can associate with batteries being re-charged. 'He abides, the comforter abides with me' is a much needed piece of theology.

Abiding is an important New Testament key word. Jesus explained what kind of 'abiding' this is. It is the state of a branch in a vine. The life of the vine always FLOWS through it. The great spiritual blessings come in that form, flowing, moment by moment, not as one single deposit. '*Hereby know we that we dwell in him, and he in us, because he hath given us of his Spirit*' (1 John 4:13). The Greek *apo* ('of') is important, meaning 'some of', literally 'out of', as in Acts 2:17 'I will pour OUT OF my Spirit' which is the same idea as pouring from a vessel (v.18), 'I will pour out' because there is more to come, not all at once but out and out and out. Eternal life itself is similar, both a gift and an endless process. God does not stock us up with a one-package delivery making us independent for ever, but imparts life in a continuous stream. Joined with Him, we live in Him and by Him like a child in the womb sustained by the maternal environment.

There does arise of course the question of backsliding or other states of decline. Because Jesus promised '*a well of water springing up into everlasting life*' does this mean everybody will always enjoy it no matter what? Does the Spirit still abide in any real sense when we turn away from God? The answer to that is the warning of Jude that God delivered Israel from Egypt and then destroyed them, and that even sinning angels were reserved for judgement, and the privileged priest Korah died for his presumption. Grafted-in branches can be broken off from the vine again, Paul reminds us. There is 'a sin unto death' (1 John 5:16) and it can overtake anybody unless they 'watch and pray'.

Every person is different and the Lord judges every case. The fact is some are judged and die (1 Cor. 11:30). We can quench the Spirit and grieve the Spirit. But otherwise 'Know ye not that Jesus Christ IS in you . . . *except ye be reprobates?*' (2 Cor. 13:5).

But the normal believer in his struggles and failure is not to be classed with these reprobates. The Lord does not leave us as easily as that. There is nothing in the New Testament as there is in the Old Testament about the Spirit of God departing from men. The promise 'I will never leave you' is perhaps conditional, but the conditions are not so intricate and demanding that the verse has no real force. It holds true through the thick and thin of a lifetime of human vagaries and faultiness.

How does the Spirit relate to us in periods when we are faithless? That brings us to the mystery of God's heart. Our relationship is one which He Himself has striven to create. He is faithful, but that does not mean we can play fast and loose, and presume upon His grace. If we do we are being very foolish and stand in jeopardy.

We ought in this connection to consider one important verse Ephesians 5:18. *It is said that the Greek tense is an exhortation to 'be being filled with the Spirit'.* That is correct; the verb is in the present continuous. But this has been almost the sole basis on which preachers have urged Pentecostals to keep on seeking new fillings from time to time, or every morning like petrol for the car. That is exactly what it does not mean. The verb is a passive describing something that happens to us not something we do ourselves, but it is in the imperative.

The only way it is possible to fulfil this exhortation is to be in a pre-condition in which we are always receiving the Spirit. We cannot re-fill ourselves. We are the passive recipients. I would translate it '*Stop keeping on getting drunk and start keeping on being always filled with the Spirit*'. How can one get into that position of constantly being filled? The answer is, *by being baptised in the Spirit.* From the moment we receive we go on receiving.

Incidentally this text *does not encourage getting drunk in the Spirit*. The CONTRAST is not between two ways of getting drunk, wine and Spirit, but between two states, drunkenness and sobriety. (Compare *The Expositor's Greek Testament*.) Drunkeness, loss of control, is the opposite to being full of the Spirit. Liquor dispossesses men of their senses, takes away self-control, but the Spirit has the opposite effect, and gives us the power 'of a sound mind'.

I'm thankful I have not heard recently the expression about being 'high on God'. God is not an alcohol or drug substitute. Every stimulant merely uses our reserves and leaves us worse afterwards. But *'the blessing of God maketh rich and he addeth no sorrow with it'* (Prov. 10:22). If that is a good translation it means God's blessings add to and enrich human strength, not merely mortgage our physical resources.

Returning to the main issue. If the baptism in the Spirit is an effect that wears off, what is the point of any of us saying we were baptised? In that case we can't say we are baptised, but only that we once were. Is this baptism temporary – a week or so? That is not what God intends or says.

When We Feel Dry

Nevertheless we can FEEL empty, flat – 'de-pneumatised' – like a pneumatic tyre blow out. When Scripture promises us constant re-filling should we ever feel empty? Shouldn't we always enjoy boundless exuberance? No, we should not. Dr Martyn Lloyd Jones in his exposition of Ephesians insists that even Paul, like other notables could swing from the heights to the depths. It is a matter of natural temperament he says, or even of health, like a woman who came to him for spiritual help, and as soon as he saw her, he being a doctor, knew she had pernicious anaemia. It has nothing to do with our spiritual state.

Paul spoke both of the mighty power of God working constantly within him but also of almost desparing of life. He said, *'we that are in this body do groan being burdened'*. 'Cast down, but not destroyed'. Peaks and troughs are inevitable since that is how human nature is.

We may have the anointing but not be aware of it all the time.
THE IMPORTANT THING IS . . . A feeling does not alter
the Word of promise. Faith is the substance of things hoped
for at all times.

How conscious is a strong man of his strength when he lies
down? He can feel as tired as anybody else. *He knows strength
only when he uses it.* Christians keep praying for an anointing,
but why? What have they done or what do they propose to do
with it? Just have emotional moments? It is not for private
enjoyment, though it does bring deep satisfaction.

Assurance

I would agree with the late Donald Gee who once said to me
that the baptism in the Spirit had given him a greater love for
Jesus; love, the essence of ultimate wonder. It is also a continuing assurance of God, setting truth on fire in one's heart –
burning conviction. A personal intimacy with Christ emerges –
not merely that of a friend upon whose door one has to knock
for a chat once a week; it brings a sense of strength, adequacy
or stature, or of a calling; an inevitable stir in the heart at
Divine things. The baptised person walks with Him, and that
is not just to church on Sundays. All this and other descriptions
apply to one and another.

What it does not mean is living in a spiritual abstraction all
day. I remember my music teacher, quite a genius, writing
poetry about snow in the only spot in his studio where the
water was not penetrating from melting snow, instead of doing
something useful about it. Spirituality does not allow us to
indulge in impractical day-dreaming.

It happens that I am mostly engaged every waking moment
with Divine things, especially the Word. I find it natural to talk
to the Lord at any moment, and have to explain I am not
talking to myself. But I am not in a state of hyper-intimacy
with God or semi-trance, my consciousness concentrated on
listening to Divine voices, preoccupied with heavenly communi-
cations. God does not talk to us all day like that. If we talk to
Him all the time, I don't know what we should say.

To be in a state of constant conscious communion with God

is not how it seems to have been with Bible worthies, and is really quite unnatural, not supernatural, or at least not Divinely supernatural. People troubled by evil spirits may experience this constant state, but God expects us to be rational and get on with our job. Otherwise it is likely to lead to a paranoid state of mind, hallucination. Some claims only reveal that imagination has taken over command. That is not what Scripture encourages in any way.

In fact *there is nothing in all Scripture suggestive of listening for Divine messages at any time*, though we should certainly be receptive and ready for when He does speak. It is presumption to expect God to speak to us as and when we decide to listen. He may have nothing to say at that moment – or for a month. His appointed organ is His Word. He has given all things we need for life and godliness there, says Peter, and only exceptional circumstances would bring us further instruction.

The prophets were never in that state. The apostles showed no sign of dwelling in a haze of euphoric abstraction. The apostle Paul spoke of 'an abundance of revelations', those expounded in his epistles, but in everyday life the book of Acts records so few occasions when God spoke to him and instructed him where to go next that one could count them on the fingers.

When God gave him direct moments of guidance they were moments in which history would be affected for ever. *Being spiritual does not mean being erratic*. We don't have to take all our random thoughts and impulses as coming from God.

There are mountain-top moments. It seems sometimes that one is being baptised in the Spirit all over again; moments when we emerge like those who have looked on God. But we cannot build doctrine on this and proclaim the need for everyone to seek such experiences regularly, calling it another filling. Altogether, apart from the anointing, the Lord has many a joy, many a revelation of His glory for us. They are times of encouragement, blessing, joy, when we stand before God, or inside the veil, or of being lost to immediate circumstances. This kind of experience is possible any time. But come joy, come sadness, He abides, the Comforter abides within.

It should help if we realise that the blessing of the Spirit is personal to every individual. The danger is to want to have the same reactions as other people, and to think that unless we do we haven't got the right thing. Phenomena can apparently have fashions. That overlooks one fact, that to God each of us is unique. God has His own 'new name' for every individual, because He allows each one to see His glory from a distinct viewpoint. What we are is how we see God. His name for us is secret and crystallises what each one truly and essentially is. It is a mistake for everybody to want to be a prophet, or healer, or visionary, or to feel inferior to others.

The anointing of God does not create disorder. We are not all cut out to take part in a public service and in that sense of 'body ministry' it is ridiculous. No leader should throw the reins away and let everybody act on every and any impulse. God has set ministries and gifts in the church, and the whole church is not equally endowed, all equally free to do whatever we want. Leadership doesn't mean presiding at a free-for-all. Like the Irishman who asked 'Is this a private fight or can anybody join in?', people are not prompted by God to interrupt, with peremptory orders from God to do this or that, bursting in any time with a song, or sermon or conducting healing or the communion. This is eccentric chaos. A leader must lead, which means like Joshua he must have the vision of the unity and order which God insists upon.

Neither does the anointing of God distract us from other matters upon which we have to concentrate. We shall not go around with God hammering away demanding attention all the time, as an interruption. There are plenty of factors operating in each human being which we hardly ever think about, blood circulation, muscle repair, anti-virus activity. The work of the Spirit may be a different kind of factor, but nevertheless it can go on without it having our entire waking attention.

The endeavour to 'practise the presence of God', as Brother Lawrence called it, picking up a straw for the glory of God, surely does not depend on thinking about God all the time as in church. Maybe Brother Lawrence was a wise old bird when he chose kitchen duties, mechanical chores, which gave him opportunity to think about God more. However some are not doing mindless jobs; maybe they have to pick up figures or facts all day, not straws which need no mental concentration.

When driving a car or walking or some automatic activity, we can praise the Lord. If our minds are free, it is a good thing to do so. I start, but often some other mental distraction breaks in. The Bible rule is *'fervent in spirit (but) not slothful in business'*.

Natural Effort

The gift and presence of the Holy Spirit does not make natural effort unnecessary. While some insist that behind every revival there is always a kneeling figure, I insist that behind every revival is a lot of hard work and attention. Both, usually.

When, as a child, I first heard about somebody being a genius, I took it they needed no study or training, but that it all came naturally like plucking complete books or symphonies from the air. Genius, it turned out, 'is an infinite capacity for taking pains'. My first impression of the power of the Holy Spirit was similarly idyllic. Our Pentecostal pastors I believed lived in an aura of inspirational independence like Moses on Sinai. They could preach without previous thought by Holy Ghost utterance, and notes would be of the flesh.

A pastor told me of his labours for revival with his church: weekly fasts and half nights of prayer, every month extra whole days of prayer, and sometimes a week of such spiritual effort. He and his churches maintained this programme for years. When I met him he expressed much disappointment at the outcome of it all. Revival tarried', what did I think was wrong? I was a little puzzled that he thought revival tarried. If his church was so ardent in prayer surely they had it already? All they needed were new hassocks!

The suggestion in my mind was that *you can't get everything done just by praying for God to do it*, no matter how persistently. He will not do what WE are supposed to do ourselves. Prayer is not a substitute for work. God has no plans to make human activity unnecessary in anything. The anointing of God frightens off no Goliaths. They have to be fought, even by the anointed.

The Holy Spirit does not make superfluous all our books which give us counsel and wisdom in the service of the Lord.

Training colleges may have their faults, and academics can become over-important, but *often the failure of ministries does not lie in any spiritual direction but in practical areas. THE HOLY SPIRIT NEVER MAKES THESE MATTERS IRREL-EVANT. But neither does efficiency in these things make the Holy Spirit irrelevant.*

I studied preaching like a concert musician refining his performance, to be a 'pulpit star' – with disastrous results. It all had to be adjusted to the Word and the Spirit, and some techniques were not accommodating to those essentials. Nevertheless I still believe that the difference between a crowd and no crowd can be a small thing in our manner, and the Holy Spirit will not constantly override annoyances which we ought to be able to correct ourselves. Bad habits are legion, I rapidly develop them and have to correct them. People at the back of a vast hall could pick me out on the platform because I fingered my tie. Read Spurgeon's Lectures!

Yet I will add that *what a man may lack in voice, manner, matter, style, gesture, appearance, oratory, knowledge vocabulary and intellect (all fields with a hundred snares in them), may be compensated by the golden assets of love for man and love for God and His Word. Love is our safeguard against inadequacy.* Two of the worst preachers I knew were successful because they oozed genuine sympathy and encouragement, always had time, an ear to listen and a hand to comfort. They were also wise and introduced others to minister the Word.

The particular colleague I mentioned happened to have churches in the toughest possible areas of two troubled inner cities with unsafe streets. In similar circumstances Christ told His disciples to shake off the dust of a village wicked and indifferent as a judgment against them.

To trouble our souls about our sowing and reaping when the field is as hard as the M1 motorway is unrealistic. All you could hope for is a flower or two in the central reservation. Jesus warned us in the parable of the sower (Matthew 13) of the great variation in results, from nothing to one hundred fold, and He blamed the ground only.

Unanointed?

Why do preachers in their pulpits and congregations at worship sometimes feel the absence of anointing? I shall offer reasons.

First, because they expect it. They suppose the anointing can come and go and has to be brought back again by their own efforts of mind and soul. If they went by the Word, they would know the anointing is there whether they think so or not. Christ CANNOT be absent when we gather in His Name. WE MUST ALWAYS BELIEVE THAT.

Second, we must not confuse loss of the anointing with other effects. When the preacher or the congregation is jaded, tired, or the message is hard to give, or words do not flow, it must not be read as lack of anointing. Congregations, especially smaller ones, do not always come together in the same state of body and mind, and that affects the general atmosphere. I never felt so un-anointed as when a three-year-old boy a few feet away squealed and screeched lustily. Forced in the end to try to take diplomatic action, I had to decide between the people hearing the child or me.

Third, the devil has a hand in things sometimes. He wants the preacher to be discouraged, and is doubly pleased if the Lord's people do the discouraging for him. However, the impression made by the sermon is not to be judged by the preacher's own feelings. I have discovered that the worst effort throws me more upon God to make up the deficiency, and He does. What I felt was a poor performance became strong in the hands of God.

Fourth, the anointing is not necessarily a feeling. It rests on faith. When we have come to a meeting thinking how well we have served the Lord and how hard we have prayed and that He ought to bless us, we are drifting away from faith in God to faith in our own righteousness. We can never deserve God's blessing in any case. Our best is poor. *His best is given not in proportion to our best but by the standard of His mercies.*

The Anointing Unfelt

Goliath is also there. There are stones to be picked up, skills to be used, faith to give us courage, positive words to be spoken, courageous action to be taken. Then Goliath will fall. He will not drop dead by shouting or singing, or go away because we utter the Lord's Name. The devil is not frightened by armies of church members marching around what they consider are their Jericho walls. Israel only did it at one city, they didn't take it as a precedent. And they had to use their swords every time, which for us means the sword of the Spirit which is Word of God, preaching the Gospel. That is our one means of the offensive. Word-power is useless unless addressed to the hearts and minds of sinners in the Gospel, which alone is the power of God. Praise is never said to be power anywhere in Scripture.

The Gospel is not the Gospel until it is preached, and then 'The Gospel is the power of God to salvation, and never until then. The anointing oil isn't permanent or visible, but the anointing is. When we act, we shall know the anointing is there.

6   The Bible and Revival Teaching

In a discussion about evangelism, somebody turned to me and protested, '*But you don't believe in revival!*'. I replied, '*Indeed I do, I believe very much in what I call revival, which is a bigger thing than what is usually meant. There's no law about what it means.*' Revival is the essence and hallmark of Christianity, and of Pentecost. Pentecost IS revival.

Let me illustrate. My house has gardens. Or, speaking personally, 500 square yards of potential backache, and also of ignorance. If I understood it all, including visitors – foxes, vandal squirrels, viking magpies, voracious snails, invading dogs (not this man's best friends), nervy doves, varied bird-table customers, the lonely fish in the pool, plus all the carnivorous insect species that have helped themselves to our blood, it would still not make me much of a naturalist. The scale is too small. I would need to study the Creator's larger world outside my fences. It takes all the earth and the heavens a thousand million light years wide to declare His handiwork.

Revival is like my garden – only part of what God does. To understand the workings of the Creator even in my garden, I shall have to go outside it. To know God, we must go beyond revival. We need comprehensive data, not limited examples. *If we confine our study of the workings of the Spirit to revival we shall not even understand revival properly. Our evidence is too narrow and selective.* There is some question begging also. We call certain events revival and then ask what revival is. If we don't know, how can we call anything revival?

There were glorious awakenings in the eighteenth and nineteenth centuries. Spectacular as they were, they don't tell us everything. If I only looked at my sunflowers and hollyhocks they would leave me with little grasp of all that is involved in nature.

The fullest knowledge of the Holy Spirit possible to us can come from one place only – the Scripture. It tells us everything we need to know, and we have ample room to make discoveries.

To begin, revival is a rare word in Scripture. Taking the King James' Bible, in its 733,693 words it is found only fifteen times, but not once in the New Testament. Most instances concern only physical recovery. In fact, the word 'revival' in the soul-saving sense does not appear in a single one of Scripture's 1,189 chapters. There is no trace of the modern idea. Revival teaching comes from revivals only. In the New Testament nothing the Spirit did was regarded as uniquely different from anything else He did. Nothing was given a more important title, and definitely not 'revival'.

Those exciting occasions we call revivals are of course God at work. The revivals of history are not unique efforts of God, however marvellous in our eyes. They are part of the Holy Spirit's work.

Revival Without The Holy Spirit?

I BELIEVE IN REVIVAL. My purpose is to create the highest expectation of revival possible. Our ideas are too small and confused, because we only study revivals themselves. The truth about revival, if it is of such major importance, must be found in the whole counsel of God, not from one or two texts.

First, however we must clear the ground. Certain Scriptures have been traditionally quoted. These are mainly from the Old Testament. But can the Old Testament provide us with Scripture for Christian revival – anything like the Welsh Revival, for example? How could it? Revival as we all agree is the work of the Holy Spirit. But until Christ came and ascended to glory 'the Holy Spirit was not yet given', says John 7:39. Holy Ghost revival could therefore not come in the Old Testament times, before the day of Pentecost. Whatever 'revivals' took place in ancient Israel could not be revivals as we know them. The only movings of the Spirit then were the occasions when He came upon the prophets as individuals, but He never once was poured out upon the masses of Israel in convicting and converting power.

In contrast, modern revival means the very thing which Israel never experienced, and could not. The Spirit moved in the prophets, but not upon their hearers as on the day of Pentecost, and as happens today. The promises to Israel don't include such a thing. The word 'revive' in the Old Testament has nothing to do with the revivals we talk about today.

Salvation was possible, of course. Before Christ many 'found grace in the eyes of the Lord', and were saved by grace. A covenant relationship with God was created, set up by faith. The Lamb was slain from the foundation of the world. His saving force back-dated itself from His work at Calvary to the times before He appeared.

But that is not the point. It is not a matter of individual salvation when we speak of revival but of God moving through a whole concourse, hundreds or thousands. The famous dictum of Jonathan Edwards runs: 'The characteristic of a revival is that a profound consciousness of sin is produced in many persons at the same time by an awareness of God.'

At Sinai the people of Israel were certainly aware of God. But they were not converted. They fled in terror. They were not even convicted of sin. In fact they sank into rank idolatry at the foot of Sinai while it shook under the weight of the Almighty. The first time God came in convicting power publicly was on the Day of Pentecost.

It could not happen before. *The keys of the kingdom which Christ said He was giving to the disciples had to be used first.* That is, the Gospel keys. It had to be preached 'with the Holy Ghost sent down from heaven' and on that day when Peter used the keys, the power of the Spirit swung open the door and 3,000 entered the kingdom. Until then revival was impossible.

This is precisely what Jesus taught. '*WHEN He is come, he will convict the world of sin, and of righteousness, and of judgment*' (John 16:8); THEN, and not until. The Holy Spirit is the Spirit of revival. In that case it is quite futile to look for examples of revival in an age when the Spirit of revival was not given. Let me say this to Bible students: any hermeneutic process by which things that could not then happen are read into the Old Testament times is obviously a curious one.

'If My People . . .'

The most frequently quoted text is 2 Chronicles 7:14: *'If my people, which are called by my name, shall humble themselves, and pray, and seek my face, and turn from their wicked ways; then I will hear from heaven, and will forgive their sin and will heal their land'*.

The previous verses explain what this meant. It referred to occasions when the countryside of Israel was laid waste by drought, pests, or cattle disease (vv. 12/13). The promise was quite plain. God would heal *their land*. It says nothing about saving souls. The conditions God laid down were that 'my people' should repent, turn from wickedness, humble themselves, pray, seek God's face. The result would be a restoration of their agricultural prosperity. This promise is in line with Deuteronomy 28, which contains nothing but physical blessings and cursings.

That is not all. The words 'my people' in this text represent the entire nation, not the Church, or even believers in Israel, but all Israel. God had chosen to call them His people. But no nation is God's people today, except Israel, and the spiritual Israel, the Church. If the whole nation repented their prosperity would return – nothing more. In fact if a whole nation repented and returned to God today any nation would have economic prosperity also.

It needs more than the Church to repent to heal a land. It needs everybody. There is no promise here that if 'my people' repent everybody else would repent. There would be no need if they had already all repented. If 'my people' needed to repent, start to pray, seek God's face, and give up their wicked ways and get forgiveness, then they were not God's people in the first place! In fact I would question whether it was His Church at all or ever had been, if it was in such a state of appalling need.

God's New Testament people are known because they have already departed from iniquity, have called, have repented, have sought God's face, and have been forgiven, according to the clear statement in 2. Tim.2:19. They could never be identified with the state of things envisaged in this verse in Chronicles. We are not perfect, but looking at the kind of wickedness which the prophets denounced, and which eventually did bring pestilence, drought and plague, how could we be so guilty and still claim to be the people of God? In the old economy things were different. By the covenant grace of God He chose to call them 'my people' though He did finally disown them according to Hosea 1:9, calling them *Lo-ammi* 'not my people'.

We must look further. There is nothing said here whatever about 'my people' praying for *the rest of the nation to be brought to repentance*. That is what we pray for in revival. ALL Israel, the entire nation, had to revive itself first before their land would be healed. The expression 'heal their land' did not remotely mean to save souls. They had come to God first for their land to be healed. God's people today pray for the nation to repent and be saved, which is right enough, but that is not in this text. It is only a promise that God would look after the state of the countryside.

I believe this promise is still for today. If any nation, Russia, the USA, Britain, or any other, ALL repented, as ALL Israel was told they must, then God would bless that nation in its economic enterprise, both in city and field. God made Israel His witness to the nations in this matter. However, Christian revival has a totally different meaning and motive. It is not to heal the land but purely to bring people back to God.

If Britain as a nation did what God said Israel must do, then there would be no need for the Church to pray for revival, for the whole country would have forsaken is wicked ways. Surely that IS revival. However that is quite different from what this text promised Israel.

There is no doubt, of course, as we have just mentioned, that a truly state-wide revival of religion would bring enormous economic benefits. And that was the aim of revival in Israel. I certainly would hope that our prayers for revival have a higher motive. Is prosperity the reason for repentance? That is all this text is about. I am quite puzzled to know how 2 Chronicles 7.14 can possibly relate to religious revival in a Christian land. It has nothing to do with Holy Ghost awakenings today.

Another text familiar to revivalism is Habakkuk 3:2, words quite fitting for Christians today: '*O Lord, I have heard thy speech, and was afraid: O Lord, revive thy work in the midst of the years made known; in wrath remember mercy*'.

It is surely obvious that Habakkuk had no concept of Holy Ghost revival as we know it. There is not a word in his prophecy which betrays the slightest notion of it. The 'revival' he asks for is something very different indeed.

The prayer of Habakkuk takes up the last of the three chapters in this prophecy. Habakkuk's concern was this. He had seen with dismay that Chaldean heathen invaders had attacked Israel. How could God allow it? He protests to the Lord. Why was God not working to defend Israel? Then God answers him. '*I will work a work in your days*'. What work? The work of the Chaldean armies which God was using for His purposes. Habakkuk is shown that the Chaldeans were the Divine instrument. God is behind this strange outbreak of wrath, it is the Divine work by which He is warning Israel. Then God will deal with the Chaldeans after they have served His purpose.

Habakkuk understands. He is stirred. He approves this strange work. That is Habakkuk's act of faith in God's mysterious providences. He sees the righteousness of God in it. Then Habakkuk declares he will trust God's judgement of Israel saying: 'Though the fig tree shall not blossom, neither shall fruit be in the vines: the labour of the olive shall fail, and the fields shall yield no meat; the flock shall be cut off from the fold, and there shall be no herd in the stalls: yet will I rejoice in the Lord, I will joy in the God of my salvation (3:17–19).

When Habakkuk comes to this point in understanding the Lord's use of the Chaldean invaders, then he says 'Revive thy work'. What work? The work God has shown Habakkuk He is doing. Habakkuk wants it kept in full operation. No longer did the prophet pray for Chaldea to withdraw, but that God would renew and revive what He was doing through them. The events he had feared he now saw must go on, and his reaction is 'Lord, keep alive what you are doing', although it was an outpouring of wrath. He had one request further '*in wrath remember mercy.*'

If this tells us anything as Christian believers it is THAT GOD IS AT WORK. It is a mistake to think He slumbers until a revival breaks out. When it doesn't even look like it, and war sweeps over the world, He is fully involved.

We often pray 'Lord revive Thy work'. No harm in that. But we don't mean what Habakkuk meant, judgment. Further we don't ask God to 'revive' HIS OWN efforts, as this prophet asked. When we pray the same words we are not asking THE LORD to revive – I hope - but we are asking Him to revive PEOPLE.

There is also the expression 'Thy work'. What we mean is Christian faith, the churches, the establishment of the truth. The term is lifted direct from this text, but Habakkuk had no knowledge of what we call 'thy work'. OUR church work has somehow come to be popularly described as 'the work of God'. But that is is not what Habakukk prayed for.

Revivalistic teaching today turns to 'revivals' recorded in Old Testament history. Spiritual renewal is found right from the book of Genesis with the Hebrew patriarchs. For example, Jacob had come to terms with God, and become 'Israel'. For years God has sought Jacob, and he called God 'the God of Abraham and my father Isaac'. But at last the Lord became his God too, 'the God of Abraham, Isaac and Jacob'. God had chosen to be Jacob's God. Then Jacob ordered his household: '*Put away the strange gods that are among you. And they gave Jacob all the strange gods and Jacob hid them under the oak which was by Shechem*'. Jacob's personal experience led him to give orders to his family and servants.

Indeed the Bible story is one of constant renewals, right through the books of Judges, Samuel, Kings and Chronicles (about which I will have positive things to say presently). Nevertheless to compare them with the wonderful movings of the Spirit in the Christian era would be far-fetched interpretation. We must 'rightly divide the Word of truth', or our use of Scripture will only leave us struggling and mystified, which is how things are with many people on the whole question of revival.

These happenings in ancient Israel were not outpourings of the Holy Spirit. That is the essential difference. Under various kings of Judah, such as Jehoash and the priest Jehoiada, Hezekiah, Uzziah and Josiah, to varying degrees the worship of the Lord was restored in Judah. It was, however, by order, not by will of the people as a popular religious awakening by any means. These events were no more than a change of royal policy. The Lord of course honoured the kings for it, and their faith enabled them to bring a measure of prosperity and security to the country for which God held them responsible. But in the vital public area, the hearts of their subjects changed little.

The Temple rites and ceremonies were restored, but during the best reigns, the state of the nation generally angered God. Isaiah prophesied during the reigns of Uzziah and Hezekiah, and described Judah as a *'sinful nation, a people laden with iniquity, a seed of evil-doers, children that are corrupters'*, and declares *'the whole head is sick and the heart faint'*. God called the land 'Sodom'. As for the ritual worship He said *'To what purpose is the multitude of your sacrifices unto me? Bring no more vain oblations; incense is an abomination unto me. Your hands are full of blood.'*

The prophet Hosea was contemporary with Isaiah and his word to Israel described it as worse than adulterous, as like a common whore. Amos and Micah followed in similar vein. Jeremiah, too, prophesied during the reign of that remarkable godly king Josiah who went to great lengths to renew the religious state of his realm. But the prophet had nothing but warnings and condemnation for the country at large.

Whatever 'revival' there was, affected the moral and spiritual state of the people very little. It needed an outbreak of the convicting power of the Spirit of God, but none was ever seen. The Kings struggled on valiantly against the inertia of faithlessness and crude ignorance and idolatrous superstition in the hearts of the vast majority of their subjects. No wonder God showed such noble-minded monarchs some degree of honour.

God was at work, nevertheless, as we saw from Habakkuk. It is evident also in the fact that the Word of the Lord moved the prophets (2 Pet. 1:21.). He was working His purposes out through it all. Indeed what He did, He did for us *'upon whom are come the ends of the age'*. The prophets spoke of things for the days of privilege in which we live, and they desired to look into them but could not. After their day a vast change was coming. And had to come, because the Spirit of God is the Spirit of renewal, but was then not yet outpoured.

But it should be remembered that when the prophets thundered against Israel they were speaking to the nation God had chosen. Their words can be taken up and applied to nations today no doubt, but the situation is not the same – Israel were the chosen people, and Britain, or America or France are not. Israel is a witness to the consequences of rejecting or following the Lord for all nations. Countries today stand condemned for their wickedness, but the answer today is in the Gospel, not in their own self-efforts to reform, not in instructions by rulers or policy of government. Judgments and condemnation, reforms imposed by law never worked with Israel, and are not the true answer today. Today's Divine answer is the Good News of the Gospel, not thunderings and threatenings. Today is the day of the Spirit, and only through Him will the world be saved.

The hallmark of Pentecost is revival-evangelism, by the abiding resource of the Holy Spirit. The enormous potency of the presence of the Spirit is only matched by the enormous opportunity. The world has been free of major war for over forty years. A new generation has arisen. The present conditions are factors affecting society never dreamed of in our parents' days.

Men and women can be reached for God, if we try. It is not the mark of a true Pentecostal church to go smugly and snugly to church week by week and hope to reach the lost for Christ, without outreach. Nothing is done without trying. Once we begin, God begins. God goes when we go. Our response too often is 'O Lord move', when He is saying to us, 'O my people, move'. That is what He is waiting for us to do. Revival rests with us, revival-evangelism.

'So then the Lord Jesus, after he had spoken unto them, was taken up into heaven, and sat down at the right hand of God. And they went forth and preached EVERYWHERE, WHILE THE Lord worked WITH THEM and confirmed the message by the signs that attended it.'

As Smith Wigglesworth said 'The book of Acts of the

Apostles was written because the apostles acted'. *There is no other power beyond the Holy Spirit*. That is enough! If you have the Holy Spirit you have all the power possible, and it is a waste of breath to ask for more power – there's isn't any more, and by the baptism in the Spirit you have opened the dam gates for that power to continually flow through your life. You have it all with the Holy Spirit. He will match every demand made upon Him.

Revival came in olden days ONLY when men preached the Gospel. It is the one fact about revival today and for ever. It is time to change our evangelical language into Pentecostal language, Christ's language – 'Lo! I am with you always, even unto the end of the age'.

As you can hear any night in American television stories – '*Le's go! What are we waiting for?*'

7 Revival – Confusion

'Revival Power'?

Need we wait for revival? Some do wait, of course, and have waited a long, long time. They know what they want. 'I want that kind of blessing'. But is it what God has in mind at present? Could He have new purposes when we are praying, *'Lord, do it again'*?

We all want God's best, which it is taken for granted revival is. But has God got a best? If He has, who is to say what it is? Who dares to mark God's work 'Good', or 'Better', or 'Best'? Can we really suppose that God excels Himself occasionally? Can we pray 'Do your best Lord'?

'He Abides, The Comforter Abides With Me'

Before the Pentecostals, it was not realised that the whole church could be permeated by power constantly: soul-saving, conscience disturbing, and even miracle power. Many still think in pre-Pentecostal terms of 'revival power' coming from time to time.

We are told often enough that 'revival tarries'. Some speak of revival as the time when God 'enters the field', as if He otherwise sat on the sidelines. What IS God doing between so-called revivals? Anything? Surely He is. For myself I cannot conceive that He isn't doing His best, all the time. If He is we ought to go right along with the thing that is happening. We may as well!

Jesus said, *'My Father worketh hitherto, and I work'* (John 5:17). That is the present continuous, not the past definite. It would be rather surprising if God reached His peak a century ago, or any other time. It is in that light we ought to look at the whole subject of revival.

'A-A-Amen!'

'Revival' is linked in my mind with my first contact with Pentecost. There would have been no first contact at all but for the cunning contrivance of my mother. She landed me in a meeting, and wished she had not. It turned out to be too special. No preaching. ALL PRAYER! For revival. Thomas B. Barrett had been there the previous week. That cultured Pentecostal apostle to Europe had described the religious revival in Norway. This, he believed, could be attributed to prayer and he had convinced everybody that England could have the same thing by the same travail. So, the Sunday evening I went, they were travailing for a long, long time.

My reactions on this occasion were the same as if I had been parachuted into Tolkien's land of the Hobbits. What time-warp had put these un-Yorkshire-like specimens ashore in our commonsense part of the world?

Actually, the pastor wanted to re-create old-time revival conditions. Hours of exposure to it should, in theory, have overwhelmed my sinful heart. I was the right material for such an effect, being soundly UNconverted. But I sat out the session with bemused superiority. Around me were people mostly kneeling, many weeping, others leading the intercession, and everyone supporting with 'A-a-amen, A-a-men'. It reminded my not-so-innocent schoolboy mind of sheep.

Eventually my mother asked 'You didn't enjoy it, did you?' I confirmed the accuracy of her discernment, negative perhaps but justified. Actually, I was secretly glad I'd been. I'd got that over for life. Also I knew now what I was missing and that every Sunday I would have a further chance of missing it. Life held that comfort at least. What I was missing I wouldn't miss in the slightest.

That first exposure to revivalism could have been lethal to my religious interests – if I had had any. But slowly the discomforts filtered out of my system. Then some months later, as much in bravado as to please Mum, I ventured again, insulated by experience against the forthcoming infelicitous hour. I knew what to expect.

I was wrong. This time I walked into my first ordinary Gospel meeting. There were no revival prayers. It was beyond all my previous (two hours) experience. I was disarmed. Something surprised my defences and reached my soul. By the time it was over I wanted to be converted. That night, in the traditional way then, kneeling at the 'penitent form' before the whole congregation, I 'wept my way to Calvary', as they used to say.

How Long O Lord?

Thus my first contact with church had confronted me with the all-prevailing, urgent desire for 'revival'. There was not only Mr Barratt's account of Norway but what had happened in Wales in 1904–6, before I was born but then well within living memory. That event had lit in English churches unflickering hopes for the same thing. It is no exaggeration to say that revival had become motive, aim, and argument for almost everything done in the church. It majored on every prayer list week after week, year after year. So immediately after being converted I joined the ranks of those marching for revival.

Before me, generation had passed on to generation the burning desire for revival like the Olympic flame. Today, leaders are still urgently calling us to take steps for revival. Some present it as if it was their original idea prompted by the approach of the year AD 2001, or received by prophetic revelation. The works of Wesley, Finney and others are once more in vogue, and what has so often been said is being said again.

For over two hundred years the cry for revival has never ceased. For instance, an Assemblies of God magazine editorial in 1953 said: '*The need for a Revival of Religion is the burning question of the hour. Almost all religious journals carry articles stressing its importance.*' Unfortunately, that writer never saw happen what he believed was absolutely vital. Thirty-two years later his editorial was reprinted by a new editor, for a new generation, word for word, in the same magazine. The situation remained the same.

There is certainly one feature common to all revivalistic literature today, namely belief that we haven't got revival. *But the main stress is that prayer is the secret.* Those who have lived long enough would like me probably to feel that there has been enough prayer to bring back the age of Wesley two or three times. I wonder whether more prayer over certain prolonged periods was physically possible. A much-quoted statement runs that 'behind every religious revival can be traced a kneeling figure.' That is impossible to prove by any research but it is likely, as kneeling figures have been common enough and somebody somewhere has always been agonising in prayer for revival. But for the entire period I have lived they have not proved to be the secret of any duplication of the events of 1859 or 1904.

It is almost a traditional mark of spirituality to ask, 'Why does revival tarry?' It represents many a regular sermon, as if lack of revival was a standard Christian failure, like other endemic sins, pride, worldliness, or envy. If we suddenly had no more pride, or worldliness or revival what would preachers do? Suppose revival no longer tarried?

Preachers and writers rebuke us because revival (their idea of revival that is), hasn't come. We are judged guilty and undeserving. New Christian failures are constantly diagnosed. Considering how gross are the shortcomings they accuse Christians of today, will we ever see what our forefathers saw? We ordinary folk now are apparently so different from ordinary folk then. Or are we?

Is it now a mark of spirituality to believe we are a long way from revival? To discern the sins of the church shows how spiritual a man is.

Looking through a 1928 magazine I read of a city being moved in a Pentecostal crusade, 1,500 people had received Christ, miracles of healing been witnessed and a large congregation established. Yet, to my astonishment, there, directly on the facing page, the editor himself wrote 'The cry of us all is for revival. When will it come?', as if we must never pretend people like us could achieve it, and whatever we see it can't be revival.

It is like the tale about the shoe city. Everybody believed in shoes, talked of having them, deplored the fact they hadn't shoes, set up committees, factories, government departments, but only one back street shoemaker made any. Everybody else just sighed, 'Shoes – ah yes, shoes. They are our greatest need. Why indeed don't we have them?'

We need encouragement. Having myself pursued this hope through decades, perhaps I might dare to bring encouragement, and learn a few other things on the way.

God At Low-Key?

Let us start logically. If there's been no revival for about a century, hasn't God done anything at all? Surely He has. If He had not there would be no born-again people nor any evangelical churches. However that is met by the usual comment: 'There was great blessing, but it wasn't revival. The Holy Spirit is at work but not in revival power'.

That strikes me as an odd view of God. We are actually praying for God to arise *and do better!* It reminds me of a prayer offered in a Yorkshire village near my home. A member rose and said *'Lord, we want you to bless us, as we are not doing very well here. There's one thing though we are thankful for, and we do praise You for it, t'other chapel down the road isn't getting even as much blessing there as we are, 'ere'.*

Is it possible that God may be so much less energetic at some times than at others? Language like that was perhaps permissible in ancient Israel before the full knowledge of the character of God was revealed in Christ. Before Christ, the Psalmist did cry, *'Awake O Lord, why sleepest thou?'*, though even the Old Testament contains enough to put that into perspective.

A charismatic I heard as a special preacher in a Pentecostal conference this year seemed still to be living in the days of that Psalmist. He said *'We must pray to clear the skies above our land, and by our spiritual warfare push back and defeat the powers of darkness. Then God will rend the heavens to come down'*. I could not keep silent, I had to lean over to my nearest ministerial colleague and remark 'All these years I've lived in the belief that Jesus had already done all that. Does God really need our human efforts to get rid of the devil for Him before He can do anything? Are we getting the victory for Him or has He got it for us?'

To speak of God rising and entering the field may be just popular expression. There are times of extraordinary soul-saving power, after all, and we can call them 'revivals', for so they are. We need not be pedantic about mere terms. But when 'revival' is given an exclusive meaning as a superior act of God we want to know where in Scripture such unique blessing is promised.

Christ HAS already defeated the powers of darkness, has cleared the skies, and has rent the heavens and come down. Such things are the absolute core of His work and triumph. That is the Gospel. Why pray to do what He has done already? This kind of talk is pre-Christian, pre-Cross, pre-Resurrection and pre-Ascension. The Spirit of revival is the Holy Spirit, and He has come into the world, the 'Another', to abide with us. He has broken through the heavens and come down. The New Testament promise is glorious. The Holy Ghost has come. No longer is God paying visits to His people on rare occasions. He abides!

There is not a trace in Scripture of a Holy Spirit who is sometimes dormant. YOU CANNOT HAVE A DORMANT WIND OR A DORMANT RIVER. It is not in the nature of the Holy Spirit to lie low. '*The river of God is full of water*', we read. If the wind doesn't blow it isn't wind. The Bible actually uses the figure and word of wind for the Spirit to show us the fact of His ceaseless activity. Bible writers bring us a picture of God 'working mightily' at all times.

Nobody will ever come to the Lord and find Him at less than His best. James (1:17) assures us of that: '*Every good gift and every perfect gift is from above, and cometh down from the Father of lights, with whom is no variableness neither shadow of turning*'. A shadow appears on the sundial as the sun climbs across the sky. At noon the shadow disappears. But God never declines or rises, and no shadow crosses the sundial of God, because the Father of Lights is always at the zenith. God never changes or varies. There is 'no shadow cast by turning', for He remains at the meridian, constantly at the height of His glory and activity.

When Things Don't Happen

Thinking about revival, it doesn't look as if God is always the same. There does seem to be 'revival power' of a special kind manifested in spectacular fashion at times, which presently withdraws and becomes quiet. My old pastor used to drum it into our heads that 'God comes in waves!' He, too, was mainly drawing this conclusion from the ebb and flow of revival. He also transferred this conclusion to church life. He warned us never to miss a meeting, because 'you never know when God might really bless us in a mighty way'. We would say, 'The Lord was present today', as if He had a prior engagement elsewhere sometimes.

The habit is to draw our expectations from past events, past revivals as the criteria for future revivals. Their rise and fall is assumed to be a Divine pattern, the norm of spiritual life. These outstanding awakenings come and go so mysteriously. But why is it?

Sovereignty Of God

The Calvinistic explanation is that 'God acts in His sovereign will'. That is perfectly true of course. He does what He wants and when He wants. But He tells us what and when in His Word, which is precisely why He gave us the Word. His Word is His intention. He has committed Himself and will never repent.

It was my sovereign will to take unto myself a wife, and I remain married all the time, whether I feel I am or not. (Some people do feel they are married all the time!). What God willed in His sovereignty was that the Holy Spirit would be with us, always. And whether we feel it or not, He is here. There would be no more rending of the heavens from time to time as occasion demanded. By the will of God the heavens are open for ever. That was His sovereign commitment.

'Sovereign' doesn't mean unpredictable, inexplicable. 'Sovereign' means free, independent and supreme. The word is unfortunately used in exactly the same sense as volatile, without consistency. A ruler can be sovereign, independent and free, but quite predictable. Being reliable in his behaviour makes for stable government. Sovereign independence can be exercised in a dependable manner, and that is how God exercises His sovereignty. He is 'faithful'.

Of course, in the area of individual lives God chooses to call whom He will to do whatever He wills and with what gifts He wills. He could hardly reveal His will for each of us separately in Scripture nor treat us all like identical machines. There will be the element of mystery in His choice, and indeed there is in even our own human choice, which often mystifies our friends. However even then His general promises apply to each one, and are the sure foundations upon which we can build whoever we are.

The Bible gives me no impression of God acting like a temperamental prima donna which some interpretations of His ways suggest. *If His 'sovereignty' means what too often it is assumed to mean, that you cannot be sure what God will do, then I am bound to ask this question – what does His faithfulness mean?* There is consistency in God, not bafflement. He does new things, but He never wanted us to be uncertain about Him. God obviously has vast and cosmic counsel which is beyond us because it has really nothing to do with us. But, we are the heirs of salvation, and in what relates to us He does not wish to leave us guessing. *'He made known His ways unto Moses; His acts unto the children of Israel'* (Ps. 103:7).

The Bible is given us not to show His power only but His sovereign will. His plans are not unfathomable mystery. The revelation of God is there precisely to assure us of God and what He will do. *The word is His will.* Many passages are written expressly to make clear to us that He is unlike the erratic and irascible gods of the pagans. He is 'a God of faithfulness' keeping covenant and truth *ABOUT HIMSELF 'to a thousand generations'*.

Revival By Good Works?

Not everybody takes the Calvinistic view that revival times lie entirely in the mystery of the Divine will. There is an Armenianist conception that human action is needed, if only massive prayer.

I may first just remark that at present there is so much general and confused talk about revival that most ordinary folk think of it both ways. I have heard frequent urgings to pray for revival combined with references to God's sovereignty. This of course is completely contradictory. You can't have it both ways.

If God does things as and when He chooses in His inscrutable mind, then it is useless talking about conditions to bring revival. We cannot say with one breath Revival comes by the sovereign decision of God, and then next say that we must get down and pray for it. Is it supposed we can alter His mind?

Coming back to our main point, the absence of revival is put down to the failure of Christians, either failure to pray, or to live right, or some other circumstance. One of the sermons I remember from my early Christian days – I can see the preacher now – gave us the illustration of a small broken wire in his wireless set. (It shocked me to learn he had such a worldly thing as wireless in those days, such was my refinement of spirituality at 14!) All reception was rendered impossible by the tiny fault. So it would be with us, he said. A small doubt, glossing over a slight scruple, a flash of temper (a flash? I was volcanic!), a little dishonesty, even our unrealised faults and so on, and we could be cut off.

From that time I ceased to look up, never sure whether everything was all right between God and me. I had too many 'little things' like that, no matter how hard I tried. I could only sigh and ask God to forgive me night by night, without hope of God ever being able to make much of me. As for seeing revival . . . ! Well, I was saved. I had that consolation. But I lived by hard labour. I was saved by grace but tried to be sanctified by works.

'Hiding Places Of Power'?

There is a frightening inference that many feel. *If God only comes forth among us in revival, how many really know Him?* Does He keep Himself half hidden most of the time? If the absence of revival is an indication of His displeasure, then for a long time God has had something against us. That expresses the secret feelings of many.

From this have sprung introspective teachings, self-scrutiny, scrutiny of others, 'congregation bashing' and general disheartenment. Who is keeping revival back? Some individuals, and certainly some churches, lose confidence in their own spirituality. One can hear and read constant criticisms. The demand for repentance is never deep enough, never heart-searching enough. There are specialists who are very penetrating, very good at pointing out faults. It is their ministry to contrast our lives and our modern churches with the glory of the past. God gave revival and thus showed His pleasure with His people then and thus also His displeasure today.

Today in column after column, accusations are laid at our door – 'worldly, materialist, unsacrificing, loveless, disunited, prayerless, unsanctified, cold, careless about the lost, without a vision', and so on. There are publications which seem to be entirely devoted to this kind of heavy-handed censoriousness.

There are shepherds with a similar dispensation for barking like sheep dogs at their flock. Every possible fault is ruthlessly considered and services are joyless, unblessed. Members go home discouraged wondering if they are Christians at all. Their only self-protection is to deflect the pulpit arrows to their neighbours. It must be others causing the absence of revival power.

Either way, the church sinks into an impossible negative attitude. While they feel so unworthy there can be no faith, and while there is no faith even less happens. Expectations shrink and die in a descending vicious spiral.

Yet, if one travels, one wonders where all these people are that are keeping back revival. It sounds to me unkind to thousands that I personally know. Something is wrong. It may be a mark of my unspiritual lack of critical discernment, but I don't see the churches so blameworthy as some see them. Maybe there are things hidden from me which holier folk can detect.

But I'm not so sure. Recently I joined a fraternal gathering of a score of ministers bemoaning the difficulties in their church. I could only comment that when I was the same age as some of them, I too had great difficulties with members, but as I grew older I was amazed how much they had improved. My church problems cropped up less and less as my birthdays came.

Here are two facts. *First, the absence of an eighteenth-century type revival in the twentieth century does not prove the church is failing, nor that God is so hard to please. All God does is by grace, not works of man. Second that what we choose to call 'revivals' may be spasmodic, but God is not.*

Doctrine By Anecdote

This brings us to an important modern issue, experiential religion, that is teaching based on experience. I have pointed out that revival theory comes from revivals. One writer explains, that 'it is to these great awakenings of the past that we must turn to understand the workings of the Holy Spirit'. For those professing to regard the Bible as the source of all truth, this is rather a startling statement.

Humanly speaking it seems reasonable enough to look at one revival and then try to bring about the same result by the same conditions. Unfortunately it hasn't always worked, because we are looking in the wrong direction to understand the ways of God. Because revivals come and go mysteriously, the glory of the independence of God is stressed. But something is overlooked – there may be human conditions which we do not understand.

For example I heard Duncan Campbell admit that he was disappointed when his workers failed to carry the revival from the Hebridean islands to the Scottish mainland, and later to the East Midlands even when using the same approach. He made suggestions as to the cause, that it lay in Christians, but this undermined his own revival theory of God breaking forth in sovereign irresistible power. If God is like that there could then be no human cause for God not working.

Prayer A Common Factor?

Reading over and over the 'revival' records I found it difficult to recognise any common pattern except one feature, which

I shall point out later. *Invariably, prayer is regarded as the indispensable element*. But Finney, for example, rode on his horse into towns where nobody was doing any praying. Church attendance was negligible and churches closed. But people came, heard and were powerfully moved and converted. One can read of times when Christian dedication to bring about mighty movings of God's Spirit was seriously lacking but revival came. In comparison modern efforts to achieve similar phenomena have been massive, and sincere. I know this at first hand. However – have similar results followed? The cry is one of disappointment.

So, further conditions are laid down for revival. Often they are so demanding that to achieve them we would need revival first. Then we would have revival! *To do what is required to bring revival would BE revival!*

But previous awakenings do not always confirm that such stringent requirements were involved. Men of no great spirituality have been used by the Spirit. James Glendenning of Oldstone, Ireland for instance. Of him Ian R. K. Paisley said, 'the one chosen as the original channel of the great revival of those early days was the least worthy and competent of all the preachers of Ulster'. Yet, through his thunderings against sin and about law and judgement he says, 'multitudes were brought to understand their way and to cry out "What shall we do?".'

Nevertheless we are inspired by every account of the work of God in the past, when multitudes were saved and the very times changed. And of course we wish we could consult the leaders of such phenomenal periods and ask them how they did it. We assume they would know. They may themselves have thought they did. But did they really know? Can their writings tell us? Some of us cannot ourselves account for extraordinary things in our own spheres of ministry, at least by accepted canons.

So, here is the crux of the matter. To turn to revivals to find out the ways of God in revival is unsafe. We shall only confirm our pre-conceptions, and may find ourselves with views which are not Bible, even about God. This is a danger we shall look at in more than one chapter of this book, *the error of doctrine based on experience*.

Today is the age of religions of experience, Buddhism, Spiritualism, Yoga cults, mysticism, Transcendental Meditation and similar experience-orientated systems. What is real and unreal in Divine gifts and phenomena? What is behind the modern cult scene? Or behind men and movements in the church introducing frequent novelties? Good Christian people getting off-centre from the Cross, wonder-seekers, brought up on a diet of experience and experience-related teaching, instead of the Word, how much is trauma, nerves and nonsense?

Of all phenomena, perhaps none is so alluring as the wonders of classic revival power. The study of it also seems fully justifiable. But do we want doctrines founded on anecdotes? There is volume after volume appearing today in the religious lists full of teaching which may sound good, but it possesses no sanction from the Word of God.

Unfortunately Scriptural exposition has a limited sale compared to testimony and especially theories identified with particular authors. OUR EXPERIENCE ITSELF, HOWEVER EXCITING, MUST BE BROUGHT TO THE JUDGEMENT OF THE BOOK. *Experience may confirm the truth, but will never create it.*

8 Revival – Pentecostal Hallmark

'A Horrid Thing'

If the Archbishop of Canterbury were to scale Nelson's Column and bless everybody in Trafalgar Square from the top, it would not shock us today like the eighteenth century was shocked when the clergyman George Whitfield preached outdoors, and when the Anglican John Wesley proclaimed the Gospel standing on his father's tomb.

When Griffith Jones, the vicar of Landowror in Wales, preached outside his own church, inspiring his curate to do the same, followed by the great Howell Harris, it brought accusations of irreverence and 'enthusiasm'. The curate, Daniel Rowlands was called the 'cracked clergyman' of Llangeitho but he and Howell Harris became historic revivalists of the principality, and by that means makers of Wales.

Such unconventional behaviour was a scandalous sensation bound to attract multitudes, and mockery and abuse of course. But it merely gave the evangelists the opportunity they sought. They gained the attention of the country, and had only to preach the Gospel. The Gospel is power, and did its own work. Thousands turned to Christ with permanent benefits to Britain.

Revivalism gave Wales three things, hymns, theology and the best educational system of its time, said Dr J. Cynddylan Jones. It gave Wales its heart. Despite the healthy social consequences of revival, the British today have a jaundiced and paranoid attitude towards religion generally. Revival especially to them would be 'a horrid thing' as the Bishop of Bristol described it to Wesley, a religious overdose, either balmy or scurrilous.

In the past the smear word was 'enthusiasm', originally

applied to religious emotionalism of a fanatical type. 'Ill-regulated religious emotion or speculation', as the *Oxford Dictionary* defines it. To some folk, of course, all religious emotion is 'ill regulated' and 'enthusiasm', because they don't think there should be any. This is another dotty trait of the non-religious, who suffer from a petrified imagination to appreciate what a meeting with Christ is like. I wonder sometimes if they will end up like the soul in Dante's *Inferno* admitting '*I did not weep, so I became stone inside*'.

Nevertheless it is by outbursts of 'enthusiasm' that true religious impact is made. Christian renewal can invigorate the national spirit. The history of America, like the history of Wales, is the history of revivals of religion. France, for example, can only be understood when this fact is taken into account – it never experienced religious revival such as that which saved England two centuries ago. On the other side of the Channel, Protestant believers had been ruthlessly suppressed. France had no remedy for the ills of its body political. Rationality and robustness of character which would have stiffened the spine of France were eliminated. It was thus that it suffered the Revolution of 1789 and the subsequent Reign of Terror, corruption and financial ruin. It is claimed that it introduced liberalism and brought Europe into the modern age, but it was a liberalism which produced war after war for France. Twice it collapsed before German aggression. It had lost its spiritual stamina and had only a primal revolutionary instinct expressed in the familiar cry 'To the barricades'.

Britain had developed what has been called a 'radical-nonconformist tradition' and responds differently to crisis. If one wants a better comparison it might be between the fanatical dementia of vast Shi-ite mobs in Iran in recent years and the cool British reaction to such provocation. However, nonconformist and social decline set in from the First World War, bringing spiritual confusion. This has kept evangelicals in a state of urgent anxiety for revival. Restoration of a lively Christian faith is daily more urgent if Britain too is not to sink into moral senility.

But what kind of religious revival? The type usually thought about is 'the mixture as before', 'the old-time religion' chain-reaction of dramatic religious outbursts across the land. But that still looks as unlikely as Britain exporting bananas. Time after time people have told us they see 'signs of coming revival', but usually it has been a mirage. Discouragement is apparent.

However, all is not dark. There are facts to face which should cheer a lot of people up. For years I personally have not seen things so pessimistically. 'Now is our hope nearer than when we believed', as I shall explain.

'Graveyard' Resurrection

It will be useful to refer to one small book which typified the outlook of the evangelical world and maybe still does. That is Rene Monod's excellent account of *The Korean Revival* (1969). It describes Christian communities in Europe as 'graveyards'. He counts only four 'revivals' this century, all in non-European countries, Korea, Uganda, Formosa and Indonesia. The best the writer can point to in the West is that 'congregations of devout and faithful Christians (are) still to be found'. He mentions 4,000 in a Los Angeles church, and isolated 'oases of spiritual life' in Paris, Vienna, Spain, and Germany. In Britain only the Westminster Chapel, London, gets any spiritual credit.

He points out that the last great revival of the West took place in Wales in 1905 (actually 1904–6), except for the 1949 Hebrides awakening which 'had no effect on the country as a whole'. Rene Monod is appalled to find only 200 in a Cathedral of 60,000 'members'. (Appalled? I would have been cheered to see so many myself!) Otherwise this writer mentions no powerful religious movements. He knew of 'extreme' sects – which could be the Pentecostals but apparently up to no good!

That is how many saw the situation in 1971 when the book was printed in English. Things then did seem difficult. In those years I was a member of a national evangelistic planning committee. Every means we could devise to get efforts under way seemed to be frustrated. 'The swinging sixties' gave us the cold shoulder at every turn. Bingo fever block-booked every available hall and venue where we might have begun pioneering, property prices were just blasting off to the Van Allen belt, churchmen spoke up for a dirty book, Bultmann and

Tillich theology undermined Christian belief – popularised in *Honest to God*, giving the nation an excuse for not believing the Gospel. The collapse of culture came with the Beatles, Rock, and drugs. What was left of our spiritual reserves were dribbling away fast.

The Quiet Revival

But, strangely Rene Monod's book has a foreword by Billy Graham, who had had more than one God-blessed national crusade in Britain, the first in 1954, which Rene Monod apparently had overlooked, as well as his world-wide ministry. At age 70, *Time* credits him with 2.2 million converts. These were tremendous efforts by thousands of churches backing Billy Graham as their evangelist. They affected the entire religious situation. Processes were sparked off which today see more than half the Anglican clergy veering to evangelicalism – *it was the quiet revival*. Statistics continued to show decline for years, but began to improve slowly. In 1987 the general trend reversed. Long before then, however, many churches had become centres of continuous conversion and blessing.

Pentecostal Revival

Rene Monod and others discounted much more – vastly more in fact. Things were happening, but not being 'classical' revival they were not given particular notice. It was not what they were looking for. Yet revival had come, the Pentecostal revival and its offspring the Charismatic movement. Its claim to be revival was not given any consideration, but it is time it was, unless we have cataracts on our religious vision.

This Korean mentioned the communities of the Brazilian Established Church in Rio de Janeiro and Blummenau enjoying fruitfulness in Brazil, but that was in fact nothing compared to the burgeoning Pentecostal movement in Brazil, and in all South America long before that time. E. H. Robertson had moved through South America at the invitation of the United Bible Societies ten years before Monod had bemoaned the absence of revival, and had drawn attention to these gathering forces in his book *Tomorrow is a Holiday* (SCM, 1959) Robertson said (pp. 103–4), 'these Pentecostals . . . alone attract the simple and poor people in large numbers. If the Assemblies of God can continue to do this and instruct in Bible knowledge, they hold the future of Latin America in their hands'.

I myself felt that the early Billy Graham crusades were a challenge to our Pentecostal claims to have received the baptism in the Spirit for evangelism, and wrote about it. I soon had a response from American Pentecostal editor and author Gordon Lindsey. I knew that the mass organisation of united church crusades backing Billy Graham as their invited preacher was different from the crusades of George Jeffreys opposed by the churches yet still filling every great hall in Britain. Gordon Lindsey then gave me the news of one lone, unsupported Pentecostal's enterprise. He had tackled President Peron for permission to evangelise in the Argentine. At Buenos Aires a crusade began which drew crowds climaxing at 400,000, and conversions resulted in 140 new churches being founded. So far as I can find, no classical revival ever had such an effect.

E. H. Robertson (no fundamentalist) only a few years later visited Buenos Aires and spoke in Pentecostal churches which were filled regularly with revival crowds. He visited one founded by an enthusiastic new Pentecostal convert which had grown to 2,000 by 1957.

One often reads challenging words that if we really get down before God as we should we might see what Peter saw on the day of Pentecost when 3,000 asked for salvation. Yet, in a book called *Holy Spirit Evangelism*, which I have authored with Reinhard Bonnke, we tell of tens of thousands coming to Christ in a single meeting. In one case, at Blantyre, Africa, this fulfilled a prophecy by David Livingstone that where he was winning individuals men would follow to win thousands. He sowed, Bonnke reaped.

In *Cry for me Argentina*, published in 1988, R. Edward Miller described his attempted crusade at Lavalle, Argentine, in 1949, which never drew a congregation despite every possible effort. Yet, within a short time he saw the preaching of the Pentecostal message break through the prejudice and the scene changed. Churches were springing up and he speaks of tens of thousands being healed who before had no idea of a living Christ. Glorious Divine phenomena, visions, miracles and an awesome sense of the direct presence of God, had been experienced across the area where he worked.

This is the account of only one man in the Argentine and there are many more. The latest information is that the churches there cannot contain the people who come seeking God. I am just adding to my Statistics File an account of a Buenos Aires Pentecostal church which was started twelve months ago and now numbers 1,600, and of Gerald Holloway, a missionary, beginning a congregation in Manila, Philippines, seven years ago which now has 6,000 attending in two venues.

Argentina is only one part of a revival whose magnitude eclipses anything ever known, not only in Latin America, but girdling the globe, persisting, increasing, possessing its own in-built power for perennial renewal. The second largest USA Pentecostal denomination claiming to be the oldest, reported an increase of 1,100 new churches and 150,000 new members in North America alone in two years. Even in England, churches I remember as having regular attendances of six, are climbing towards the thousand mark.

Pentecostalism is capable of thriving without leadership, and therefore is hard to deal with by persecuting governments. Its natural habitat is underground. It can persist against the most obdurate hatred in any country on earth. It is not worried about organisation, therefore is not vulnerable; it is a spontaneous fire breaking out in a thousand places at once. In this respect, and in other respects we trust, Pentecost bears the same hall-mark as first-century Christianity. There is only one way to describe it, and God uses Joel to say the words, 'I will pour out of my Spirit upon all flesh'.

The River Flows

People used to pray for 'showers of blessing'. Today the river flows. This revival is no mere religious excitement breaking upon an area and then after a while leaving the ground dry and waiting for another downpour. A hundred years ago they spoke of the necessity for regular revivals as the proper pattern for church growth, but one now has to think in entirely different terms. The Times of extraordinary public interest and what Finney called 'excitements' will come, but they will come simply because the ocean-tide of the Spirit is irresistibly flooding in across every shore. IF WE ARE STILL PRAYING FOR 'A' REVIVAL WE SHOULD REMEMBER IT WOULD BE PART ONLY OF THE WORLD-WIDE PENTECOSTAL REVIVAL HAPPENING NOW.

There was not a single person calling themselves Pentecostal when many older people with us today were born. Yet in 1986 statistics spoke of over 250 millionCharismatic-Pentecostals. In view of this one wonders how much more extensive such Christian success would have to be before we stop asking, 'Why does revival tarry?' Is it tarrying, or is it just not what some people think revival is? If this is not revival, what is?

Here is a revival that does not pivot on a revivalist figure, such as Whitfield, Evan Roberts and the rest. The Pentecostal movement has never had a world-figure or even a national leader. It has the original characteristic of Christianity: *'And they went forth, and preached everywhere, the Lord working with THEM, and confirming the word with signs following'*. In many, many places, ordinary people are filled with the Spirit and faith, reaching out with joy, and finding revival forces within themselves as they witness and work. Here is not only the Christian hallmark, but the true hallmark of Pentecost – evangelism.

If we want revival this is it, and it is useless looking for a different, non-Pentecostal revival. If Britain or Europe is to experience spiritual restoration, God has shown us the way He is working, and unless we work along with Him, we shall struggle. Revival tarries when we do not accept the revival God sends.

Why It Tarried

The tragedy is that it was rejected in the first place. Outstanding evangelical leaders in Britain, men of calibre and godliness, who believed in revival power nevertheless either stood aloof or opposed the Pentecostals when experienced leadership was needed. To look through old files of excellent Christian papers it is saddening to see illustrious names at the top of graceless attacks upon Pentecostal believers. One does not need a very good memory to recall the surprise when a Pentecostal writer was given space in the columns of any Christian publication.

Someone once challenged me, 'You can't blame those outside the Pentecostal movement for its shortcomings'. It dawned on me, with a sense of shock and dismay that I could only give one answer: 'I'm afraid we can. Those not in the movement are responsible for much in it or not in it. They ought to be in it. That is the very thing that went wrong. God desired the entire evangelical world to be part of the Pentecostal witness. Regrettably many refused to have anything to do with it. And we needed them.'

I confess that my heart aches as I look back. Could we have had a revived church and nation before the First World War? Or was God's revival rejected looking for a different one? If it had been recognised that this was the end-time promise of the deluge of the Spirit with the gifts of the Spirit and had ministered as Jesus did to the sick, and if the hundreds of fine churches had swung into mid-stream of Holy Ghost blessing, no Pentecostal church would have been necessary. And – I tremble as I wonder – what effect would a nation-wide Pentecostal revival touching the entire life of Britain have had upon the future course of events and of international conflict?

What happened? Instead, *religious decline accelerated at the very moment when this revival was turned down by the churches generally*. That was inevitable. This was the new thing of the Spirit for the age of change – the vastest changes humanity had ever known. The pattern of European thinking was changing, and the Pentecostal style was created for the new era and by it, a new way for a new era. The old axe would not go to the root of the tree. God knew the shape of things to come, and gave tools for the task, but they were left unused until too late – or is it too late?

Only 'One Winter'?

In his novel *One Winter of the Holy Spirit*, Tom Davies describes the Welsh Revival and represents Evan Roberts as saying God has shown him that what was happening was not just for Wales, but was to cross every ocean and continent. He may well have said this, I do not know. But Evan Roberts' words in fiction or actuality, are true. The revival was to have a global embrace. In some strange providence of God the little land of Wales was chosen as a place to play a vital role in the world-revival of Pentecost already touching forty times more people than the entire Welsh population. The last revival in Britain was a bridge between the era of classical local revivals and the charismatic-Pentecostal world revival.

Mrs Penn-Lewis put her finger on one reason. She wrote that one of the outstanding features of the Welsh Revival was that

Much importance is attached to the work of the Spirit . . . 'Heretofore the work of Christ has been the all-important truth to the exclusion to a large extent of the doctrine of the Spirit. Much emphasis has been laid on receiving Christ, scant stress on receiving the Spirit'. Now however the question coming to the forefront is: 'Have ye received the Holy Ghost since ye believed?' There were thousands of believers in our churches, who like the disciples St Paul met at Ephesus, had received Christ, but had never received the Holy Ghost. The present (Welsh) revival, however, whilst not obscuring the doctrine of the Cross, has brought into prominence the doctrine of the Spirit.

In that case the Welsh Revival was embracing at last the secret of constant revival, and was moving into the present age of world-Pentecostal revival.

Mrs Penn-Lewis also wrote:

The Pentecostal character of the awakening in Wales is unmistakably clear . . . the wider fulfilment of Joel's prophecy is at hand. Undoubtedly we are in a new era of the world's history, when we may expect supernatural workings of God such as have not been known since the days of the primitive church (*The Awakening in Wales*, p. 63).

This was surely a prophetic insight, now fulfilled, showing the link between the principality of Wales and the movings of the Spirit across the face of the nations today.

Pentecost

The fire in Wales drew many, like Moses in the wilderness, to *'turn aside and see this strange sight'*. Among them came Dr F. B. Meyer, Dr G. Campbell Morgan, the Rev Alexander Boddy, and Squire Cecil Polhill. Another was the American Baptist Holiness preacher Joseph Smale. The latter returned not only to pray for revival in his town but also determined to hand over the reins of services to the movings of the Spirit and the promptings of the people as in Roberts' meetings. He saw this spontaneity as the essential pattern of revival. A visitor to Smale's church was Frank Bartleman who had corresponded with Evan Roberts and drawn a promise from him to pray for Los Angeles.

Dr Meyer visited the USA and also stirred up interest, and even more effective was Dr G. Campbell Morgan's written account, and S. B. Shaw's booklet *The Great Revival in Wales*.

In April 1901 a handful of Holiness believers had enjoyed the first Pentecostal shower and had spread the word widely. After six years it was, however, not widely noted. Nor was it when the famous Azusa Street, Los Angeles, meetings began. It needed a fillip. That fillip came with the news of the Welsh revival through Drs Morgan and Meyer, Frank Bartleman, Joseph Smale and others.

Those who had been in Wales discerned that the same Spirit was present in Azusa Street. Mrs Elizabeth Pisson in San Francisco heard of the Welsh Revival and declared she heard the Lord saying, *'This is not a Welsh Revival, this is the beginning of a world-revival. Wilt thou not be a factor in world-revival?'* Frank Bartleman wrote, long after his first visit to Azusa Street, *'The present world-revival (Pentecost) was rocked in the cradle of little Wales. It was "brought up" in India, becoming full grown in Los Angeles later.'* His reference to India concerns the marvellous Pentecostal manifestations in the work of Pandita Ramabai, not as a result of her hearing about Azusa Street but following the news of the Welsh Revival.

End-Time Revival

Another vital link between the Welsh and Pentecostal revivals
was provided by two other men, Pastor Thomas B. Barratt and
the Anglican clergyman Alexander Boddy. Both were deeply
inspired by the Welsh happenings. Mr Boddy later heard that
Thomas Barrett had been baptised in the Holy Spirit after
meeting people from Azusa Street in New York. He wrote to
him and eventually met him in Norway. The Rev Boddy then
invited him to Britain. In Mr Boddy's parish the Pentecostal
blessings fell and from there the main thrust of Pentecostal
ministry began in this country. Squire Cecil Polhill also gave
the work the weight of his own influence and help, recognising
that what he saw in the Alexander Boddy conventions was a
continuation of what had happened in Wales.

There are, of course, those who want nothing to do with all
that the Pentecostals stand for. Nothing yet ever had universal
assent. But the situation as I write in 1988 is that the teaching
of the Holy Spirit as presented from the beginnings of the
movement, has reached everywhere in the Church. Born-again
believers generally know the need of a Pentecostal experience.
The Baptism in the Spirit is a renewing force beyond anything
ever previously taught or experienced. *Understanding is clear
that this is what Christ promised and that this baptism is part of
normal Christian life*. It is not the acceptance of a doctrine or
theory such as the Keswick teaching, but is an objective blessing
with an objective sign, speaking with tongues.

One reads the gripping accounts of past revivals where fire
fell in the dark discomforts of the pre-technological age. As a
boy, I often wished myself there in the early Methodist class
meeting or revival 'love feast' in some cottage or country chapel
lit by candles or oil lamps, warmed by a wood stove, to which
humble folk had come through winter weather, singing the
meaty hymns of the revival. I used to imagine God could not
do today what He used to do because those kind of people
no longer existed. They were of a different mould from my
generation, and more easily brought into salvation, but my soul
burned with the glory of such accounts.

However, behind me as I write is a file drawer, packed with

figures and stories collected over the last few years, of incredible movings of the Holy Spirit in this space age, enough to fill this and several chapters. Indeed the college libraries are swollen with histories and statistics pouring in from every continent every day, of what God is doing in supernatural power.

When did Whitfield, Wesley, or any such worthy men speak face to face with 100,000 or 200,000, or half a million, or more? Spurgeon is famed because he preached to 6,000 night and morning in the Metropolitan Tabernacle, every Sunday. But today is an age of the super-church. Ten thousand is not the peak, but figures soar into several ten thousands of members, and one in Korea of over half a million.

We know that criticism is possible, especially that the number of people coming forward to receive Christ in no way is reflected in the strength of churches. This is both true and not true, depending on vastly differing circumstances. Yet it has always been so. Great concern was expressed about the 'low quality' and swift falling away of Finney converts, some declaring that only one in ten continued their Christian life. It was reported some time ago that the D. L. Moody campaigns yielded even less percentage of church members than the Billy Graham crusades. But comparisons based only on church membership are perhaps not the way God sees things at all.

Again, when I was a boy, reading of Hudson Taylor, and living in Hull I went to gaze at the cottage on Drainside where he lodged, and every time I went to my church I walked past Kingston Square where he worked with a doctor. What burnings within my soul the story of that heroic and godly founder of the China Inland Mission stir up! But this is the new age, when Pentecostal fire has fallen in mainland China, and reports stagger one's imagination as the fire of God leaps from heart to heart and village to village, reaching millions where once early missionaries were glad to reach individuals, but without whose work nothing would now be done.

The time has come for which great men worked, laboured and prayed. They sowed, we planted, but now God is giving the increase. The mighty gifts of the Spirit adorn the hand of the Church. She is His bride to be adorned with all the Bridegroom's gifts, ready for His coming.

'Some will say, "This awakening in Wales should shake the world!" Yes and it will shake the world within the limitations we see following the first Pentecost'. (*The Awakening in Wales*, p. 70)

9 Revival – Evangelism

There may be evangelism without revival, but there can be no revival without evangelism; although not everybody will agree perhaps.

There is a passage by J. Cynddylan Jones which I have written out slowly and by hand, to savour it, from Mrs J. Penn-Lewis' *The Awakening in Wales*. It carries high sentiments but there's something about it from which my instincts shy away.

> Revival is independent of all human organisation, straight from heaven. Missions are not revivals. Men can organise the former, not the latter and it is a pity the distinction should be overlooked. Man's method of saving the world is by costly and complicated machinery – salvation by mechanics; but God's method is vital energy – salvation by dynamics.

Much of this may be true . . . but on what authority is it said? How much of it carries the authority of Scripture, and how much is opinion, or how much is simply popular sentiment? The tenor of this is echoed constantly and it seems to me that Revival has produced its own theology and no theology has achieved greater dogmatism. It also produces some obvious questions. We must look at them.

Are Missions Revivals?

For instance, if revival is independent of human organisation does God only bless us when we are UNorganised? And is it true that 'man's method of saving the world is by costly and complicated machinery'? Why this concern about money anyway? Is cost a consideration against the eternal destiny of one soul? What is money for? But how many efforts to save the world can afford costly and complicated machinery? Certainly not mine! Nor the efforts of most of my colleagues. In a lifetime I have participated in none either, unless Billy Graham's crusades are described in those terms. In fact thousands of evangelistic endeavours are made by Pentecostals in which cost and complicated organisation are minimal – by choice!

'Missions are not revivals'? Certainly some are not. They are more like recruitment campaigns; 'sign on the dotted line'. I have heard 'Gospel appeals' conducted which reminded me of days long past when I earned my living as a qualified member of the Incorporated Society of Auctioneers and Landed Property Agents. Like this: 'Is there another? Who'll be number six? Six? Thank you yes, now seven, seven, yes, will anybody make it eight, eight, where's number eight?. . . . Have you all done? Ah – thank you number eight, eight, and now who'll make it nine anybody. . . .'!

With a bland message about the 'way of salvation' meaning no more than the way to heaven, and hopes for the help of the Holy Spirit but without fire – a mission is not likely to be a revival. Not long ago a minister wrote to me asking if I didn't think it wrong to advertise a 'Revival Crusade'? I replied as follows: *'Tell me why it is wrong and I'll tell you if it is wrong. I don't know any law about it, and there is certainly none in Scripture. Is a crusade by definition not a revival? Doesn't God like crusades? Can you tell me what revival is – and is not? Isn't it a matter of opinion?'*

I am aware that organisation can run to extremes. A colleague remembered George Jeffreys in one London area with a quartet of workers. They booked a hall and went ahead despite the general disapproval of the churches. In a few weeks the result was that people in numbers running well into four figures came to Christ, leaving a permanent church of over 500 members. In contrast, some years later my friend supported a non-Pentecostal crusade in the same hall. He said that months of 'complicated and costly' preparation found him and every member of a dozen committees carrying a heavy file of documentation as the main basis for expected results. His own church gained nothing from it.

If the Spirit of God is at work then some organisation is necessary, *'Bring of the fish which ye have now caught'*. This is an applicable Biblical principle. It ought not to be that *'their nets break'*. One of the most God-blessed evangelists was Stephen Jeffreys, who between the two world wars saw conversions on a scale greater than in any Welsh revival service, as well as mighty miracles of healing. Indeed Stephen was converted in the Revival and his Crusades (called campaigns then) must certainly be considered an extension and continuation of it, wherever he went, in America, England, South Africa.

However Stephen organised nothing, and results were dissipated. It was revival without organisation – *unfortunately*. His brother George sometimes took over from Stephen and with a genius for organisation conserved the results, as well as those from his own crusades, from which has come one of Britain's main Pentecostal groups today.

Nevertheless cost and machinery do not quench the Spirit, and may sometimes be the only way. Evangelistic endeavour loses nothing of the 'vital energy of salvation by dynamics' which Dr Jones demands, for the sake of spending money and making proper arrangements. What else are church offerings for?

Further, God has given evangelists as His gift to the Church. They should get on with their job. I don't know how any evangelist can do his job without conducting missions. His is a missioning work. Evangelists and missions go together, and can hardly be separated, so why not revival also?

'Preach The Word'

I mention revival again because I have no choice if I talk about evangelism. They cannot be separated. THIS IS THE ONE COMMON FACTOR IN REVIVALS – PREACHING THE WORD, OR IF YOU LIKE, EVANGELISTIC EFFORT. I don't know of any classical revival of the past without evangelism. That is all most revivals were, missions, evangelism, some man's enterprise and boldness. The sweep of God's power was rarely spontaneous but came by preaching. *The revival began and existed in the soul of an evangelist.* Over the door of the George Whitfield Memorial Church, Gloucester, is carved, *'The love of Christ constraineth me to lift up my voice like a trumpet*'. And George Whitfield was a Calvinist! Revival went where he went, to the last flicker of his life as, holding a candle in his hand, he preached from the upstairs of the house where, in the morning, his kneeling figure was found.

Usually, by some means, often the visit of the evangelist himself, or some other related event such as a plague, or crisis, a public excitement was created and crowds came together. The causes of revival must include the causes which created the excitement and the crowds. Then comes the evangelistic message. Causes of interest may be numerous, and may simply be the social conditions. But the immediate cause of conviction and conversion has never been mysterious, as if a cloud unexpectedly descended from heaven. It has always been the Word of the Gospel – evangelism.

The Word itself is power. *Where the Gospel is preached there is no need for Dr J. Cynddylan Jones to worry about the 'vital energy of salvation by dynamics'. It will be there exactly as Scripture says – 'The Gospel is the power of God unto salvation'.* It is not the power of God only in times of revival, but at all times. Paul knew that wherever he went he would go *'in the fullness of the blessing of the Gospel of Christ'*. And why not? Christ commanded us to go into all the world and added, *'Lo I am with you always, even unto the end of the world'*.

I wonder, if Christ is with us always, who are we to make a distinction between one Christian enterprise and another? Especially I ask, are we to put a premium on NO enterprise? Are we to value only a purely fortuitous religious upheaval? Does God despise evangelism, and only bless us when we organise nothing, and shun the sacrifice involved in 'costly and complicated' effort?

The presence of Christ is surely all anybody can ask, and that is guaranteed, in full measure, never in varying degrees.

To think about the great awakenings of the eighteenth century or any other time, is to name certain men who preached the Word. Whitfield, just mentioned, was himself actually called 'The Awakener'. Revivals followed preaching, first and foremost, even when praying was not too conspicuous. I do not mean preaching to a hundred long-converted sermon tasters at a bourgeois event called a Gospel meeting. I mean preaching to unconverted crowds. Whitfield preached even at fairs.

Reading that Evan Roberts sat with his head in his hands for a couple of hours in a service letting the Spirit move, I suppose there might well be such meetings. But not normally. And it happened too often maybe with Evan Roberts. The 'Word' which converted so many was often the message of the Welsh language hymns only. A strong criticism of the Welsh Revival was its lack of the Word of God, making the latter part of it more a revival of Welshness and emotion, and its fires burned down too quickly.

A Welsh nationalist spirit was a factor in this wonderful period. God can use that kind of thing. Efion Evans says of revivals in general: 'Many factors were involved, sometimes singly and separately, at other times unitedly . . . remarkable providences, sacramental occasions, revival reports, fast days, prayer meetings, as He willed.'

The Welsh revival came at a critical time when the Welsh language was beginning to feel the heavy threat of English and of English immigrants. The chapels and the hymns had always been the stronghold of the language. The crowds which came in were bound to have sensed that this was an invigoration of the bastions of national culture. The chapel, the language, the hymn-singing added to the fervour and the willingness to accept the revival.

If by 'revival', we mean 'revivalism', that is reliance upon powerful outbreaks of contagious emotion, then, generally, it cannot be organised, that is true. But is that a recommendation of it, or a criticism? Is it a proof of a Divine event when something is beyond control?

Previous Welsh Revivals followed in the track of preachers, such as John Elias, Christmas Evans, Daniel Rowlands, Howell Harries, David Morgan and Humphrey Jones. Humphrey Jones' human and emotional input was so great that after three or four months, in 1859, he was a nervous wreck and never could preach again, rather like Evan Roberts in 1905.

Efion Evans in *Revivals* (Evangelical Press of Wales, 1986) declares: ' . . . *supremely it was the preaching of the Word which He (the Holy Spirit) especially countenanced. Jonathan*

Edwards, the Tennents, George Whitfield, John Wesley, Daniel Rowland and others like them were called and equipped primarily to preach, and it was in the capacity of preacher that each was most signally blessed and most widely used'.

The Word Of The Cross

John Elias preached from a bedroom window to thousands on the day of a horse race that gathered crowds. Some said they felt the ground rock beneath their feet as his *hwyl* rolled like thunder across the multitude. It was a message of denunciation, full of the terrors of judgment, like that of Jonathan Edwards' famous revival sermon, 'Sinners in the hands of an angry God'. *But central to all revival preaching was the message of the Cross. It had to be, or there was no message.*

Mrs Penn-Lewis speaks of prayer circles for power to win the world, of which there were thousands at the close of the nineteenth century. She says that God said, *'I am ready but My children are not. Before it comes they must preach the Word of the Cross, the message of Calvary'* (*The Awakening in Wales*, p. 20). She says, *'God Himself cannot send Revival until the Gospel of Calvary is proclaimed'* (p. 21). She believed also that preparation for the revival had come from India in 1903 with millions of booklets world-wide stressing the Word of the Cross (p. 22).

Pentecostal theology and evangelism always has been Cross-centred. If the Pentecostal movement ever begins to decline it will be by weakening its understanding of Christ crucified. I think maybe it could swing to supernaturalism, wonder-seeking, rather than away from the miraculous, but it could lose its vision of Calvary. The first attack of Satan could be a subtle temptation to preach healing, preach the gifts of the Spirit, preach church growth, preach praise, preach worship, preach morals, but to leave the death of Jesus aside.

I heard George Jeffreys preach scores of times. He and his brother Stephen were the courageous pioneers of the laying on of hands for Divine healing in Great Britain. I never heard him preach on healing once, but every sermon clung closely to the theme of a crucified Redeemer.

This is the central theology of true Pentecostalism, though I am not so sure that every charismatic, or even every Pentecostal, stands so close to the Cross as was once so common. This swing away from its true axis is being pushed particularly by his songs for worship, which first began when praise passages from the Psalms – obviously pre-Calvary – began to take the place of redemption songs. Thankfully, sermons have usually been more redemption centred than the worship.

The value of the Old Testament cannot be over-estimated – it is God's Word. But it is not God's final Word. That came in Christ. And that Word became the Word of the crucified one. The way Paul puts it in 1 Corinthians 1:23, is rather startling. *'We preach Christ crucified'*, using the present participle for 'crucified', which put literally in (un)-English is 'We preach Christ having been crucified', or 'We preach Christ he has been crucified'.

That is the thing about Him. It is not only that He is God the Son, or the flawless Man, or anything else, but this, that He is the wounded one. He is that today. A man has been married, but what happened at the altar signifies very much on his Golden Wedding anniversary – he'd better remember! What happened at Easter AD 30 is the truth to dwell on about Jesus. He is Jesus of Calvary, the crucified One.

The cry of Jesus from the Cross, *'It is finished'* (John 19:30), is similar to *'It has been finished'*. That's the state of things today. There's nothing left to do, no conquering, sweating victory for us to struggle for. The work stands prepared and complete before us. It is not our hymn-singing and shouting that will scare the devil away. Christ emptied Satan of power long ago when He personally grappled with the devil for us, something we cannot do.

The more I have considered over these years how the death of Jesus saves us, the greatest mystery of all perhaps, perceived slowly by the best of us, the more my thoughts gravitate to that crisis in human history. I cannot worship, or preach, or pray without the Cross. *I cannot live without the Cross – my hopes of mercy and acceptance rest entirely there*. I may as well try to read in the dark. The Cross makes meaning of meaninglessness, including my own life.

He died for me. *The death we all avoid, He did not.* He sought out death to pursue death. He tracked death down to destroy him that had the power of death. He cornered death, entered into death 'tasting death for every man', waged the great war on that dread foe in realms beyond our knowledge, and emerged three days later the eternal Victor, the final fate of death settled. There can be no come-back for the devil or for death his weapon. Christ has drawn out the serpent's sting; 'O death where is thy sting?'.

Before His death Christ called Himself 'the Son of Man'. Everything He said relating to His death was in that name. After His death, in the 'Revelation of Jesus Christ' (Rev. 1:1) John speaks of Him as 'the Lamb'. The view of Him on the Throne is the Lamb. He is the Son of Man bearing battle scars, a Lamb as it had been slain (Rev. 5:6). The One we worship is not one who was crucified but overcame it and forgot it, as when perhaps we had an injury years ago. The One who was *'brought as a lamb to the slaughter'* still is, and always was – *'slain from the foundation of the world'.*

In some way beyond our understanding that fact, that One, known as the Crucified One, has become the focal point of all things. That is the one great fact of existence. Not to assume it in our Gospel, in our worship, is to miss the Throne itself. There is no throne of power and glory and might and majesty except the Throne of the Lamb.

In some way beyond our understanding the barb and bitterness of our wickedness is buried in His heart, for ever. Evil is swallowed up in the mercy sea of His infinite being. He knows evil – our evil, the stench, taste, tang of it. He came so close to me that the apprehension and shock of sinfulness, the knowledge of what I have done, communicated itself to Him, and He relieved me of it and shielded me from the realities of it, and from Hell.

Knowing such things, what else can I talk about? Knowing such things WHAT ELSE CAN THE HOLY SPIRIT TALK ABOUT? He takes of the things of Christ and reveals them. *He only blesses what we say about Jesus, and the great thing about Jesus is His Cross.* His Cross was the victory of both Good Friday and Easter Sunday morning. He rose from death by the power of His Calvary conquest, not merely from brute miracle power. He rose from death because He tackled and overcame death by dying on the Cross. It was a new kind of death, a death from which resurrection was certain, the death only one Man ever died.

If we want to sing of power and might and majesty, we know nothing of it, and have never been shown any whatever, except on earth in the Cross and Resurrection. Any other glory we imagine, but His we can see: 'My glory all the Cross'. If we divorce glory and power from the Cross we confuse it with the pomp of kings and the pageantry of those who wade through blood to a conqueror's throne. It is not that at all. It is a new glory known only to those who draw near to Calvary. *There's* might. *There's* majesty! AND *THERE'S* REVIVAL POWER. No message like that on earth can so move men, and that is what has always moved men in every revival.

Power To Conquer Earth

It can be salutary to go back to historical roots. The Pentecostal outpouring came at the beginning of the twentieth century following the intense desires and prayers for power to evangelise the whole world before Christ came – which was anticipated this century, by the year AD 2000. The understanding of the baptism in the Spirit had never been too far removed from 'power'.

The history began with the teaching of Wesley and perfect love, and developed into the Holiness doctrine, which presently came to be called 'the baptism', or the 'cleansing baptism', the idea being that holiness and sanctification brought power. Even when it was regarded as 'the baptism with the Holy Spirit' to empower, as Dr R. A. Torrey eventually showed it to be, the preliminary requirement was considered to be holiness – no baptism of power without a perfect walk with God.

But which must come first? Holiness or the baptism? Are we to be holy by our own efforts and so merit the Spirit? We would have to be pretty good! *The truth is there cannot be a perfect walk with God ever, without the baptism in the Spirit.* Why? Because that perfect walk is not merely religious and moral, but is also evangelistic, a witnessing life in obedience to Christ's command. *'Without me ye can do nothing'* Jesus said. Therefore the baptism in the Spirit must be given prior importance, and be prior to all other blessings.

What Jesus finally said before His ascension is of the greatest significance.

> Wait for the promise of the Father, which ye have heard of me. For John truly baptised with water; but ye shall be baptised with the Holy Ghost not many days hence. Ye shall receive power, after that the Holy Ghost is come upon you: and ye shall be witnesses unto me both in Jerusalem, and in all Judaea, and in Samaria, and unto the uttermost part of the earth. (Acts 1:5,6,8).

Therefore the command to wait for the baptism in the Spirit and the commission to evangelise are absolutely one. It is a single package – power and purpose, baptism and evangelism.

If there is a hallmark of Pentecost this is it – evangelism. Those who seek merely to become 'spiritual' and concentrate their ministry, or church, or personal life on developing the state of their own soul, or their little church, with constant use of the gifts, prophecy, tongues, words from God, healing and so on within their own assembly life, without evangelism, are heading for elitism and stagnation.

Further, holding Pentecostal services, having a good time, good meetings, and so on, relying upon natural accretions to the fellowship, represents failure to recognise the main purpose of the Spirit and the Church. The Spirit is not given for mere fellowship, however much fellowship is spoken of in the New Testament. The Spirit is given for soul-saving.

Increase must not be left to chance. It should be the purpose, organisation and aim. Everything must be geared to it. Let a church be attractive in itself, but it must do more than be nice and welcoming. It should be propagandist, opportunist, driven by zeal as Paul said, 'that I might by all means save some'.

Pentecostal Purpose

At the time these words are being written one question is receiving much attention. *Why has not the Charismatic movement, now twenty years old, made a greater impact upon Britain?* It did produce the House Church movement, which today is stirring itself in more evangelistic style I believe. This substantial Brethren-Baptist-Apostolic offshoot added Pentecostal teaching to ideas of church order, which they believe are an important Scriptural pattern, by which alone revival could come. Its original growth was fairly swift, as Brethren-Baptist-charismatic groups naturally 'gelled', coming together by mutual experience with some additions from other church memberships attracted by the apparent successful growth.

Its 'restorationism' was described in an article as 'no longer preaching a desperate evangelism, but proclaiming a community of love'. 'Desperate evangelism!' I wonder how Paul would react to that? Discussing matters with one leader who took his entire membership of 250 into a House Church denomination, out of his Pentecostal denomination which had pioneered it over many years, he declared 'We don't go much on evangelistic campaigns. We just have good meetings and people come'. He was evidently of a different spirit from the evangelising Pentecostals which had laboured to create his church in the first place.

Nevertheless change is taking place. That is inevitable where there is real experience of the baptism in the Spirit. It must come to that. More recent figures claim a good proportion of House Church new members brought in had had no previous church adherence. There was stress on apostles and prophets but not on evangelists in the church order, but the genius of evangelism is too much part of the baptism in the Spirit not to come out.

Evangelicals are stronger now in the final years of this century, and the Charismatic movement must take some credit for that. The impact of Charismatic revival is not negligible by any means, especially in the Anglican communion.

In the minds of many who only think of religion in terms of the Anglican church, a Charismatic vicar is simply one who wants to turn the seats around, and let people wave their hands to kingdom choruses. This is a caricature no doubt. He is not usually seen as a parish visitor intent on bringing people back to Christ. But . . . we shall see.

A series of magazine articles by well-known leaders all came to the same conclusion, that the Charismatic movement has so far failed to be evangelistic. One leader with world-wide Charismatic interest expressed to me the same conclusion when I discussed the issue with him. I recall meeting an American Episcopalian Charismatic who had set up a commune of some 200 or more families, but had by becoming a cloistered community shut themselves off from evangelistic opportunity.

This seemed to me a powerful criticism of the idea of a Christian commune, apart from it having no encouragement in Scripture. A question I put to him on what evangelism they did revealed that they ran a musical group which rendered a background of Gospel songs in a restaurant. Strangers might be counselled for salvation there. For the many churches who had lost these 200 families it must have been disappointing to see such a small Gospel outreach to justify it.

Gifts – Or Work?

At first Charismatic Anglican churches (and others) were Charismatic in the church hall only, not in the regular services. This has been largely corrected. But often it appears to be still a 'charismatic' approach, in the actual meaning of the word 'gifted'. The interest is in spiritual gifts. But, on Biblical grounds, I would say that the gifts may be exercised without the baptism in the Spirit. At least, this was the case before there ever was a baptism in the Spirit in Old Testament days. And some who have exercised gifts, such as healing, have claimed to have been baptised in the Spirit much later. Among these were fine Christian folk like the 'Peculiar People'.

The baptism in the Spirit with its essential basic sign of speaking with tongues has one major purpose: power for witness.

The acceptance of the Holy Spirit in British main-line churches has not thrown up too many evangelists or campaigning ministers as yet. Those who have come forward are prominent because they are such rare birds. They have generally ministered within their own circles of church folk, a ready-made clientele, mostly for healing, and have not rung the bell on the front door of ordinary non-churchgoers in any notable way.

But speaking of historical roots, while some Pentecostals in the beginning were imbued with evangelistic zeal, not all were. If mistakes are being made now by the neo-Pentecostals, they were made originally by the classical Pentecostals, though 'one thing we learn from history is that we don't learn from history'. They had missed the point. Original Pentecostal groups all over Britain for years concentrated on deepening their own Christian experience.

Without doubt it was the impact of the Jeffreys of Wales which began to change this. The Welsh revival had left this legacy in their souls – reach for conversions.

Despite the fact that we as humans are often slow to pick up the cue, the world picture is exhilarating. If any proof was needed that the Pentecostals had something from God, and that it is the 'power' for witness which Jesus promised, it is there in large quantities. Even before any Pentecostal denomination was formed in Britain it had already begun training and sending out missionaries, some of whom died on the field. So long as true Pentecostal fire burns, it will eventually prompt the purposes for which the blessing was sought a century ago, to evangelise the whole world before Christ comes.

Combine Harvester Reaping

Writing the book called *Holy Spirit Evangelism* with evangelist Reinhard Bonnke, I have perused masses of information about his work which he talks about having to be done with a spiritual combine harvester, not a sickle. This harvester quite recently had the shape of his mammoth marquee seating 34,000 people. But it has now proved uselessly small, as he would need half a dozen such tents to shelter the vast audiences of the last two years.

He himself is making every endeavour to produce evangelists

with a powerful faith ministry like His own. And, significantly for all I have written in this chapter, he insists that the message is the Gospel of the Cross, not healing, and that that Gospel, set on fire with the Holy Spirit, can save the whole world. I believe it.

10 Renewal

I couldn't believe it. I had set out to buffet through the churning North Sea near my home in the north-east hoping to swim to the next wooden groyne – seventy yards. Year after year, this mighty triumph eluded me, despite all my practice! And now, this time, here I was, I had swum to the end of the whole sea-front of the town.

My self-congratulation overwhelmed me. But I knew the Lord was smiling at me and saying, 'I told you so'. He had in fact. After years of negative reading many books, the Bible had begun to grip me, and I came to Psalm 119. It opened out. Verse 50 is the heart of it: *'Thy Word hath quickened me.'*

This verse excited me. It summed up something I knew had been happening to me, a definite rise in the temperature of my previously tepid faith. Things I never expected had taken place. This verse explained them and I knew they would go on happening. *'Thy Word hath quickened me,'*

Physically I had not been a robust specimen, my ministry argumentative, my home drab, my church half empty, my pocket emptier, but it was all changing. So, I wasn't surprised at this changing too – after trying since childhood, I could swim, and swim! I had strength I didn't have even at twenty-one. *'Thy youth is renewed like the eagles'* (Ps. 103:5).

That was some time ago, but, getting older, to maintain undiminished energy I simply read more. The Word is 'My medicine and my health'. Pore over the Word and power pours over you. Jesus said, 'The Words I speak unto you they are life' – not just ancient documents for the purposes of literary and historical analysis.

What the Bible urges upon us is – itself. The more I opened it the more it opened itself to me. It told me I must know it better and lay aside my learned theologies and discover the things it stressed. First one thing, and then another began to come together all over the Book, like pre-set patterns and series of bright lights.

One thing I saw that it was all about was the very thing I had begun to enjoy, *RENEWAL*. No other book contains anything like it. In fact, it begins with an ending and ends with a beginning. The end of the Creation story starts God on a renewing process. Genesis 3. The Divine programme develops from that point, to be completed in Revelation with the beginning of a new heaven and earth. The entire Book is a picture of God ceaselessly at work, initiating, restoring, bringing new life, despite human inertia and intransigence.

We became, through our sinfulness, the unburied dead, 'but you hath He quickened who were dead in trespasses and sins'. The world will never become 'the late great planet Earth', because He will make all things new.

God is a revival, the Spirit of renewal, not merely a hard-to-be-persuaded giver of spasmodic revivals. He never stops. In our timidity we only pray 'Lord send "*a*" revival'. A revival. You may as well look at the Amazon and beg for a bucket of water. The heathen used to ask God to make springtime come again. Asking God to 'revive Thy work' is like praying Him to make the grass grow. What else do you think He does?

Sometimes traditional ideas are like struggling in a tank of treacle. When surprising events occur, conversions and healings, our customary explanation is that they are acts of 'sovereignty'. There is not a word in Scripture to support such talk. That is philosophy, not Bible. The Bible presents us with a quite different truth. *Whatever God does, He does to show us what He is like ALWAYS. That is God normally, not exceptionally.* God's sovereign acts reveal His eternal faithfulness, a known constant.

To read Scripture as a mere chronology, a record of what has happened, is not faith. Faith does not mean believing in the historical accuracy of Scripture or its inspiration. Faith is to read Bible as a testimony of what God IS, what always happens when God is around, and to live and act upon it.

The past predicts the present. The rabbis believed the Scripture was inspired, but their reading 'was not mixed with faith', Paul said. They dismally failed to discern that the object of the

Scriptures was to reveal the everlasting character of God and to encourage them to step out boldly in dependence on Him.

The will of God alone makes anything possible, but faith makes everything possible for us within His will. We have no power over God, but we can have the power of God to execute His will. His sovereign will is set out in the great promises of grace. *Revival is His will, now, and always, not when He makes a sudden new decision.* He made that decision long ago and it is for permanent realisation.

His supposedly occasional works are never actually *'one-off'* events, but *start-off* events. They are initiations, or would be if we took the cue. The first person I ever put my hands upon for healing, was healed. I stared incredulous – what on earth had I done? I was a Bible college student sent to preach where I could do little harm, to a congregation of two dozen student-proof hardies. I operated with 1000-watt bright hopes but my miracle expectations were an example of the perfect vacuum.

I had never seen such a thing as an instant healing, before. 'Sovereignty' – did that completely explain it? Actually I think it did, on this occasion. But that was too spiritually theological for me. I think I took it as beginners' luck, coincidence, anything.

It never entered my head that God had taken the initiative in an act of personal encouragement, to show me what He would do if I co-operated. It took fourteen years for the fact to penetrate my murky comprehension, until His reviving determination at last moved me.

That's God. Here is the basic rock of Scripture. Perhaps I can look at an outcrop here and there.

Renewal begins in Genesis 1:2

'*The earth was without form, and void, and the Spirit of God moved upon the face of the waters*'. For God a cold lifeless universe, without love or laughter, would never do. His mind flowed with creativity and inventiveness, beautiful things, blue seas and white breakers, plumage among the verdure, elephants, dragonflies, glittering icebergs, mountains in the mists, clouds in the sunset.

The Lord took light and water and mud, shaped them,

stepped back and said, 'Very good'. The joy in His voice went ringing on, the symphony of nature, in the waterfalls, windsong and birdsong, thunder thrown from crag to crag, in the rolling drumbeat of oceans on endless shores.

The first humans heard the Voice echoing in Eden. *He had revealed Himself. The renewing Spirit, the God of all future springtimes – in His element, creating, maintaining, multiplying, restoring.*

However, I've begun too late. Creation is recent. Long before that, we read about: '*Christ, a lamb without blemish or spot: who verily was foreordained before the foundation of the world*' (1. Pet. 1:19–20). Or as Revelation 13:8 says, '*the Lamb slain from the foundation of the earth*', confirmed by Jesus when He said, '*Thou lovest me before the foundation of the earth*'. Things had been going on a long time before time.

What was going on IS going on. What is that? The Father loving the Son, and the Son laying an ambush for evil, even before it existed. The world not then born was already lit with Calvary's light.

But God rested on the seventh day – briefly. Unfortunately the embryo human race, Adam and Eve, fatally damaged the genes of its own spiritual and moral nature. The Fall of man reversed the Divine pattern. Instead of renewal and life came decay and dissolution. '*By man came death . . . the law of sin and death*'. And what about God resting on the seventh day?

God did not rest because He was exhausted. 'Ceased' is the word. (see N.I.V. Genesis 2:2 note.) But when the first cry of distress comes from Eden He immediately responds. There is work to do, work for a Redeemer. The seduced pair and their Seducer stand before Him. His original intentions are jeopardised as the storm breaks over Eden. The image of God in man is distorted in the disturbed waters. But He has stood ever since with outstretched sheltering wings 'till the storm of life be past'.

After Christ had made a cripple well at the Pool of Bethesda, or Bethzatha (see John 5), He reminded His critics of how God had broken His Sabbath rest to come to the relief of man. The authorities, devoid of feeling for the cripple who was now healed, were only concerned that Jesus had fallen foul of their multitude of legalisms and they charged Jesus with Sabbath breaking. *He replied, 'My Father works hitherto, and I work'.* God worked on His seventh day of rest (John 5:17).

After man realised his Divine image was shattered, he began attempting to create his own image, aping God. We improve our circumstances but not ourselves, making ourselves miserable in comfort. But the story of the Bible is of a God who never gives up on us to let us make the best we can of a bad job. His intentions are unchanged. He determined, come what may, all the way from Bethlehem to Golgotha, to do what He set out to do. He chose us and called us and *'did predestinate us to be conformed to the image of his Son'.*

What He did for a world without form and void, in six days – which did not cost Him anything, He began doing for mankind but at inconceivable cost. He began in the Garden of Eden and is found also in the Garden of Gethsemane. Unrelenting in purpose, prostrate with awesome groaning and 'strong crying and tears', the driving energies of God were set to re-make man in His own image. *'And we know that, when he shall appear, we shall be like him'.*

The God of the Bible is the God of the Gospels
In the Gospels the God we read about in the Old Testament stands before us. He is the Door which opens for a little time and we see eternity, and what is always going on there. In Christ is the picture of a tireless one with ceaseless aims. What He was then is what He always was and will be. What Jesus was in AD 30 God is from eternity to eternity. We just cannot accept the idea that 'Renewal' began in the 1960s. You cannot have anything to do with God at all without being subjected to His renewing Spirit.

For a vignette, look at John 4. At the point of exhaustion, Jesus sits at a well. A woman comes alone, trying to hide the fact that other village women will not associate with her because of her loose life. She is the worst possible contact, but it is enough. A few words, and soon Jesus creates high drama and unforgettable truth appears. Down from the village come the men, in white, for the heat of summer sat on the countryside. Jesus sees them, as a harvest already being reaped and says,

'*Say not ye*, <u>There are yet four months to harvest? behold</u>, *I say unto you*, <u>Lift up your eyes, and look on the fields; for they are white already to harvest'. They looked up and saw half the town reaped by a mere woman</u>.

It was not four months to harvest, but possibly harvest time very soon. It was summer, for otherwise he would have found water to drink on the journey. 'Four months to harvest' was their saying '*Say not ye?*' It was equivalent to the Spanish '*Manana*'. There could be no 'tomorrow, tomorrow and tomorrow' with Him. No waiting for the weather, but 'in season and out of season' the harvest was there. Here at Sychar, an unpropitious moment, an alienated race, a despised little woman, a forbidden social tradition, and for Jesus they add up to a grand total of THE DAY OF SALVATION.

Read the prophets and the tragedy of Israel

There we discover Him still totally concerned, displaying a grace that can never exhaust itself. His patience would make us impatient. There's Hosea, for example, a mouthpiece for His heartcry

> How shall I give thee up, Ephraim? how shall I deliver thee, Israel? how shall I make thee as Admah? how shall I set thee as Zeboim? Mine heart is turned within me, my repentings are kindled together. O Israel, thou has destroyed thyself: but in me is thine help. I will ransom them from the power of the grave: I will redeem them from death: O grave, I will be thy destruction (11:8, 13:14).

Does anything there suggest a God of sudden bursts of mercy? Is that a God who moves by fits and starts? '*All day long have I stretched forth my hand to a wicked and gainsaying people*' (Isa. 65:2. Rom. 10:21). Jeremiah stresses God's uninterrupted attentions to His people in a phrase characteristic of his prophecy, depicting God as 'rising up early', 'again and again'. We read '*From the thirteenth year of Josiah even unto this day, the three and twentieth year, the word of the Lord hath come unto me, and I have spoken unto you, rising early and speaking; but ye have not hearkened. And the Lord hath sent unto you all his servants the prophets, rising early and sending them'* (Jer. 25:3,4).

We see His ever-active love for Israel as He brings them out of Egypt, walks with them in the wilderness, campaigns with them in the Promised Land, anoints leaders through the centuries, is exiled with them in Babylon, protects their return as a remnant, sends Christ from heaven to them, and then to the apostles, and still, when they were scattered to the four quarters of the world He declares His intentions to preserve their race. He has never forgotten to be gracious. *What He WAS with Israel declares what His character IS*. He is incapable of inaction, of needing to stir Himself.

As for us, is God only to move when we make heavy appeals, as we are told we must if we are to see revivals? He declares *'I was found of them that sought me not'* (Isa. 65:1). He is always moving, and moves us in the process – eventually. He is a volcano of love, breaking forth upon us whenever and wherever He can.

Here is the central fact of all experience. 'Lo, I am with you always, even unto the end of the World' (Mark 16:20)
This promise is absolutely unconditional. It does not wait upon our perfection or sanctification or upon our unity or anything else. He is with us, and there's no way to alter the fact. We can do nothing about it, either to bring it about or stop it. *'For where two or three are gathered together in my name, there am I in the midst of them'* (Matt. 18:20) – and note, He said that in the context of people with differences between them. That's when we need Him near. He is not God for perfection conditions, easily put off.

Think about the Holy Spirit
Jesus said, *'I will pray the Father, and he shall give you another Comforter, that He may abide with you for ever'* (John 14:16). This theme is repeated in John's first epistle (1 John 3:27) the abiding presence of the Holy Spirit, unfluctuating, unwavering. The man baptised in the Holy Spirit is not just a person that something HAS HAPPENED TO, but a man that something IS HAPPENING TO though he may not even realise it. He is

'being filled', moment by moment. The conditions are the mercy, grace and faithfulness of God, not Christian merit.

Consider some of the best known Scriptures
Romans 1:16: '*the Gospel of Christ . . . is the power of God unto salvation*'. When is it? Sometimes, when there is revival? The answer is, every time it is preached, as we read in Romans again (15: 28/9): '*I will come by you into Spain. And I am sure that, when I come unto you, I shall come in the fulness of the blessing of the Gospel of Christ*.' How so sure? Sure of his own integrity? He had 'no confidence in the flesh'. He knew one thing. God never changed, and that revelation was given for those who serve Him. He is to them the faithful unchanging one.

In both text and context throughout the New Testament we have the picture of the power of God at work as an ever-present fact. '*Strengthened with all might, according to his glorious power, unto all patience and longsuffering and joyfulness*' (Col. 1:11). A power that ebbed and flowed, or gradually dissipated itself would hardly characterise the eternal Spirit. If OUR renewal was the purpose, it would hardly do for it to depend on us. *Have we to renew the renewing power?* The answer is '*For it is God that worketh in you both to will and to do of his good pleasure*' (Philip 2:13). Paul speaks about '*the effectual working of his power . . . strengthened with might. . . . according to the power that worketh in us*'. (Eph. 3:7,16,20).

The whole truth of the matter is expressed thus: '<u>the renewing of the Holy Ghost: which he shed on us abundantly through Jesus Christ our Saviour. The inward man is renewed</u> *day by day*' (Tit. 3:5, 2 Cor. 4:16). The Holy Spirit is the Spirit of renewal, like an ever-flowing river which does not wait upon our renewing it, but comes with freshness to renew us.

'Revival' in the New Testament is linked with regeneration
'*You hath He quickened who were dead in trespasses and sins*'. If revival is mentioned anywhere in the New Testament, this is it. Then we '*pass from death unto life, receive everlasting life. The last Adam is made a quickening Spirit. God who quickeneth all things*'. These are the kind of revival expressions in the

Christian Scriptures. Conversion is revival as the New Testament knows it. Whether the conversion of one or thousands, it is the same Spirit of revival or renewal at work. Revival is tested by He who works, not by statistical results. It was revival on the day of Pentecost when 3,000 repented, and revival on the Damascus road, when Paul repented.

Read right across history and learn what God is
We can take the greatest encouragement. The story of man is steady decline. The story of God is restoration. Man rises to a civilised level, then sinks back again: 'Thou turnest man to destruction'. It shows in our art, always the expression of an age. The classical age comes, and then returns to primitivism, again and again. It is happening at this present time with undeveloped crudity foisted upon us while art becomes Art, a sacred name.

We can expect it. The difference today is that in our intellectual pride we make a virtue out of godless decline and hail primitivism as an advance. But, somehow the creative instinct of beauty returns, and the unseen workings of the creative Spirit eventually sponsor true and fresh loveliness.

It is the subject for a long thesis. We might simply glance at the movings of God in the Christian age. The church became sometimes the devil's church, and the Word of God was banned. But Wycliffe shone, and Tyndale wrote, and Luther defied the devil, and a new warmth crept into Europe. The reformed faith came, then the early evangelicals, and the holiness movement, and the Pentecostals. 'Revivals' featured in all these developments. They are part of the great revival of the last days, part of its texture. 'A' revival is a moment when THE REVIVAL FORCES OF GOD always at work burst forth in noticeable local vigour. Revivals are not scattered movings, but part of His universal work.

The Truth About Revival

There is the view that the truest form of Christianity is seen only in revival. Other forms are regarded as an alloy of flesh and Spirit, human effort bringing human results. That there can be inferior Christian situations is obviously possible. When the 'works of the flesh', in pride, exhibitionism, self-promotion and other egotistical motives actuate Christian service, it must be distinguished from revival.

But it is grievous to me when sincere Christian service which does not burst forth in the full flower of public approval is denigrated. Anxiety for God's best is admirable, but judging what is best is another thing. It can deteriorate into censoriousness. We may look for faults where there may be no faults.

Here are my conclusions:

1   *There can be no true Christianity which is not revival.* Christianity is revival. Revival is its hallmark. In all Holy Spirit activities revival is not confined to the notable occasions. It is the same God of renewal at work everywhere. The Sower Himself spoke about unequal results from the seed (Matt. 13).

2   *We may decide to keep a special term for occasions when there is an outstanding surge of religious interest and repentance, for convenience of description.* We can call it 'a revival'. But the danger is to despise everything which does not enjoy equal public response, as if it represented an inferior form of Divine activity, or suffered from an admixture of human effort. This is a gross misunderstanding of the operation of God. The activity or intensity of the Spirit is not to be judged by the scale of its impact upon the world. The Holy Spirit has only one intensity. He will never dilute Himself.

3   *The word 'revival' has been used in an exclusive sense which is misleading, and reflects on the true character of New Testament faith and the work of the Holy Spirit.* Revival is an acceptable term if used in a *general* sense for all the renewing work of God. Dr A. Skevington Wood comes nearer to this concept than most. He says, '*The definitions of revival are legion. Every book on the subject has supplied its own. The many attempts to crystallize the meaning of revival in a single statement represent variations on a theme. There are no serious discrepancies*'. His book *Baptised by Fire* goes on to recount many a story, differing widely, some personal, some public, which he regards as instances of revival. He is right. He speaks of the Holy Spirit as the source of every kind of revival. That

is how it should be seen – revival, *'variations on a theme'*, and the Holy Spirit is that 'theme'.

4 *However, if I could, I would drop the use of the word 'revival'.* It creates the necessity to compare one Christian happening with another, and that is odious. Revival is not a Biblical term, and has gathered to itself meanings which are not in Scripture. It represents a particular (and confused) theological outlook which is not always encouraging. We are always trying to define it, which is ridiculous since it is our own word – surely we know what we mean by our own word? It being our own word we have no authority except our own to declare what it means. We should speak according to the Word of God and take our understanding of the way the Spirit works from no other source.

5 *'Revivals' as commonly spoken of are part of the revival which is Christianity* – more particularly, Holy Ghost, Pentecostal Christianity. Lesser or greater degrees of the manifestation of the Spirit are hard to judge, and may be due to lack of faith, or to quenching or grieving the Spirit, but not always.

Revival is not exceptional, but normal. Lack of revival is abnormal. *We must believe this, and believe that God is with us and working with us at all times.*

11   'To Whom Will Ye Make Me Equal?'

Nothing astonishes me more than when I see somebody healed – especially when the Lord assures me it would happen. My astonishment, however, is not that it did happen, but that I had so little to do with it – nothing at all really. I lay hands on somebody but even a child could do that, and sometimes I do nothing at all.

I don't feel very much either. When a person has pain it may register in my hands. That is a peculiar thing and nothing I sought or expected. There is warmth and even heat, otherwise simply the spiritual and physical glow of the Lord within and around me. Normally one is only aware of that impossible-to-describe assurance suddenly there, as if Somebody had said 'It is all right.'

I don't DO the healing. At best I only hand it over by the simplest act possible, from the Lord, as did Peter and John to the cripple at the Gate Beautiful of the Temple.

Now this is all a mystery but there is a very important issue here.

Healers And Healing

Begin with Paul. With him it was an important point that all the Gifts were 'by one Spirit', the Holy Spirit, including the 'gifts of healings' (1 Cor. 13).

So, consider this. We know that the healing ministry of Jesus was also by the Holy Spirit. *'God anointed Jesus of Nazareth with the Holy Spirit who went about healing'*, said Peter. Further, it is by the same Spirit today that God heals through us as He did through the disciples. He stated, *'Without me ye can do nothing. Verily, I say unto you, He that believeth on me, the works that I do shall he do also; and greater works than these shall he do; because I go to the Father . . . and I will pray the Father, and he shall give you another Comforter, that he may abide with you for ever'* (John 15:5, 14:10–16).

The 'works' of Christ in John are consistently manifestations of Divine power and glory, the Holy Spirit at work. They are the works of God, not man, therefore they are not just preaching the Gospel though the proclamation of deliverance is all part and parcel of Christ's works. The preaching of the Gospel is essential for such works to follow.

Now if Christ healed by the Holy Spirit, and the church heals by the Holy Spirit what conclusion can we draw? Does this put men on the same level as Christ? Are we Christs, when it comes to healing – and other wonders? That is an important question. Does this make us equal in power with Christ?

Pentecostals would have dismissed the very thought as outrageous. A tramp might use the same electricity as the king but it doesn't make him a king. Using (or being used by) the same power as Christ does not give us equal rank with Jesus. Nevertheless this doctrine is blowing in the winds today. It is being said that we are gods doing what Jesus did. It is a frightening heresy. Authors could be quoted, but our attack is not personal but only on this teaching. New Age teaching is that man is part of God and must realise his godhood in his higher consciousness and mind-power. We must resist that doctrine in whatever form it comes.

Distinction With A Difference

The greatest distinction exists between Christ working and His servants working. Having the same Spirit of power no more makes us Christs than our having a body of flesh like Him makes us equal. We are not substitute Christs. The entire

Church is only His body, and He is the Head. We are not level with the Head, but members of Christ.

It must be realised that *Jesus and the Holy Spirit have a different relationship than we have with the Holy Spirit.* As the Second Person of the Trinity He is one with the Third Person. Their oneness is that of God alone. His works were done through the Spirit and with the Father, but He had an independent authority which we know nothing about. We are dependent upon Him, as our mediator with God. The sovereignty of the Father and of the Spirit was also His sovereignty, although as Man he was obedient. What He willed He did. *We can only do what He wills.* He healed in His own Name, by His own authority, an authority in which His Father concurred as one with His Son. We only heal in His Name, subservient to His will.

The error comes from 'freelance' sources. Pentecostal churches have doctrinal statements which protect them to some extent from gross error of this kind. But not all who profess Pentecostal beliefs are subject to such theological discipline. They are a law to themselves, which is not the New Testament doctrine situation. 'Covering' by one pastor or one person is certainly not good enough and was not the kind of thing known in the early church. Regrettably some have brought deserved criticism upon themselves, and this is one cause, that that they act as gods in God, Christs in Christ.

Here is perhaps the commonest example: some say that the Word of God (from the Bible) is '*as powerful in our mouth as in the mouth of God*'. Apart from it being mere quackery, it is is an awesome claim. The most obvious question is, on what grounds is this statement made? It is so far-reaching and significant that we would at least assume the claim has the most explicit backing of the Word itself.

Instead, the Bible indicates the very opposite, God said: '*My word that goeth forth out of my mouth shall not return to me void but it shall accomplish that which I please, and it shall prosper in the thing whereto I sent it.*' Dare any man say the same thing, even it they do use the words of Scripture?

If they do, it is presumption and quite mistaken. It supposes that the sentences written in the Bible are some kind of abracadabra, with their own secret potency, formulas for power, like a magic spell. One need only repeat them and the wonders take place. The Bible, however, is not that kind of book.

It is not the power in the words, but the power in the one who speaks them which is all important. God said, 'MY WORD which goeth forth from MY MOUTH . . .' not anybody's and everybody's mouth. That is not to say that we are without authority. Elijah, for example, said, 'There shall be neither dew nor rain these years, except by my word' (1 Kgs. 17:1.). This he could say because the Word of the Lord permitted him. The essential thing was that Elijah could preface his dramatic edict by quoting the source of his authority: '*As the Lord God of Israel lives, before whom I stand*'. God has sent him to say this, otherwise he would have made a fool of himself.

In the New Testament Peter spoke with confident authority when he healed the sick and raised the dead, and so did Paul (Acts 3:6, 9:40, 16:18, 14:8). Jesus gave His disciples some authority and power (Luke 9:1). It was not total, to say anything God says about anything, but only to do certain things – *in His Name. He did not mandate Lordship to them, certainly not over other people, nor comprehensively*. A man has no comprehensive authority even over his wife, for he and she are both subject to Christ. The Apostles never acted with the slightest sign of such arrogance, as if they were Christ's vice-regents on earth. They did not reign as kings, as Paul hinted to the Corinthians, knowing that '*a servant is not above his Master*'.

We cannot take just ANY authority we like to ourselves simply by repeating God's words, much less equal authority with God. The idea is senseless. *We only have authority when He gives it.*

There are many conditions to be considered, not just knowing what words to say. A parrot can repeat words; we must not be human parrots. That would be as fatuous as the Tibetan prayer wheel carrying the prayer endlessly 'O the Jewel in the Lotus bud'.

There are such considerations as the situation itself, whether it is covered by the promises of God, and whether it is His time, or His will. There is also the little matter of our own spiritual state. Are we saved? Are we working with God or for our own ends and purposes – pride, egotism, self-glory and satisfaction, self-vindication, exhibitionism, or even just to make a living? An infinity of factors differentiate a man from God. Merely saying His words does not eliminate that difference.

'He whom God hath sent speaketh the words of God'. If anybody else tries they will not be God's words at all even if taken from the Bible. When Christ spoke it was effective BECAUSE HE WAS GOD. It was not the potency of mere language that did it, but the Holy Spirit performing things because GOD SAID THEM. When we say God's words they become our words, not His, true as they may be.

God said, *'Let there be light'*, and there was light. *There was no potency in those four words themselves*. Anybody can say them – try it! The Spirit of God carried out what God said at Creation. The first creative act, was determined from beyond time by the whole Godhead. Father, Son and Spirit acted together in full understanding of an eternal design.

To suppose we can achieve the least marvel just by repeating His words, at any time, is childish superstition. We couldn't even say 'Let there be light in the garden shed', never mind throughout the solar system. It doesn't happen even on a human level. Unless I were expressly given authority I could not command London to switch on the Christmas lights, much less God. Having the words does not give us authority.

That which is peculiarly Divine can never be ours. Godhood is not transferable. *Nothing can ever make men Divine*. To reduce the distinction between men and their Saviour represents a gross heresy. It is a misuse of Scripture, beside a vast over-simplification and over-emphasis upon faith. The power of God is granted to men, but it does not make them anything more than men. Their spiritual blessings are great and their status that of the children of God, but they remain for ever men. God remains alone, and shares His essential Deity with nobody. Royal authority does not make commoners royal. Being 'partakers of the Divine nature', nor more makes men gods than partaking of our breakfast egg makes us chickens.

If we were gods, it is a strange thing that all the New Testament writers carefully avoid any such language. The nearest they ever get to it is to say that we are adopted sons of God. Language must not be forced. The relationship between the Godhead, as between the Son and the Spirit are great mysteries not to be forgotten when we consider our own relationship with God. It is utterly different.

One cannot build doctrine on a phrase, especially such a far-reaching doctrine which turns Christian truth on its head. Scripture contains enough to explain chance phrases. To suppose that the sons of God are little gods puts a strain on even the phrase itself, never mind the rest of Scripture which we must take into account. One preacher is quoted as making his congregation shout over and over '*I'm an exact duplicate of God*' (*Seduction of Christianity*, p. 83). In charity one can only excuse this blasphemy as representing a vast ignorance of all theology and the most superficial acquaintance with Scripture.

God is God alone, and beside Him there is no other. 'I am the Lord: that is MY name: and my glory will I not give to another' (Isaiah 42:8). This explicit claim of the Lord to be a Being utterly beyond all others, comes in many forms in Scripture. God asserts and re-asserts that He has no duplicate, because it is of the most fundamental importance.

It was expressly for this very purpose the Bible was written, to destroy all thought of rivalry, false gods (human or otherwise): 'casting down imaginations and every high thing that exalteth itself against the knowledge of God, and bringing into captivity every thought to the obedience of Christ' (1 Cor. 10:5).

To claim Deity is part of the Old Religion of Satan. The six chapters of Isaiah from 41 to 46 hammer at this very thing, using the word 'I' 126 times stressing the singularity of God as opposed to all others who presume to speak in personal authority, and 46 times he says 'I will' as opposed to all other wills. Here are some phrases:

'To whom then will ye liken me, or shall I be equal? saith the Holy One, I am the first, and I am the last; and beside me there is no God. Is there a God beside me? yea, there is no God: I know not any. I have formed thee; thou art my servant. THAT CONFIRMETH THE WORD OF HIS SERVANT. I am the Lord and there is none else, there is no God beside

me, I am God and there is none like me.' These are only some
of the phrases drawn from those chapters.

And this is added for those who are mad enough to seek
equality with Him (47:10, 11, and 48:11, 12): '*Thy wisdom and
thy knowledge, it hath perverted thee, and thou hast said in thine
heart I am and none else beside me. Therefore shall evil come
upon thee. For mine own sake, even for my own sake, will I do
it; for how should my name be polluted? and I will not give my
glory unto another. I am he; I am the first, I also am the last*'.

I emphasised the quoted words '*That confirmeth the words
of His servants*', because they correct all misunderstanding.
When God sends us and permits us to speak in His name, we
are SERVANTS, not equals, and God alone can confirm what
we say, and then only when He permits us to say it, or sends
us with the message – as with the Gospel. Then He alone can
confirm it.

Never, but never, can we place God in the position of doing
what we say because we simply say it. *We can only do or say
what He has previously declared He intends to do*. That is also
the meaning of power to bind and loose – we can only loose
what He has loosed.

Our position is a simple and reverend one – we are allowed
to share in a small measure in His mighty acts as He performs
them, because He likes to bestow this joy upon us.

The Lord is self-existing, has underived life in Himself, alone
has immortality, and is removed from His creatures, even those
born-again of the Spirit, by a gulf of infinite distinctions.

What we are is explained in Scripture by terms which clearly
do not elevate us to gods. We are nothing without Him, we
read, We are 'in Him', hid in Christ, temples of the Spirit, co-
workers with Christ.

Again, though we are anointed with power it is not as Jesus
was for He alone is 'THE Anointed One', Christ. What we
have is from Him, and we depend of Him constantly for it.
Only the High Priest is fully anointed, and all other priests
have only a touch of oil upon ears, hand or feet. We may have
the same Holy Spirit but not as He, for '*God giveth not the
Spirit by measure unto Him*', even in His earthly state as Man.

The mystery of the Incarnation is here. To define in precise language the infinite level of the Son of Man above men is impossible. It is not a matter of degree but of creatureliness before their Creator. CHRIST AND THE GIFTS OF THE SPIRIT.

Now some have wondered whether Jesus healed by the gifts of the Holy Spirit. The answer is that He did not. Apart from the Scripture just quoted there is the rest of the passage: '*God giveth not the Spirit by measure unto Him, The Father loveth the Son, and hath given ALL THINGS into His hand*' (John 3:34/5). It was not doled out to Him in gifts, but everything was His at His will. The Lord did not speak with tongues. That is a sign-gift, and He needed no sign-gift because of His complete possession of and unity with the Spirit of God.

There was the mystery of the Son in His complete oneness with the Father and the Spirit. All that they did together is a transcendent experience beyond our knowledge. His relationship with the Father was a thing apart. He never even prayed with the disciples, but always alone.

Under the anointing of God, knowing His will, one may say to deaf ears, 'Ears, be opened', and they are opened, and in my own ministry it has happened many times. But the reason for this is not that we have independent authority and that merely mouthing the same words or sounds as Jesus must have the same effect. It is because He promised to honour obedience and faith.

The voice of Christ will raise the dead, He said, but we have no such unique underived authority. In fact that has particular comfort for some of us when asked why some are not healed to whom we minister. The answer is of course why should ANY be healed through mortal men? But that won't satisfy. The ultimate answer to why we don't bring wholeness to every patient is, *that we are not Christs*.

He had no failures. He healed everyone to whom He ministered. But some He left alone even when the power of God was present to heal. He knew what was in man. I do not, and therefore touch everyone unless the Spirit says no. It is not a case of God's will, but of circumstance. If God's Word was as powerful in my mouth as in His there would be no failures.

There were moments when He healed all their sick of all

their sicknesses (Matthew 4:23). This signalled the measure of His compassion, and power. It had to be seen He was like that. He worked perfectly, so that we might have confidence in His love to go forth in His name among men.

Whatever theology makes of Christ becoming Man, it cannot take away from the fact that He was God incarnate. If there were no differences in His works and ministry and ours it would be the greatest of all problems. His relationship with the Father and the Spirit was never surrendered, and was never ours. Though He was Man, He was also the Word. We are still men, only permitted to do His works by Him and in His name.

We can only be very humble that we are permitted to do anything in His name when the greatest born among women (as Jesus called John), thought it a privilege to unloose his shoe latchet, John worked no miracle, we read.

God help us to watch our language, and not fall as Lucifer fell because he wanted to make himself equal with God, to ascend to the Throne of God.

12   Pentecostal Healing

Bible Roots

Innocentia, a woman of high standing, was dying of breast cancer. The Lord spoke to her in a dream, telling her to stand with the women at the baptistry and ask the first newly baptised woman to make the sign of the cross on her diseased breast. She did as instructed in the dream, and the sign was made. At that moment the cancer disappeared. The doctor however was unimpressed and became sarcastic and angry.

The only unusual thing about this story is not the healing itself. It is the fact that it comes from the immortal Augustine, fourth-century Bishop of Hippo, the greatest mind of the church for centuries. He had previously declared '*Miracles were not allowed to continue till our time, lest the mind should always seek visible things*'. He changed his attitude later, and admitted that '*if I kept merely to miracles of healing and omitted all others . . . I would have to fill several volumes*'. (see Spencer D. Gear, *Pentecostal Evangel.*)

I have before me recent attacks on Divine Healing by American and English Calvinist ministers. They state that the great Augustine said that miracles had ceased, which he did, until he changed his mind. If they knew of Augustine's retraction their books would be dishonest. If they didn't know, then their scholarship is at fault.

Bible readers could never be blamed for believing in Divine healing. Of course if anybody doesn't want to believe, a little ingenuity can always get round it. But there is an awful lot about it in the Bible to get round. Why would God put so much in Scripture about His power to heal, to be read for 2,000 years, if He meant to do no such thing?

I do accept that it is not so easy for some Christians as the Church has developed a tradition of non-miraculous Christianity. *But the New Testament faith itself is for body as well as soul.*

Unfortunately the Christian heritage has become a palimpsest overwritten with later doctrines lacking the supernatural element.

Something has changed his situation, however – the recovery of understanding in the Third Person, the Holy Spirit. This is the Pentecostal contribution. That is, not merely charismatic interest, or Divine Healing, but the entire scope of the power of the Spirit, as we shall explain.

Of course people knew about physical religious effects long ago, but always associated it with Revival. Revival was the time when that kind of thing happened. God's power was simply revival power and came at such seasons only. Revivals came and went. Otherwise manifestations were not looked for, certainly not in physical demonstration. Power was occasional, when the revival conditions were right. Believers in the past would have found it hard to think of God acting in power at other times.

It was rarely if ever realised that the Word promised power in the church AT ALL TIMES – constant revival. That was a truth which awaited the humble folk who began the Pentecostal movement to point out. Until then anything beyond revivals from time to time was never visualised. But, even from the days of Wesley, teaching was moving closer to an understanding that the Holy Spirit (revival power) is an abiding presence.

What The Holy Spirit Is

It can clear matters considerably if we get our basic theology right about the Holy Spirit. Who is He? Genesis 1,2 gives us the first clue: *'And the Spirit of God moved upon the face of the waters'. He is there when we see things happen, and when we do, we know Who He is – the Holy Spirit.* Power-signs alone do not display His presence, but He is God in action here on earth. He is the Holy Wind. He is identified by wonders, the Third Person of the Trinity, the God of Pentecost.

So – the 'revival' power of the past turns out to be the Holy Spirit, and *that Spirit has not to be sent, for He has already been sent, and continues to proceed from the Father and the Son*. The abiding presence of the Holy Spirit is the abinding presence of revival power.

This is a truth that had to be recovered. How was it? The Holy Spirit leads into all truth – *leads us*, not suddenly dumps us down where all the truth is. It was a historical process. First the Reformation. The Scriptures were put where they should be, and faith was seen to be the key to Christian life. But Reformation teaching gradually became an arid, lifeless orthodoxy until the Pietists (1670) reacted and stressed experience and love for Christ. However, they neglected intellectual doctrinal elements which provoked an intellectual attack on supernatural religion. The Church replied, defending the supernatural and bringing it to the forefront.

The stage was ready for the evangelicals of the eighteenth century who brought all these developments together – Reformation truth, the Word, faith, experience, love for Jesus, and the supernatural, plus their own contribution, public evangelism.

In the old revivals physical reactions were common, such as prostrations and tremblings. It became easy to think of God working supernaturally. That independent-minded man, John Wesley, also caught a vision from scripture of a 'second blessing', a greater thing. He was open to the supernatural. Wesley believed in the power of prayer to effect healings and relates instances in his Journal, even that he prayed for his horse.

Wesley died just before the nineteenth century, but Wesleyanism strode rapidly forward, and with it also the 'second blessing' teaching which developed into the powerful Holiness movement. Bible-based holiness naturally stressed the fruits of the Spirit. From the fruits to the Gifts of the Spirit including healing was not a great step.

Divine Healing became widely accepted among evangelicals. Dr A. B. Simpson, founder of the Christian and Missionary Alliance, wrote in '*The Gospel of Healing*' (1888 and 1915): '*Healing is not the whole Gospel, nor perhaps the chief part of it, but it is a part, and in its due relationship to the whole, it will prove to be, like the Gospel itself, "the power of God to everyone that believeth"* '. He goes on to state that other gifts than healing may be claimed: '*To a greater or lesser extent the gift of tongues has been continuous in the Church of Christ, and along with many counterfeits has undoubtedly been realised in the present generation'.*

'Seven years of silent enquiry are required for a man to learn the truth', said Plato. In the Church it took seven times longer. A century ago when healing was talked of, it was only thought as a special gift to rare individuals. Mrs Woodworth-Etter, who had at first resisted her call to evangelism because of the strong disapproval of women preachers, came to a point in her diary in the later decades of the nineteenth century where she said, 'Today the Lord gave me the gift of healing'. This remarkable evangelist had some of the most extraordinary revival-type meetings I've ever heard about.

In St Louis, Missouri, in her 8,000 seat tent, thronged day and night for five months, unprecedented signs and wonders took place: visions, trances, healings, prophecies, tongues and mighty conversions with powerful social and city-wide benefits. Some healings were even greater than one reads of in the New Testament. Dangerous and criminal opponents were transfixed and quelled by 'the awful presence of God'.

There were other godly folk experiencing power-signs. The Church of God of Cleveland records in 1896 that 'many afflicted people were healed' in an outpouring of the Spirit. (*Like a Mighty Army* p. 26). In 1888, a Scot, John Alexander Dowie (1847–1907), emigrated to the USA and founded the Christian Catholic Church with a community in Zion, Illinois, where Divine healing produced further outstanding evidence. Dr Dowie's ministry brought help to the sick so regularly that it was an answer to most of the objections which could be brought against it. John G. Lake is a noted name and there were many more.

Among others was Reader Harris, KC., founder of the Pentecostal League of Prayer, who published testimonies of healing in the paper *Tongues of Fire*. However he preached against speaking with tongues, declaring it Satanic. A victim of his own propaganda, he believed stories of tongues-speakers' excesses, which were repeated over and over for decades by others. He removed the name 'Pentecostal' from the title of the League of Prayer.

Apostolic gifts had long been in view. In a sermon 'A More Excellent Way', John Wesley said that the gifts had been lost 'not, as has been vulgarly supposed, that there was no more occasion for them because all the world was become Christian. This is a miserable mistake. The real cause was that "*the love of many*", almost all Christians, so called, "*waxed cold*". The Christians had no more of the Spirit of Christ than other heathen . . . this was the real cause why the extraordinary gifts of the Holy Spirit were no longer to be found'.

So, Divine healing was known before Pentecostals came on the scene, and was practised in America, Britain and Europe. Mainly, however, it was confined to born-again believers, spiritual preparation being considered necessary and ministry would be generally private. After the Welsh Revival, Evan Roberts visited the continued prayer meeting at Gorseinon and anointed the sick with oil privately. He also exercised the gift of prophecy. The famous Smith Wigglesworth ministered to the sick in his Bradford mission before he was baptised in the Spirit.

The Pioneers

When the Pentecostals came on the scene they introduced healing into their evangelism. This was a new thing. New Testament evangelism bore this hallmark and so has Pentecostal evangelism from the beginning. They engaged the devil and his oppressions in combat publicly, as Christ did, and Peter, Philip and Paul, believing healing was not merely a bonus blessing for the converted. Acts begins with the words: '*The former treatise have I made, O Theophilus, of all that Jesus BEGAN both to do and teach*'. The word 'began' (Greek *erzato*) indicates a beginning to be continued, healing and teaching.

Jesus, we read '*went about healing all who were oppressed of the devil*'. This is the work He began, and which He will continue. *Not one line indicates He would stop*. Matthew records that He went nowhere without healing, in synagogues, out in the country and streets, among foreigners, great multitudes following Him (4:23–25). That was the style of His ministry. That is what He intended should go on, through His Body the Church. Christianity must never change.

Pentecostal evangelism sprang out of the Welsh Revival, during 1904 to 1906. The two most outstanding products of the Welsh Revival were without doubt the Jeffreys, Stephen and his younger brother George, as well as Edward and William. After revival fires had settled down, some retained too much fire for the chapels. The Zions and Bethesdas wanted to re-establish their normal respectability. Exuberant converts felt bottled up. These 'Children of the Revival', *'Plant y Diwygiad'* began getting together in prayer meetings especially with news of Pentecostal revival. One venue was Maesteg, and there Stephen received his Pentecost. In 1910, George Jeffreys was also baptised in the Spirit in the old Duffryn chapel as he said. George became a student at the first Pentecostal Bible School, Preston, under Thomas Myerscough, a Brethren filled with the Spirit at Alexander Boddy's Sunderland Convention in 1909.

After leaving Preston, in December 1912 George went to preach at the Maespicca Farm, Cwmtwrch, Wales, where with much sacrifice, converts of the revival had built their own house of God. George recommended his brother Stephen as a preacher, though he was then still a pit worker. On Christmas day Stephen went 'for a day or two' which stretched into seven weeks of extraordinary power. It became obvious that a new revivalist had appeared – the Welsh revival's new arm.

During that time, in Pen Y Bont, Radnorshire, a young girl asked Stephen to visit her home to pray for a diseased bone in her foot. There and then her foot was cured, and the same night she played the hymns in the service. The possibilities must have crossed Stephen's mind though little healing then took place. The city-shaking effects of his signs-following ministry had to wait another ten years. A turning point appears to have been 1922, in Grimsby, where, beginning with a house-meeting at which his host's painful bowel complaint was visibly healed, he was soon attracting thousands, mainly because of his healing ministry. Later George joined him as a Bible teacher to the converts.

The Jeffreys had previously had many good campaigning years. But increasingly the dynamic revival effect of the Holy Spirit in healings became evident, especially after a six-months tour of the USA in 1924. From that time an aggressive surge of evangelism took place. Both brothers boldly carried the Gospel with signs following up and down Britain, and also abroad with mass Christian healing services never seen before.

This was the introduction of healing to the British public in the face of fierce disapproval and cynicism. Its novelty, no competition, as well as the poor state of medical services then, gave the Jeffreys a field day. Thousands were converted as the Gospel was preached. Stephen especially was 'against sin', and made that thunderously clear. Such campaigns created scores of new churches. By this means the Pentecostals arrived permanently on the British scene.

If healing is not of God, it is a remarkable thing that from it came the ever-growing hundreds of churches outstandingly dedicated to winning people for Christ.

The mighty signs and wonders of the Jeffreys naturally meant that churches full of new converts looked to them for healing, rather than to their own young pastors (who were often *too* young). Healing, of course, became an important article of Pentecostal belief, though a lesser one in practice. Pastors did anoint with oil those who requested healing, but for many it was more in hope than expectation – they hadn't 'the gift'.

The idea of having 'the gift' remained until that generation had largely passed away, but James 5:14–16 is now seen to be very important. No gift is required. Having preached in hundreds of churches and tested the congregation about healing, I found an average of at least ten per cent of people had been healed within the previous twelve months. Far more are healed today in regular Pentecostal services than ever I saw as a youth, and other spiritual gifts also operate wherever the full Gospel is proclaimed.

In The Word

Pentecostal pioneers were originally evangelicals with the deepest love of the Scriptures. The Jeffreys and Smith Wigglesworth in Britain and others in North America only believed what they first saw in the Word. Preaching to thousands George Jeffreys would hold the Bible in one hand and point to it with the other. I recall vividly his habit of shaking it above his head with both hands and thundering 'I tell you by the authority of the Word of God'. His sermon to 10,000 people on 'Preach the Word' still makes an impact on me across the wild waters of the years. The fire of the Word kept these pioneers warm when the whole world tried to freeze them out.

'Healing Epidemic'

Since the Jeffreys made the public aware of supernatural healing sixty years ago, there has taken place exactly what Peter Masters calls a 'Healing Epidemic'. Even evangelism for some is simply healing, a Gospel with the Cross at the verge, not central, attracting wonder-seekers instead of God-seekers. Countless forms of healing are promoted with an estimated one 'healer' for every thousand people in Britain, especially psychic and hypno-psychic healers, jumping on the bandwaggon, some mere money grabbers. Spiritualists and psychics have almost 'cornered the market' and organised themselves. Pentecostals are often considered to be newcomers, and some churchmen warn people that the parish priest must be first consulted!

The Charismatic church world has its own healing innovations but 'classic' Pentecostals continue their witness for Biblical healing through the power of the Holy Spirit. There could never be anything superior to the miracle-working power brought by simple faith in Christ, compassion and the power of God.

Campaigning in Spain, for example, I discovered that every village has its psychic healer to which the populace resort as to the doctor. My own meetings in Britain attract many who ask whether I think they have the gift of healing, and are puzzled when I say there is no such thing. Cigarette-smoking Cockneys who have never been to church in their lives, mediums, church members, folk who 'felt their hands tingling' when I ministered to the sick, clergy, pastors, spiritists, irreligious people who have 'seen something', usually in the night, ask me what such an apparition means, I know what they think it means – 'the gift of healing' (it can be quite lucrative!). But the 'Irreverend' George Canty replies 'It means you had pickled onions for supper'.

Psychics and spiritists are probably the best known healers among the public generally as Christian healers are Christian, preach and have choruses and hymns. The public prefer seventh sons of seventh sons! Some just believe they were born with healing in their hands, like a Londoner who played Beatle records as he massaged his patients. One lady told me she was 'learning to heal at a spiritist church down the road, and was getting quite good at it'. She added ingenuously 'Some come for healing who are ridiculous. Honestly – they expect miracles!'.

Some years ago I was invited to contribute as a Pentecostal to a healing conference. My Pentecostal approach (the original), healing by the Holy Spirit, to my astonishment was considered a novelty. One practitioner spoke to us of relaxing and meditation, including wiggling one's toes. The Prince of Wales has suggested that holistic methods should be considered. Some read feet as a guide to ailments and treatment. *The Star* newspaper took photographs and interviewed me for their pages but published instead a piece about a man who healed dogs.

The King's Touch was much believed in by one or two monarchs and by the crowds that came to them as part of the 'Divine right of Kings'. In China Zhao Xuexhong practises the ancient art of *gigong*, concentrating one's '*qi*', a kind of force like laser that 'unclogs the *jingluo* (meridians)'. The Communist government denounced it as witchcraft, but now science argues over it like over acupuncture. Zhao claims 45,000 out of 50,000 cured in four years for the type of ailments he says he can treat, according to *Time*, May 1988.

Healing, Christian And Christ's

All this demonstrates that sickness is an intolerable burden upon mankind and that belief in non-medical cure is universal. Even witch doctors are given official status as part of native culture alongside 'Western' medics. There is an ineradicable instinct to look beyond man for help. Human nature is still a stranger to sickness. The Fall brought suffering, man being made originally in God's image to enjoy Divine preservation, and the nostalgia recurs.

The commonest religious question of all is why God allows sickness. But He has a name, *Jehovah Rophi*, the Lord who heals (Exodus 15:26). It is one area where some suspicion of Divine power still survives in the common mind, keeping the door ajar where the Gospel can come in.

Christ gave the church a threefold commission. Preach, teach, heal. That was His ministry and He called us to shoulder it with Him. He gave healing authority to His disciples and those who were to carry His Gospel 'to the end of the age'. Now. . . . WHY? That is the critical question.

This is the Bible answer: *The purpose of healing is just healing because God hates sickness and is troubled when His children languish.* It is certainly not a mere proof of something. Obviously it has the effect of confirming the faith, but that is incidental. Divine healing is simply a facet of God's undeviating concern for us all. It is not everything, but it is something.

To suppose that miracles were given merely to establish something or other sounds to me rather cynical. Was that the reason he healed people – with His mind on some ulterior purpose than people being well? Did He view the suffering crowds as just an opportunity to strengthen an argument? Did he exploit their need for His own different purposes?

This callous doctrine of God not really concerned about the sick as sick, but finding them conveniently useful, suggests a Divine exploitation of suffering.

The reason He healed is plainly stated. He had compassion. He came to '*destroy the works of the devil, and went about healing all who were oppressed of the devil*'. With Him it was not a situation to cash in on for some personal objective. Healing a woman bent over with spinal trouble, He gave His own reason. '*OUGHT NOT this woman, being a daughter of Israel, whom Satan hath bound, lo, these eighteen years, be loosed from this bond?*'. *She ought to be* – not because the Church or the faith or anything else had to be founded, but because Satan had bound her, just that, and to Him it was intolerable.

Natural human reasoning thinks God gives miracles as Christian confirmation. In fact they *are* confirmation but the mistake is to assume that is the reason why God gives them. Believers frequently ask God to heal the sick 'to get glory to Your Name'.

Well, that's what we want, of course. But is He of the same mind? His thoughts are not ours.

How much is that kind of faith worth which is based on what people see – on miracles? According to John 2:23–25, Jesus did not believe in the faith of men who believed because they saw His miracles. He wanted them to believe for higher reasons than wonders. Christianity does not rest on a kind of Euclidean QED – miracles follow the sermon therefore the sermon must be true.

Just one thing healing did prove. Jesus loved the people. That is the way they took it, and the way the Bible talks. The supreme hallmark of Christianity is compassion, and Pentecostal healing must carry the same impress, healing with no strings attached. Healing is a love gift. Just that; not filling pews, not Divine polemics, not Christian evidence, and certainly not for the preacher to make a name for himself, or a career, or money. It is no evangelistic gimmick. It is purely that God loves us.

Jesus, anointed to heal came into the world because 'God SO loved the world . . . !' All He did was for love, real love, not religious love. Nothing of the 'evangelical smile'. He came reckless of His very life to stretch our His hands in pity to the wretched.

Far from wanting this to be a witness to His identity or His teaching, He even told people not to say anything about their healings, and omitted to tell some grateful people Who He was. He saw the travail of His soul and was satisfied. His love! 'It brought my Saviour from above'.

Parents don't lavish care upon children to prove they love them. It does prove it, but that is merely by the way. Children could point to their parents' care as evidence of their love, but it would be a poor sort of parental attention meant only to prove their love to them or the neighbours.

God is good, we are 'evil' Jesus said, and BECAUSE God is good He gives good gifts, not for any other reason whatever. It is totally disinterested concern. *He no more heals the sick to prove something than he forgives to prove something.*

The thought that Christ would love us enough to physically die for us but not be interested enough to do anything for us physically would startle even a child's logic. It is a thought not found in Scripture.

As a Pentecostal evangelist, my job is to be an extension of the hand and voice of Christ Jesus. By nature a Yorkshire north-easterner from the hard times, I need this love of God shed abroad in my heart, God's love – HIS love, not my love for Him. *When His own love channels through me then I shall be driven as He was, to have compassion as He had for the weary, harassed, sick, and hopeless.*

What sort of love is it that merely preaches the way to heaven when people's lives are a Hell of misery now? His compassion was His compulsion. Kenneth Copeland said a curious thing. *'Love is not a feeling, and a feeling is not the evidence of love. When the Bible said that Jesus was moved with compassion, He was not moved by the feeling of compassion'.* (*Voice of Victory*, vol 16 no. 9 p. 8.) He uses 'love' and 'compassion' interchangeably, but they are different words. 'Compassion' certainly does mean feeling. The Greek word explodes with it. It describes the physical disturbance of a man's heart, bowels and kidneys. It means Christ saw sick people with a sense of shock. He is touched with the feeling of our infirmities.

For Him He 'needs must' heal. Healing wasn't given as a sign, but it became one. It reminds people of Jesus. Would Jesus be recognised without it? Is he NOW recognisable without it in some hard Gospel which has no comfort for the sick? That alone is the true Christ who is the same yesterday, today and forever.

13 Inner Healing

All Is Not Gold . . .

The first wonders performed by Moses before Pharaoh were easily imitated by the sorcerers of Egypt. Pentecostal Christianity has no monopoly of the supernatural today. There are imitators.

If wonders are all we want, we need not be Christians. There are wonders of a sort outside the churches, and also 'of a sort' inside churches. Christianity is not primarily for wonders but for far deeper needs. Jesus came to bring forgiveness, love, assurance, power over evil, not the power of psycho-kenesis or extra-sensory perception. We want contact with the living God, not with the dead. There are people curious about life after death who have no idea that there is Life *before* death. Jesus stands at the centre of the scene – everybody's scene.

Modern life, with all its rationalism and materialistic brain-washing has not changed our need for some kind of religiousness. It shows through everywhere in astrology, spiritualism, witchcraft, and other forms of popular sorcery. Satanism has increased its British adherent-victims to 16,000 today. Television and cinema screens cater for a huge public appetite for the supernatural, and even for space fantasy which is a cry for unknown mysteries. Parapsychology draws vast interest in such forms as Yoga, Transcendental Meditation, mind-power and eastern quietist religions. The hard-headed world of business and even law-enforcement are resorting in such directions for help.

While some evangelical Christians still cling to a non-miraculous, non-healing theology, in a world like ours the challenge to Christianity is overwhelming. After all the Bible presents on its very face a miracle Gospel however ingeniously a negative theological mind re-vamps it. It looks to the average person as if there has been a drastic U-turn in Christian belief if it is no longer what it was in the beginning.

Conducting evangelism in Spain I discovered that a non-healing Gospel cut little ice. The Catholic church has at least kept people's minds open to the supernatural, though it is mixed with superstition. One curious outcome is that every village has its psychic healer to whom people resort as they would to a doctor, and some have powers that go beyond natural explanation. One can fight superstition. But for a thousand years the whole nation has conceived of Christianity as miraculous. They read about it in the Gospels and cannot avoid seeing it as a possible source of miracles and healing.

If anybody wants to approach the Spaniards and other people with a Gospel stripped of its original miraculous element, they will limit their success. Christianity to them is an age-old unchanging religion and in that they are right. Even though their beliefs are also mixed with gross non-Gospel ideas they think of God as being able to do what He used to do. That is an outlook true Pentecostal evangelism can start with at least.

My Gospel is miraculous, enabling us to challenge both psychic healers and superstition. The Gospel should be 'not in Word only but in power and demonstration of the Holy Spirit'. We are not mere doctrine-mongers. To see strong men weeping, hugging us with joy, and women leaping and crying out *'Gloria Deos!'* because their limbs were moving again and pain-free, never struck me as being anything but the New Testament continued.

Wonders have two origins, particularly healing, Christian and non-Christian. They are not always distinct, but should be. Non-Christian expedients may be used by Christians to achieve results, without realising they are the same techniques as sorcery. The only safeguard is the Word of God, not results. Once put our foot outside Scripture and we shall be on a slippery slope. *Before miracles can be taken as the hallmarks of Pentecost, we need hallmarked miracles.*

The subject is vast with many side issues, and has produced many books. At my elbow are works on hypnotism, Satanism and witchcraft, Christian titles like *The Hidden Dangers of the Rainbow* by Constance Cumbey, Texe Marrs' *Dark Secrets of the New Age*, Hunt and McMahon's *Seduction of Christianity*, books by Roy Livesey, Donald Bridge, Basilea Schlink, Arthur Longley, J. Stafford Wright, Dr Martyn Lloyd Jones, Peter Masters, documents issued by the USA Assemblies of God and so on, as well as the writings of John Wimber, Yonggi Cho and others which they severely criticise.

Some writers are mainly concerned with prophecy, and the purpose is to show that there are false miracles and miracle workers which presage the coming of Anti-Christ. Even if their prophetical views were mistaken, and if these pseudo-signs do not anticipate the dark days of world domination by Anti-Christ, it does not alter the danger to which they alert us.

We must take seriously Paul's warning about 'doctrines of demons' and Christ's prediction: '*False Christs and false prophets will arise and show great signs and wonders, intending to lead astray, if possible, even the elect.*' Exactly what deceiving the elect means is becoming evident, and is perhaps more alarming than we thought.

If They Speak Not According To Thy Word

The 'classic' Pentecostals were the first to bring the truth of Divine Healing to the public at large, long opposed by both modernist and evangelicals. It was in the Word they discovered it and they believed it whether they had seen it take place not. From the Word they took their teaching and practice. There was no changing of fundamental Christian faith. For the vast millions of 'classic' Pentecostals healing remains a simple matter of prayer, faith, and the gifts of the Holy Spirit. No thought of special secrets or techniques is found in all their literature. But of course claims of new secrets attract.

Along these general lines perhaps we could take up instances involving the gifts and workings of the Pentecostal Spirit.

Divine Healing

A great deal of material can be put together from Scripture concerning sickness and healing. The numerous instances of Divine cures are not put in the Bible just to be spiritualised.

They create an expectation of physical healing, and if that expectation is not valid it is certainly natural.

The causes of sickness and the conditions of good health are made clear throughout the Bible. Repentance and faith are always emphasised. Ordinances such as anointing with oil or laying-on-of hands are themselves obviously too simple to be techniques and are mere symbols of faith.

However, novelties have been introduced. Healing has been made the subject of more than one new method, some completely opposite to one another. There is Positive Confession. That method of healing contradicts Praise-healing. Positive Confession means healing by 'confessing'. 'I am well. I am healed'. But Praise-healing reverses the procedure by confessing the sickness and praising God for it. Though, of course, you praise God for it in the hope that soon you will be healed and won't have it to praise God for! We will come back to the entire question of Positive Confession presently.

Many excellent believers have taken freight on board which in innocence they do not recognise as spiritual contraband.

Freelance Ministry
A colleague has handed me a brochure advocating 'Inner Healing' and asked for my comments. It will be useful in this chapter.

The promoter of this ministry (or 'Christian Ministries' as it is acclaimed) is a freelance charismatic, which is not unusual when innovations are put forward. Also he began inner-healing ministry because of certain experiences which he describes, particularly an unexpectedly good meeting with many prostrated and healed – perhaps no more than is normal in many meetings, but exciting to him, a novice in such things evidently.

In euphoric surprise he interpreted what had happened to mean God had a new work for him, and apparently a new teaching. Prophecies were also made which encouraged this impression. He then 'sought direction', which is always a point where things can go wrong, especially when we have a direction in mind.

The long and the short of it was that he stepped out in the direction of inner healing. This foundation for a ministry arising mainly from things that happen, is wrong, as Dr Martyn Lloyd Jones points out in his exposition of Ephesians chapter 6. A new direction, with a new teaching, should never arise except from the Word of God itself – the Word must be the initiator, not prophecies and impressions and blessing. It is sad when lovely Christian folk step away from the Word, especially to do a sincere work.

There are two preliminary comments that should be made. *First, some innovators are content with their own authority*. They cast aside dependence on the body of the Church and some even attack what they call denominationalism – a word I am not sure they could explain exactly. It expresses their prejudices mainly, or sometimes a desire for their own solo authority.

The organisation of Christians into groups, large or small, denominations or fellowships, is never condemned in Scripture. But some things are condemned, such one-man parties, rejecting or standing apart from oversight. To operate without the checks and balances of other Christian leadership, setting up private ministry independently of established disciplines is certainly a breach of Scriptural principles. It is lawlessness and division.

The Pentecostal bodies exist to ensure personal and theological discipline. God has raised them up for this vital purpose. They take to heart the apostolic warnings about the infiltration of false teaching and strengthen their gates against it. There is no sign that this has brought about deadness, but some mistake stability for stagnation. The Pentecostal denominations are each a battalion, united in God's army to win the world for His Son.

The other comment is that *experiences which come upon us unexpectedly should be very carefully evaluated by Scriptural standards*. They must not themselves become the foundation for innovative teaching and practice. Some feel superior not only to 'denominationalism' as they call it but also to 'tradition' in the church, that is the sound doctrine they stand for.

Counselling

Counselling has become a major industry in recent years. It seems to follow the trend in the world at large, largely because of the popularity of psychology, particularly in America, where the trend is for everybody to have a psychologist like having a doctor.

'How to counsel' is offered to us in all kinds of forms, and college diplomas in pastoral psychology for ministerial ordinands are becoming almost an essential qualification. The subject offers opportunity for inexhaustible reams of writing, attempting to classify all the hang-ups and weaknesses of human nature and propose an analysis, and verbal instruction formula to rectify them. There are as many counselling systems as there are counsellors. No doubt it has been known to bring help. Testimonies are always forthcoming for almost anything.

But in all honesty, what has this to do with the Gospel or with the New Testament? Spiritual counselling is becoming a substitute for the Gospel and the power of Christianity. Two-thirds of those who take psychological treatment get better. So also do two-thirds of those who do not take the treatment. I also hear that suicides are higher among psychologist practitioners than in any other profession, which seems to be an acute commentary.

May I also say by way of preliminary that Freud's psychological theories on which spiritual counselling is often based, might have been invented to undermine Christian faith. Freudian theory is behind 'inner healing' practice, with talk about 'consciousness' in various forms. Psychology and psychiatry have largely created the need for themselves, and the more 'Inner Healing' is practised the more it seems to be needed.

If what the New Testament says is true, psychology and counselling should play a limited part in Christian life. Instruction in the Word of Life brings life. The promise of God's strength, guidance, power, peace, victory, deliverance, through faith and prayer has always covered Christian needs gloriously until these last twenty or thirty years. Of course, pastoral help and advice can often be given, and in complicated issues might take up considerable time.

Some insight into human nature can often shorten discussion, and a wise man is one to consult. But after long years of pastoral work I rarely found it useful to spend hours in cross-questioning and talking with church members. Interminable accounts of feelings and reactions or what has happened to people, and delving even further into the forgotten past by psychological methods is completely strange to the Bible. The Scripture tells us to leave the past behind.

There IS deliverance in Christ. He is all-sufficient for our daily walk, even if we are as beset by stress and old memories as was St Paul or Peter. Paul could claim in the words of one translator, 'He maketh my way a constant pageant of triumph'. We sing, 'He is all I need', so why walk off to the psychiatrist's or hypnotist's couch? Talk is not the answer. It is faith in Christ, and perhaps a course in 2 Corinthians.

Inner Healing by Counselling

Inner Healing is outlined in a brochure before me. Briefly it is as follows. First patients will be 'slain in the Spirit'. That is prayer is made and the patient falls to the floor prostrate. People still retain their faculties in that state, so sometimes they are brought into a deeper 'rest'. In this semi-conscious state their inhibitions can be by-passed, and then their subconscious memory can be probed. Old hurts or sins can be brought to the surface when the controls and resistance of the patient are overcome.

How this helps is not shown, nor what is the cure, but presumably it is by other Inner Healing methods, visualising Jesus dealing with it in the past. This is practised, for instance, by Mrs Rita Bennett, wife of Dennis Bennett one of the first Charismatics. Jesus is projected back into the situation, to cleanse the past.

The brochure describes this state of mental openness as 'resting in the Lord', and being laid prostrate by the power of the Spirit as 'God's rest'. Let us say at once, that it has nothing to do with what the book of Psalms means by resting in the Lord. No Psalmist meant by it lying down half asleep. It is trust.

When Joshua is mentioned in Hebrews as giving Israel rest it does not mean he brought them into a state of suggestiveness and passive semi-consciousness, but into the Promised Land by tremendous campaigning activity through faith in God. The brochure quotes Matthew 11:28–29: 'You shall find rest for your souls'. If anybody interprets that to suppose that Jesus had any such thing in mind as people in a comatose state being psychologised, then one despairs of their Bible understanding.

It is also assumed that after conversion and new birth – after receiving salvation in fact, people are still not really delivered. Things that happened in childhood, or even before birth are still to be reckoned with, repented of, and forgiven. Apparently to be born again a new creature in Christ Jesus has not really affected a full radical change. The first birth experience has to be repeated. Is that Bible? It would sound as if the words 'ye must be born again', mean not only birth from above but also to go through the birth experience again from the womb, the very thing Jesus made it clear He did not mean when talking to Nicodemus.

Are we to think that until lately when charismatics discovered Inner Healing that people were not fully set free? All these centuries, right from the apostles who never dreamed of such methods, have people missed such a marvellous thing?

The brochure states: '*we can actually "talk down" a person into a state of twilight rest . . . called the Alpha mode. It is the state used in hypnosis and auto-suggestion (which) we do not use*'. In fact that is exactly what IS being used, whether it is called that or something else. (See '*The Science of Hypnotism*' by Melvin Powers.)

The frightening reason offered by the brochure is that patients '*do not use the many conscious and unconscious defence mechanisms which we often see when people are fully "in control"* '. These controls are in fact part of our natural God-given nature, mental soundness, for God gives a sound mind. Breaking down natural defences in a person's mind to intrude into the memories of a born-again believer is not remotely Christian.

God said '*Your sins and your iniquities will I remember no more*' (Hebrews 8). Therefore what need is there for a practitioner of Inner Healing to visualise Jesus going back into some sinful moment of a believer's past to remember it? It may be in accord with atheist Freud but not with Christ.

John and Paula Sandford, quoted by Hunt and McMahon from '*The transformation of the Inner Man*', said, '. . . search out the whole history of the person . . . Frequently resentments (have) originated either in the spirit in the womb or at birth'. Such probings are patently absurd. In fact the mind conscious, subconscious or unconscious, does not register such events. Any scenario recalled under the 'Alpha mode' twilight sleep or hypnosis is written-in by suggestion. By the identical means non-Christian hypnotists have caused subjects to recall events before they were even conceived, or in previous lives, as evidence of re-incarnation. Which is the *reductio ad absurdum* for this whole practice.

Inner Healing focuses mainly on childhood and its buried memories. The Freudian idea is similar. It assumes that what took place in the formative years became irresistible in the adult. Freud created the theory of the power of the forgotten past, or unconscious mind. It is an unproven hypothesis.

Even more doubtful and completely anti-Christian is the idea that our lives are pre-shaped or determined by what we have forgotten. Doubtful Freudian speculations about this have been accepted by educationalists and sociologists, and many politicians believe that we are hapless victims of our childhood beginnings. It has shaped atheistical forms of socialism.

That we are affected by childhood experience is to some extent true – but we are not hapless. We retain the power to determine our own lives, especially when we have received Christ as our Saviour and Lord. When Christians fall into these errors via 'Inner Healing' they find an excuse for their fears and habits in the contents of their unconscious mind, and blame their failures on other people or forgotten circumstances which compel them to do what otherwise they would never do. But they are then in a quagmire from which there is no release. This is not Bible.

The Gospel promises '*Sin shall not have dominion over you*', when Christ reigns within. Paul speaks about the human bias towards sin (Romans 7), but does not suggest inner healing as a cure. He simply says. '*Who will deliver me from this body of death? Thanks be to God, through Jesus Christ our Lord*'.

When a patient's forgotten situations and hatreds and supposed suppressed reactions are dug up, *they may not even be real*. They are invented either by the subject or by suggestion, and become real to the patient. If he believes that such a thing happened, whether it did or not, it may, and sometimes does leave him worse than he was. Problems are *created* by the inner healing process, not found by it. Can they be eradicated? They are likely to be carried subsequently in the *conscious* memory where they are more potent. They are seen as past failures capable of affecting their behaviour again – or of excusing it. The ability to forget is not a weakness, but one of God's mercies. To remember too much leaves us neurotic.

The major popularisers of Christian inner healing, such as Agnes Sanford and Ruth Carter Stapleton (sister of former President Carter), and the Jesuits Matthew and Dennis Linn could hardly be relied upon for sound theology, and indeed found no particular difficulty in other religions.

Biblical Christianity and Biblical salvation are not deliverance by psychology. Redemption and forgiveness cannot be achieved by mental therapeutic methods. *Paul declared that our faith would stand in the power of God not in the wisdom of men.*

The apostles never resorted to psychological processes to bring deliverance to darkened minds in the first century, nor have evangelicals for centuries. Have all these people been deprived of a necessary ministry? Why was it never explained in Scripture if psychological probing is needed to bring about true forgiveness and deliverance? Has the Gospel lacked the power to cleanse the personality of guilts, fears, resentments and sins because nobody had explored converts' minds in twilight sleep?

Or have we in 'Inner Healing' an implicit denial of the Scriptures? The Gospel is a promise of total deliverance, total cleansing and forgiveness, total new birth and the creation of the new man: 'The blood of Jesus Christ God's cleanseth us from all sin', said John. Was he mistaken?

New methods within the general scaffolding of Christian truth are on offer to bring about effects which Christ said He alone could bring about. It is another Gospel, and another kind of salvation.

Physical Healing

First we know many sicknesses are self-induced, or psychological – psychosomatic as they say. If the mental state can be changed, and a new attitude adopted, health may follow. But it may not . . . we can produce illnesses in our bodies by our attitudes but we can't easily reverse the process, and cure ourselves by correcting our attitude. Therefore it is ridiculous to say that Divine Healing only cures psychosomatic illnesses, for medical science itself cannot cure them anyway. They are miracles of God.

But God heals more than sicknesses brought on by mental or spiritual conditions. There are infections, physical failures, broken and twisted bones and so on. Only God can handle these things. Therefore it is vital to rely upon him in all our healing ministry. Suggestion won't do. Most of the people healed in my own services suffered from complaints no psychologist could handle, much less a person like myself not trained in medical psychology. Last week in my London service, for instance, a woman was healed of a cataract, normally requiring a new lens implant.

Inner healing may be a showy wonder but often cures only what it first explains needs to be cured. Bible promises cover far more than that. Healing services are not for showmanship. People come before us, clutching at anything to be rid of their misery and pain, perhaps with cancer, emphysema, heart conditions, crippling diseases. The only possible way to look upon them is with absolute pity and love. They are not there to be convenient subjects to display our powers and bring applause or satisfy a public craving to see wonders. Jesus never exploited the sick to bring glory to Himself. He didn't always say Who He was, and often wanted the miracle kept quiet.

Most people coming forward carry no spectacular ailment and may be healed without it being in any way observed. Healing meetings are not for excitement, but compassion. One way to overcome this drawback and keep congregations on their toes is to be dramatic oneself, and acclaim 'You are healed!', or some such theatrical words.

This is not the hallmarked healing of the New Testament. It is not Pentecost. I do not hesitate to say 'You are not healed' if I know they are not – and sometimes I do know. Then one can involve everyone in more ardent prayer and I can look further into things and encourage a patient to ask, seek, and knock.

Despite the advances of medical skill, sicknesses remain awfully prevalent, but not more so than the goodness of God. We may see only a percentage healed, as so few are in a state of mind and spirit in which God can help them, but for all whom I have seen relieved I am deeply grateful, and remain certain that God wants everybody well. He is never against it.

So long as God answers prayer I am ready to pray, and by the encouragement of the Word and the countless people restored, I could never wish to give up. There is the real, and the unreal need not make Divine Healing untrue.

14 The Kingdom and Demons

One of the most stimulating times I remember from my earliest days with other pastors was spent on the Isle of Wight. For three days we studied Scripture regarding the Kingdom. I have read and searched much more since, but some today write as if we had never heard of the Kingdom before and had overlooked that subject, considered to be the most important of all subjects. It suggests we had not understood what Christianity really was until now.

Certain novel Kingdom ideas have also been introduced, which for the life of me I cannot find in Scripture at all. One writer professes to tell us what on earth is this Kingdom and suggests dismantling the entire organisation of the Church and its ministry! Another substitutes a message about a 'community of love' for evangelism. Others believe that there are immortal Christians, and that they will take over the world government and hand it to Christ.

Amid such confusion, before I write about a Kingdom sign, I ought to try to clarify the basic facts about the Kingdom.

Outside To Inside

The first three Gospels contain the message of the Kingdom. *That was Christ's own message.* Actually that is remarkable because Christ did not come as a Messenger, as Mahomet and Buddha claimed they were. Christ Himself IS the Message, and He spoke of Himself synonymously with the Kingdom. Our message is Christ, we are His witnesses, as Paul emphasised and as Jesus commanded (1 Cor. 2:2, Acts 1:8). Jesus proclaimed the Kingdom; we proclaim Christ, who is the King.

Now Matthew, Mark and Luke DESCRIBE the Kingdom, from the outside, including its people, laws, conditions, blessings, resources and power. There are Kingdom principles, but we have always accepted them, regarding them as simply Christian principles. The first three Gospels, which contain practically all the Bible's teaching about the Kingdom, are the door into the Kingdom landscape.

Then the Scriptures change. From John's Gospel onwards we WALK through the door INTO the Kingdom. John tells us how, by new birth. (3:5–6).

He then says nothing more about it. Why? The explanation is simple. Thereafter the New Testament writers talk *from INSIDE*. The Kingdom has come for them and they cannot point to it being in it. '*The kingdom is taken by force*' (Matt. 11:12). The Gospels tell us *about* the Kingdom, and the rest of the New Testament is written from inside it to Kingdom citizens.

The Kingdom does not occupy a prominent position in apostolic teaching, especially among the Gentiles where it would have been misunderstood as a rival to Rome. But it is there. The Kingdom gives us another view of what salvation is. Evangelical emphasis has quite rightly been upon the great Christian truths, particularly those developed in the writings of Paul. The first three Gospels do not supply much material for evangelical doctrine.

The result is that ordinary evangelical doctrine and the Kingdom have only loose links. In fact sometimes the Gospel of the Kingdom has been described as another Gospel for a future dispensation. That is a gross error, for there is only one Gospel, though it has many aspects. So, how could the Gospel and the Kingdom be linked?

There is an all-important event linking the times of Jesus with the times of the Apostles. The bridge between the message of the Kingdom and the message of salvation, historically is the day of Pentecost. That is the key to the New Testament teaching of both salvation and the Kingdom.

If we make the Kingdom our central truth it throws everything out of focus, including the Cross, which must be central. In many new worship songs of the Kingdom the supreme truths of redemption and the atonement are a missing note. The whole counsel of God means the entire Word of God, not three books, but sixty-six. We must constantly read all of them to keep a proper theological balance.

Kingdom Power

The Kingdom of God is a Kingdom of power. What is this power? When Jesus declared that the Kingdom of God had come among us, He pointed to its power by casting out demon spirits. What was that power? He tells us that He cast them out BY THE FINGER OF GOD – that is the Holy Spirit. There is no other power. It is not the Kingdom which gives us power but the baptism with the Spirit. That 'anointing of the Holy Spirit' is how Jesus cast out devils (Acts 10:38).

This He later spoke about, identifying Kingdom power, promising His power by the baptism in the Holy Spirit. We have 'Kingdom' power only when filled with the Spirit, even if we don't call it Kingdom power.

Kingdom Sign

We can now turn to the Kingdom sign: '*If I with the finger of God cast out devils, no doubt the kingdom of God is come upon you*' (Luke 11:20). This important verse follows a statement by Jesus about the kingdom of Satan (v.18). The two kingdoms are the ultimate expressions of good and evil. Therefore when Jesus appeared, Lord of the Kingdom of Light, the King of Darkness mobilised all his forces for the most decisive battle of all time. His dark Kingdom was about to be crushed, and there was a multiplication of those troubled by demon power. But in any case, superstition and occultism were rife, as today.

Those who stress the powers of Satan and create belief in possession, prepare the way for Satan to enter people's lives. The Gospels talk about 'casting out' demons. (Greek *ekballo*). Demon-possession (Greek *daimonizomai*) is a state mentioned a dozen times almost exclusively in Mark and Matthew, only once in John (10:21), the case of the Gadarene madman, his personality lost behind that of the foul legion. Acts 8:7 says, 'Unclean spirits, crying with loud voice, came out of many that were possessed with them'. (Greek *echo* – 'having' spirits).

Not every case was alike. Paul cast out a spirit of divination from a girl who constantly followed them (Acts 16:16), but she did not exhibit the signs of total control. An evil spirit troubled

King Saul and gave him fits of murderous violence, possibly because he had opened himself to it by his venomous hatred of David, but he could otherwise be quite sane. The devil 'entered into' Judas Iscariot (John 13:27), but he did not become a raving lunatic.

Lunacy is not always demon possession. Alzheimers' Disease, for example, explains dementia in some cases. Scripture distinguishes between the one thing and the other: *'diverse diseases and torments, and those which were possessed with devils, and those which were lunatic, and those that had the palsy'*. The distinction is made particularly plain in Matthew 10:1: *'He gave the power against unclean spirits, to cast them out, and to heal all manner of sickness and all manner of disease'*. They did not *cast out* sicknesses.

Complications arise in two directions, however. How does Satanic power operate? Can Christians be possessed?

Occult Or Non-Occult?

First, for people to have demons is a very small part of Satan's activity. Too many Christians have an unhealthy fascination for demonology, and forget the general evil in the world. Occultism is a very small part of Satanic operation. He works from outside not from inside, by promptings, temptations, pressures, evil suggestions and engineered circumstances, not by everyone 'having' demons. Why did not Jesus otherwise cast out the 'spirits' of pride, egotism, and soon out of the disciples if spirits they are as some believe?

Some have forgotten that the devil does not usually work by any manifest demon power. That is comparatively rare. This had led to the most grotesque types of deliverance ministry, as if we were never safe unless constantly being exorcised.

One of the questionnaires which I have, by a charismatic Anglican itinerant, seeks to isolate cases of demon oppression, possession, or 'demonisation'. It contains forty-nine questions, with sub-questions, one with nearly 150 sub-questions.

Demons are associated with such sins as pride, egotism, worry, adultery and most other sexual deviations, and if a dead body has been touched, or there has been a serious accident.

Theological cross-examination is included about belief in the Virgin Birth, Biblical inspiration, and other fundamentalist points and the state of relationship with parents, family, and outsiders, and also about such feelings as love, rejection, apathy, introversion, dreams, fantasising, fears and so on. Why didn't Paul cast out the demons of bad relationships between Syntyche and Euodias?

This ministry turns the simplicity of the Gospel into a fearsome, complicated system. To be forgiven, patients must expose their naked heart and soul to the counsellor, answering all questions 'honestly and correctly'. The questionnaire is designed to help people confess every conceivable sin in detail, back into the past, or the deliverance ministry will not be effective. Forgiveness apparently rests with the effectiveness of the ministry of the counsellor. A fee is required for this service. This is '*another Gospel*'.

It is further explained that those having demons (of almost anything, every weakness or fault names a demon), may begin hissing, spitting, wriggling, coughing, making animal noises and so on. In a meeting led by this particular man (Winter 1988) Christians were on the floor barking like dogs 'manifesting'. In other churches Spirit-filled and godly men acted like snakes on the floor. 'Mucus' and gagging are also a sign of a demon.

So many conditions are listed as a sign of people having demons that nobody escapes. In one of the pieces of literature used there are eleven pages of closely printed questions by which the presence of demons can be exposed, naming every common failing. In the services sickness was also regarded as demon-effected. Everybody must have a demon!

Spirits are named, though not named in Scripture. Spirits of striving, criticism, childishness, immaturity, hardness, and scores more are named. Everything which constitutes less than perfection, is named as a demon. One brilliant scholar foolishly told an audience of children they all had demons. But as Theodore Roosevelt said, 'Every reform movement has a lunatic fringe'.

Such questionnaires are an intrusion into the privacy of a man's soul. NOTHING MORE DEMONSTRATES THE ERROR OF THIS TEACHING THAN THE ABSURD AND

ELABORATE PROCESS INVOLVED. Is this how the Gospel was ministered through the apostles? It is a crude, revolting, and dangerous method of deliverance far removed from the forgiveness offered in the New Testament. It is like a foreign religious system. The glorious Gospel declares God forgives both sin and sins, and casts out Satan when we come to Christ.

There is constant reference in Scripture to sexual sins, and to unbelief (see 2 Peter and Jude), but they are never related to occultist power. *Scripture describes unbelief and sin as 'the works of the flesh'*. It never mentions a demon of adultery or demon of gluttony, or even a demon of alcoholism. Nobody can blame lust on 'having a demon'. They are responsible themselves.

Paul has a long passage concerning these evils (Col. 3:3–10). 'Mortify therefore your members which are upon earth; fornication, uncleanness, inordinate affection, evil concupiscence, and covetousness which is idolatry: in the which ye also walked some time, when ye lived in them. But now ye also put off all these; anger, wrath, malice, blasphemy, filthy communication out of your mouth. Lie not one to another.'

His instruction about conquering these evils is not exorcism, nor are they explained as the work of demons. Paul's simple words are 'Put (them) off', or 'mortify' (Greek *nekrosate*, put to death), and then (v.10) 'PUT ON the new man, seeing ye have PUT OFF the old man with his deeds'. The new man, Paul says, is 'renewed in knowledge after the image of him that created him.' The renewal of the Holy Spirit overcomes besetting weaknesses.

There are other passages similar as in Romans 6:12: 'LET NOT sin reign in your mortal body, that ye should obey it in the lust thereof'. He puts the onus firmly on believers, never on demons, and the cure is victory in Christ by self-control, not by coughing up demons in a deliverance meeting. Peter simply says '*ABSTAIN from fleshly lusts*' (1 Pet. 2:11), which would be a useless command if a demon was responsible.

A teenager phoned me in terror long after midnight. She had been told at a deliverance meeting that she had a demon of finger-nail biting. After their attempts to expel the so-called demon the habit remained and she was horrified to think she still had a devil controlling her. One thing she could have been sure of – if the major sins of fornication, uncleanness, and covetousness are not attributed in Scripture to the power of demons, finger-nail biting certainly is not.

Just as surely other human weaknesses are not the be equated with possession, such as depression, smoking, drinking, moodiness, nerves, or gluttony – was poor Billy Bunter demon possessed? Bible characters display many failings, cowardice, lying, murder, envy, arrogance, deceit, and so on but Scripture does not usually relate them to devils.

Satan lurks behind all evil, but not always in direct action. Demons don't need to lead some people astray. Isaiah says we wander off in our own way. James declares, '*Every man is tempted when he is drawn away of his own lust and enticed*' (1:14). He specifies this: anger, filthiness and excessive evil, which James declares can lead to death (1:19–21).

According to Scripture, Satan may be allowed by God (only), to touch and bring sickness, as he did Job, or pressurise us, as he did Jesus on more than one occasion, or lead us to speak evil foolishly, as he did Peter, or to hinder us in our circumstances, as he did Paul, or bring us martyrdom as the saints in Ephesus, or deceive us with false teachings (Jude's entire epistle warns us about this), or even destroy as by death as Peter warns us (1 Pet 5:8). Death is his worst role but in that matter God is our protector when we walk in His will (Heb 2:14, 3 Tm. 4:17). *But in all these ways, Satan is an external foe, never internal*. He attacks us, but is not attached to us nor does he control or dominate us.

We can '*give place to the devil*' (Eph. 4:17). In that particular context Paul refers to sinful anger, where an evil intent is involved. But it is more than that. Giving place to the devil is described as '*falling into the condemnation of the devil*' (1 Tim. 3:6). *That is, being condemned for what the devil is condemned for – pride*. There is also (v.7) the 'snare of the devil' (i.e. to fall into reproach). Generally we can slip into a state where WE give the devil power in our lives. '*Know ye not that to whom ye yield yourselves servants to obey, his servants ye are to whom ye obey, whether of sin unto death or of obedience unto righteousness*' (Rom 6:16). Yet even this state is not possession and is nowhere associated with it, AND EXORCISM IS NEVER SAID TO BE THE CURE. Satan has no power except what he draws from those who yield to his will.

'Resist the devil and he will flee from you', just as he fled from Christ (James 4:7). It was obviously in the minds of the apostles that the devil can come to us. Scripture shows the ways to resist, not by superstitious melodrama, barking orders at him and assault by words. The devil attacks with 'fiery darts' against which our faith is the shield, and he can come to us with 'wiles' against which the 'whole armour of God' is proof (Eph. 6:11, 16).

This is where our 'wrestling with principalities, powers, and spiritual wickedness' is involved. *When we are attacked what do we do?* The means of response given in Scripture are: by truth, righteousness, the Gospel, faith, salvation, the Word, praying FOR all saints (not against the devil directly, in hand to hand combat which is impossible) (Eph. 6:10–19).

Before we think about setting out in spiritual warfare we should take note precisely how Paul thought of it and the means he saw could be deployed. It is easy to make up our own campaign methods against Satan which may be worse than useless. Kingdom authority does not consist of singing, praising and shouting – such strategy is not mentioned in the New Testament. One of the peculiar things about the New Testament is the little that is said about worship.

It may be difficult to say what relationship a person has set up with the devil. Some talk about Christians not being possessed but 'oppressed' by the devil. The only reference to such a state is in Acts 10.38: Jesus '*healed all that were oppressed of the devil*'. 'Oppressed' is a strong word meaning 'exploited' or 'tyrannised'). This tyranny is sickness, in that context, not 'having' a demon.

To avoid criticism some Deliverance Ministry men insist they never use the word 'possessed', but nevertheless they indicate that a person is in some way dominated by Satanic power, physically and mentally. *But it is that very state the Bible declares is met by the Gospel at new birth, and not by services of exorcism.*

We are warned not to 'give place' to Satan. If we fall in with temptation along a certain line, we weaken ourselves and Satan is strong in our weakness. But this does not mean we 'have' a demon. Habitual sins do not need a demon to keep them going anyway – the Devil can let the habit look after us. In fact THOSE WHO WISH TO BE DEMON POSSESSED, AS IN VOODOO AREAS, FIND IT FAR FROM EASY.

The apostolic method for sinning believers was never exorcism. *The answer was to pray for them, or 'restore' them* (Gal. 6:1), (Greek *katartizo* make fit, mend, or prepare), not by casting the devil out, but by loving encouragement and counsel: '*Of some have compassion, making a difference: And others save with fear, pulling them out of the fire*' (Jude v.22,23). Also 1 John 5:16 says: '*If any man see his brother sin a sin which is not unto death, he shall ask, and he shall give him life for them that sin not unto death. There is a sin which is unto death: I do not say he shall pray for it (that sin)*'.

Satan draws attention to himself when he persuades Christians they need Satan to be cast out of them. Too many give testimony to him and his works, rather than giving praise to God. The very services in which people gather to find the Lord and see His power at work, are subtly taken over by Satan as a stage where he can manifest his power – or pretended power. Evil spirits are called upon to manifest and reveal themselves, a practice unknown in Scripture. Our work is to call upon the Lord to manifest His presence.

Now here is one of the shocking dangers and effects. Suggestible subjects are mesmerised and frightened by this teaching. Given a list of ways demons will manifest, and a list telling them what weaknesses are demonic, those persuaded they have demons will act the part, hoping to be set free.

Further, once people suppose they have a demon, getting rid of it is another. Exorcism is not always a success. Many people are left far worse than they were. One of my colleagues went to preach in a Welsh church and was met at the door by a member saying 'You are not coming here to preach are you? Don't you know that we all have demons here?' This followed a 'deliverance' campaign.

The Wicked One Toucheth Him Not

Nevertheless demonology must be treated with seriousness. The sense of evil spirits once found among African animists, or ancestor-worshipping Orientals, is plaguing the West today. It has been imported with eastern religions and occultism.

Some tell us that only Christ and the apostles could expel resident evil spirits. This is simply not true even historically, never mind Scripturally. Having just read a current book by a London minister which attempts to prove exorcism was only for apostolic days, I am encouraged, the arguments used against casting out demons are so feeble.

Anyone should at least HOPE Mark's account is for us today when Jesus said, 'In my name shall they cast out devils'. There are devils enough to be cast out, and only believers can do it. *But the glory of the Gospel is that when we belong to Christ we are invulnerable.*

The very meaning of salvation involves deliverance from Satanic power. Arnold Bittlinger (*Gifts and Graces*), says that Christian conversion makes a clear break from demon power, and there is no evidence of any further work of deliverance. There are only two kinds of people, people with the Spirit and those without. 'In his comparison with paganism the point Paul is making is that a Christian CANNOT be violated in this way' (p. 16).

Paul said he was sent to the Gentiles '*to turn them from the power of Satan unto God, that they may receive forgiveness of sins and inheritance among them that are sanctified*' (Acts 26:18). He wrote to the Ephesians (2:2–5) '*In times past ye walked according to the prince of the power of the air, the spirit that now worketh in the children of disobedience, but God . . . hath quickened us together with Christ*'. Therefore 'with Christ' we are immune from Satanic domination just as He is. *That is what salvation means.*

To Colossae (1:13) he wrote, '*He hath delivered us from the power of darkness and hath translated us into the kingdom of his dear Son: in whom we have redemption through his blood, even the forgiveness of sins*'. Two tenses are used, 'He . . . delivered us' (past and complete) and 'we have . . . forgiveness' (present and continuous). There are no hidden sins lurking in the unconscious. *In fact Freud's idea of the unconscious is never found in Scripture.*

Light cannot mingle with darkness: 'In Him is no darkness at all'. Satan is the Prince of darkness. When Jesus was arrested He said, 'This is your hour and the power of darkness' (Luke 22.53). Paul talks about '*the rulers of the darkness of this world . . . spiritual wickedness in high places*' and '*ye were sometimes darkness, but now are ye light in the Lord: walk as CHILDREN OF LIGHT*', and also said, '*Ye brethren are not in darkness . . . we are not of the night nor of darkness*' (Eph. 6:12, 5:8; 1 Thess. 5:4, 5). '*Ye should show forth the praises of him who hath called you out of darkness into his marvellous light*' (1 Pet. 2:9).

Paul then wrote, '*What fellowship has light with darkness? What accord has Christ with Belial? For we are the temples of the living God: as God said, "I WILL LIVE IN THEM, and move in them, and I will be their God"*' (2 Cor. 6:15, 16). '*If we say we have fellowship with him while we walk in darkness we lie* (1 Jn 1:6).

If God is within us and also a demon, then has God been overcome or does God agree to 'have fellowship' with the devil? God sharing a house with an unclean spirit is utterly impossible, and even less possibly could a demon cast out God or subdue Him. '*GREATER IS He that is in you that he that is in the world*' (i.e. Satan) (1 Jn 4:4). THE SONS OF GOD ARE LED BY THE SPIRIT OF GOD AND CANNOT AT THE SAME TIME BE LED BY A DEMON.

Christ 'hath shined in our hearts', so would a dark spirit relish being with us who 'walk in the light'? John, in Chapter 1, verse 4 said, '*The light shines in darkness and the darkness has not overcome it*'.

The position of a child of God is impregnable. Jesus spoke of an unclean spirit leaving a man, but returning and finding it empty and in order, so he returns with seven more evil spirits and dwells there (Luke 11:24–26). The warning is that the unclean spirit returned BECAUSE the house was empty. *Demons only come into empty houses, not occupied houses.* The previous verses (21–22) describe casting out the devil and

God entering a house. But a believer is not an empty house. *'Know ye not that your body is the temple of the Holy Ghost which is in you, which ye have of God?'* (1 Cor. 6:19).

Further, *consider the relationship between a child of God and Christ*: *'Christ in you the hope of glory'. 'Know ye not that Christ is in you?' 'I live, yet not I, but Christ liveth in me'* (Col. 1:27; Cor 13:5; Gal 2:20). Arthur Longley quoting the above Scriptures, reminds us that Jesus said that a kingdom divided against itself would fall, and adds 'It would be impossible to have a house more "divided" than the body of a Christian occupied by the Spirit of Christ and an unclean spirit at the same time'. (see *Christ Made Satan Useless.* p. 87). He says there would be conflict in which a person could die.

'I am sure that neither angels, nor principalities, nor powers, nor anything else in all creation will be able to separate us from the love of God in Christ Jesus' (Romans 8:38/9 – RSV)

'For God hath raised us up together, and made us sit together in heavenly places in Christ Jesus. In whom ye are builded together for an habitation of God through the Spirit' (Eph. 2.6 and 22). So, if a Christian has a demon the demon is with him seated with Christ in heavenly places! *'Your life is hid with Christ in God* – with a demon also? I have always remembered an assuring sermon as a schoolboy, and the illustration of a huge lock on a farm door, which shot a bolt home with one turn of the key, and then shot it further with another turn. We are in Christ, and Christ is in God. A safe, in a strong room. But if we have a demon, hid with Christ in God, does God need somebody to cast it out?

Hallmark Of A Pentecostal

Contrary to the notorious and dangerous film *The Exorcist*, children cannot have demons. They belong to the Kingdom of God, Jesus said, *which Kingdom is in absolute opposition to the Kingdom of Satan*. It applies also to the children of God: 'Every Spirit that confesseth not that Jesus Christ is come in the flesh is not of God. Ye are of God, *little children*, and have overcome them; because greater is he that is in you than he that is in the world.'

'*The Devil cannot lord it over those who are servants of God with their whole heart and who place their hope in Him. The Devil can wrestle with, but not overcome them*' (*The Shepherd of Hermas*).

15 Deviations

The Last Days

The expression 'last days' was used by Peter, Paul, John, Jude, James and the writer of Hebrews. They meant their own days, as well as the years immediately before Christ's return. They all wrote with the possibility in mind that Christ could return in their times.

For example, 1 John 2:18: *'Little children, it is the last time'*. Peter told the crowds on the day of Pentecost, *'This is that which was spoken by the prophet Joel: And it shall come to pass in the last days, I will pour out of my Spirit . . .'*. When James (according to the Authorised Version) said, *'Ye have heaped treasure together for the last days'*, the Greek word is *en* – IN the last days, their own day.

John says, *'as ye have heard that antichrist shall come, even now are there many antichrists; whereby we know it is the last time'*. By no means can anybody ignore the warning by saying we are not yet in the 'last days'. History moves from crisis to crisis, or as has been said 'in a perpetual state of catastrophe'. Last days are always with us. Satanic forces will create world-confusion and use it for evil. He is the typical Anarchist behind global chaos and break-down. His strategy is to produce a Satanic scheme and foist it upon people looking for a new order while they are still in a state of disorder.

The apostles had a major anxiety. It was the corruption of the pure doctrine of Christ. Even Christ Himself said, *'Beware of false prophets, which come to you in sheep's clothing but inwardly they are ravening wolves'*. *'There shall arise false Christs, and false prophets, and shall shew great signs and wonders; insomuch that, if it were possible, they shall deceive the very elect. Behold I have told you before'*, Paul said, *'After my departing shall grievous wolves enter in among you, not sparing the flock. Also OF YOUR OWN SELVES shall men arise, speaking perverse things, to draw away disciples after them. Therefore watch and remember . . .'* (Matt. 7.15, 24:13; Acts 20:29–31).

Peter added his voice: *'There shall be false teachers among you, who privily shall bring in damnable heresies, even denying the Lord that bought them. Many shall follow their pernicious ways'*. The Greek original, which I would paraphrase as follows, is more forcible: *As there used to be false prophets, so now their role will be taken over by false teachers, who will craftily propagate destructive opinions among you* (2 Pet 2:1). Jude says such men 'crept in unawares'. Somebody called them 'creeps'.

The entire letter of Jude, who was the half-brother of Jesus, is concerned with nothing else but preserving the faith from the corrosion of new ideas. He had put pen to paper eager to talk about something different but felt this matter of false teachers was more important. His denunciations are some of the fiercest in the New Testament.

We shall be caught off-guard if we suppose these perversions of the faith are a thing of the apocalyptic future and cannot be insinuated into our churches. The battle between truth and error has always gone on. The strength of the Church has been weakened more by heresy than by any direct opposition.

The Camel's Nose

The apostles saw deviation would come from within rather from without the Church. The best believers, 'the elect', could be deceived because the means is not a frontal assault but a small, apparently Christian variation, emphasis, or novelty – the camel's nose in the tent. There have been a series of teachings in popular style books, mostly experience-related, with authors who bring no back-up from any responsible authority but themselves. One does not like to condemn them outright, because they have an element of Biblical truth, and the writers are themselves godly and sincere. But there is some edging away from the clear road of truth, and this can eventually create a major diversion.

Sometimes ideas can come from contacts outside the church.

Some success training methods employed in business courses can appear adaptable for spiritual purposes. A friend who is a Pentecostal church elder found himself listening to a 'spiritual' seminar, which he recognised as being taken direct from an ordinary business management course with which he was familiar. Yoga for example is recommended widely in secular fields. But the Lord has His own 'methods' and wisdom. Only by persistent reference to the Word can the subtleties be recognised.

Thank God For Cancer?

Other deviations arrive as some individual's brain-child, born out of a too-swift acquaintance with a text. To mention one example: *there is teaching that we should praise God FOR everything, even for evils which befall us or others*. It has a beguiling appearance of advanced spirituality, but is quite muddled. Of course testimonies can be produced, but praising the Lord IN FAITH produces good results, even if this teaching is extreme.

There are times when we should rejoice because we suffer. That is in persecution, glad that we are counted worthy, as Jesus said and about which the apostles were glad in Acts 4. *Rejoicing in such a case is not because we have trouble, but because by it we serve God*. It is a privilege to be associated with Christ and suffer for Him. The joy is this, that it brings us into a relationship with Him which we cannot achieve any other way.

That, however, is not quite the situation when other evils assail us. When a precious child has cancer, or a son becomes a murderer, or a daughter is raped, we would be putting on a false face to praise God for it. It hasn't a shred of Bible to support it. Certainly nobody shouted hallelujahs in Scripture *because* sicknesses or loss plagued them. Job did not, nor does any Psalm suggest such a thing.

For example, Habakkuk had had dialogue with the Lord, and understood what He was doing. He then knew that there would be distress – fig trees would not blossom, vines, olives and fields became fruitless, sheep and cattle were lost. But even in that rare circumstance, where God was behind this distress, Habakkuk did not thank God FOR it. He said 'THOUGH' . . . 'Though (such things happen) . . . I will rejoice IN THE LORD not BECAUSE of distress in the land.

It is a mere mouthing of words, lip-praise to say – 'I thank and bless you O Lord because my mother was badly injured in that accident'. Our hearts are not thankful surely? What is wrong here? It is the same thing as we see in other innovations – *saying words with the mouth as a power-formula*, believing speech itself is potent. This is a subtle deviation from Scripture, carrying a Christian air, but in essence a magic rite.

New Age Pantheism

Two or three years ago a Canadian friend took the trouble to send to me '*The Hidden Dangers of the Rainbow*', Constance Cumbey's thorough investigation of New Age. I scanned it and put it by. The movement meant nothing to me then, but it has given me deep concern since.

Many British believers have heard of New Age. But in October 1988 the BBC were sufficiently aware of it to broadcast interviews with New Age leaders and with their Christian opponents. Religious bookshops carry an increasing number of works on the Rainbow.

There are, however, countless groups, teachings, cults, embraced by New Age. Basically it is a unifying movement for non-Christian ideologies. Some New Agers claim Christian sympathies, but only insofar as Christian and New Age aims have a superficial similarity. What is it? Nothing less than the same thing as that which happened in Eden. Man made in God's image was tempted by Satan to be as God by his own effort. It is also another tower of Babel attempt to create a new world reaching heaven without God, all speaking the same religious language.

The New Age plan, according to several investigators, is for the global village with one government and one religion – a syncretism of all religions. It is obvious that many people are working in the direction of New Age aims, often without realising it.

When an Archbishop dialogues with Hindus, Buddhists and Moslems to find common ground, he is on dangerous New Age grounds. When Quakers find common cause with Buddhists, when Christians adopt the practices of meditation, mind-power, Positive Confession, Inner Healing, Word-power and mysticism, they are moving on to New Age ground.

New Age wants to bring together all religions and mind-related cults which offer humanistic self-salvation – anything which gives people mind-power or word-power to change themselves or their circumstances. It is a direct challenge to Christianity which declares '*There is none other Name under heaven given among men, whereby we must be saved*' (Acts 4:12).

Prophetical writers are predicting a coming world ruler will emerge from New Age. Texe Marrs, one-time US Air force officer, and university lecturer, head of Living Truth Ministries, Texas, has quoted over 600 statements by New Age leaders which he says indicate their plan for one-world religion and government and the intention to eliminate 'every vestige' of Christianity (*Satan's Plan for a One world Religion: 'Dark Secrets of the New Age'*).

Richard A. Bennett (Cross Currents International Ministries) states that Robert Mueller, from a Roman Catholic family, Assistant General Secretary of the United Nations, has advocated a one-world government and a one-world religion, influenced by the Buddhist U Thant, UNO Secretary. It includes pantheism, Hindu reincarnation, and the belief that we are part of God. He suggests that in the coming New Age millenium the planet should be called 'Brahma' ('planet of God'), that is, God is the planet. The Krishna movement, and Seung Moon and his 'Moonies' or Unification Church, a syncretist religion, are typical parts of what is happening to eliminate all differences, especially Christianity.

The Christian expectation of the Millenium when Christ reigns is met by the New Age promise of a millenium with other Lords but Christ, and created by mankind with their newly discovered godhood. Also some Kingdom teaching also speaks of Christian believers themselves bringing in the Kingdom ready to hand over to Christ. Scripture tells us that God the Father alone will give the kingdom to His Son.

The teachings grouped around New Age are fundamentally pantheistic and humanistic, but often linked with spirit-power and mediumship, and the occult in general.

Countless theories exist which relate to world-soul, or universal-force as a source for new potential and higher consciousness. Some see in world-consciousness the explanation for evolution. Teilhard de Chardin, the Roman Catholic theologian-scientist, has been quoted in this connection.

There are some strange ideas, such as the Pyramid theory. The pyramid shape gathers the world-energy, and so some sleep or sit in pyramid-shaped rooms, and use pyramid shaped receptacles for preserving foodstuffs.

A comprehensive list of New Age-type developments would need a whole directory. A typical phrase is 'create your own destiny', which is in essence an invitation to throw off trust in God. Atheism could be included, Scientology, Christian Science and 'Christian' spiritism. The mind-sciences, psycho-cybernetics, holistic medicine, reincarnation (karma), psychotherapy and hypnosis, Self-esteem, self-success-motivation programmes, Higher Self, Positive Mental Attitudes (PMA) (used in some business training schemes), Possibility Thinking, word-power, and so on, will give some idea of current direction and trends.

New Age began to take shape with Madame Blavatsky (1880–1949), a spiritist medium, but the spirit's instruction was not to become a public movement until 1975, when the Plan for taking over the world could be revealed.

Some of the teachings generally incorporated today include that God is the creation, we are part of it and gods ourselves, that the human mind possesses 'supernatural' powers, that world unity comes with world-consciousness teaching, that all religions have basic common truths and can be syncretised, that evolution is a correct science and is shaping the New Age, that healings are possible by mental attitudes and word techniques.

New Age is described by some investigators as sympathetic to abortion, artificial insemination, genetic control, euthanasia, compulsory limitation of families, personal life subordinated to a world directorate, no private ownership, no money – only credit cards. It speaks of Christs, such as the Lord Maitreya, the fifth Buddha (Jesus), and the Moslem Imam Mahdi with Lucifer as the high ruler.

New Age is the age of Aquarius, with the concept of the planet swinging into juxtaposition with new influences from the stars, the moment of change when we must all be part of the great Universal Mind.

Offered to us as they are, they would not lure many Christians aside. But they come sometimes in Christian guise, Satan as an angel of light, the enemy as a friend, or wolves in sheep's clothing as Jesus said. Not only they do appear Christian but also they are spoken of as science.

Sorcery

In an American airport a loquacious young man insisted on my taking a large volume as a gift. I said I was not interested in a new religion. He replied 'This is science, not religion'. It was in fact another eastern mind-system. So 'religion' and 'science' meet. Hence comes the scientific development from physics to metaphysics, interest in psycho-powers, parapsychology, psycho-kinetic ability, extra-sensory perception, psychical research and so on.

Daniel, from his life in Babylon 2,500 years ago, has something to teach us apart from his dreams. He was forcibly drafted into membership of the magicians' circle in Babylon. They were crystal-gazers, necromancers, astrologers, all feeding on the fat of the land, food which Daniel refused. He stood in danger of his life, but steadfastly held fast to Jehovah, even though far from Jehovah's promised land, Israel. Through his faith both Nebuchadnezzar and Darius came to acknowledge the supremacy of his living God, the God of Gods, King of all the earth. This acknowledgement came about through the defeat of the sorcerers as Daniel proved the Lord was God.

Sorcery may be hard to distinguish from Divine manifestations. In *The Practice of Pentecost* I showed that *the Gift of Discernment was not so much detecting an evil spirit in a person, as in doctrine*. We now need this Gift in operation. *'Beloved, believe not every spirit, but try the spirits whether they are of*

God; because many false prophets are gone out into the world'
(1 John 4:1).

Christians sometimes feel uncomfortable with certain situations. It is an instinct, a revulsion which they cannot explain. It could be a mere prejudice, but it is as well to 'try the spirits', for *'many deceivers are entered into the world'*.

'Try The Spirits'

John showed how some spirits could be tested. *His method was to compare their teaching with the truth of Christ being 'IN THE FLESH' Incarnate. The incarnation, God in the flesh, is the point of contest between Christianity and sorcery.* God in Christ, God in Man, is the perfection of Manhood. Through Him we all may become 'temples of the living God', receiving the spirit which is not of the world but of God. *'Truly our fellowship is with the Father and with His Son Jesus Christ'* (1 Jn. 1;3).

New Age-type teaching is that God in the flesh is not the truth but that we are all part of God. It is a case of fellowship not with the Father but with material existence, cosmic forces. It denies the Father and substitutes the world-spirit for the Spirit of God His Son Jesus Christ. It is happening today in all manner of consciousness systems. There are contestants for our minds, God and the devil.

I have included in this book looking more deeply into the vital relationship of God Himself with human flesh. *I have showed that speaking with tongues by the indwelling presence of God is a powerful sign of that reality.* The Pentecostal experience, receiving the Spirit with physical signs, is the answer to all higher-consciousness teaching, and a safeguard. Having the Spirit we don't need the world-spirit. We do not tune in to the infinite, as Trine said. 'Where there is the real, Satan has his counterfeit'. The devil anxiously tries to create a non-Divine power out of human minds, because the present-day outpouring of the Spirit is such a serious challenge to him.

The devil works by sleight of hand, however. None of us knows everything, and new ideas are attractive. If New Testament apostles had to warn their own converts, we today should be alert. He comes with a whisper, a word, a Scripture used in an unusual way, as he did with Jesus.

But *'whatsoever is not of faith is sin'*, and that means faith in God *not faith or faith in a method*. The likely approach would be in fact to direct faith away from God directly to the method. Those earnestly seeking to serve God and demonstrate His power to the world could well be the first target of attack. Methods will appeal to them which need examining, however. Prayer techniques, miracle formulas, mind science, and so on may be a substitute for the straightforward prayer of faith which bends to the will of God.

There is the 'fourth dimension' teaching. I'm very glad that some people's hearts are holier than their theologies. Fourth dimension teaching is a genuine attempt to encourage faith in prayer and to explain the apparent wonders in non-Christian religions.

The theory is as follows. Behind the visible lies the invisible, (true). This is described as 'the realm of spirit'. (This is only partly true; see my book *In My Father's House*). Next, this realm is regarded as the realm occupied by the Spirit of God, the spirit of man, and the spirit of Satan. (This is completely mistaken. Jesus said, 'In my Father's house are many abiding places', and not all spirits occupy the same 'world of spirit'.) Then it is explained that by proper means anyone can exercise control over this world of spirit, just as we can the physical world. (Again incorrect. It is a serious deviation from Biblical truth.)

Fourth dimension teaching believes that the realm of spirit can be manipulated if people have the right means. Besides Christians, others can control the world of spirit, including false prophets, and Transcendental Meditationists, Buddhists, and the new Japanese religious-political cultists Soka Gakkai. (Soka Gakkai has been shaken recently by moral accusations against its leader Mr Ikeda, who was called by a former prime-minister Kakuei Tanaka a 'sutra-chanting Hitler. 'Sutra-chanting' is word-power, by which the spirit world could be affected).

Visualisation

Fourth dimension teaching is that just as Buddhist healers can tap into the resource of the world of spirit by their necromancy, the Christian can also tap in by prayer, if we have the right technique. The technique is similar to Soka Gakkai and other manipulators, namely by visualisation, and by word-power. This means conceiving exactly what is wanted, and using the formula of the Christian to obtain it. Praying in the name of Jesus, and having faith, is however regarded as much more potent in that realm, it is said, than Buddhist prayers.

The theory could be dangerous. For Christian people, however, it simply attempts to explain what happens when you pray in the name of Jesus to the Father in faith. It is a theory about its mechanics only. The essential thing is not the theory but the right approach in faith and in Christ. This brings the answer from God.

The real danger lies in the assumption that God can be controlled like a spirit-world element by use of the right system or expedients. In fact God is a Spirit, but He is not in common lodging with all other spirits or spirit elements. He is not to be compared with other gods or spirits in any sense. If they can be manipulated by visualisation and conception, God cannot. We cannot have power over Him, and He is not open to human control. Our attitude must always be one of absolute humility before the sovereign Lord of heaven and earth.

However, ideas in our heads may be hopelessly wrong – do any of us have perfect beliefs? God hears prayer in the name of Jesus even when we have odd notions about how it works. Miracles prove nothing much. They certainly do not prove our methods or theories are correct, but only that we have proper faith. God is gracious, and answers prayer in Christ's name despite the fourth dimension theory, not by it.

But the idea of a realm of spirit to be controlled by a technique of visualisation and conception, has too many resemblances to oriental metaphysics for occidental Christians. If Soka Gakkai Buddhists, with seventeen million members, use this method to produce results in the spirit world, and Christians do the same, where is the uniqueness of the Christian faith?

Where is the God of Israel? Is He really sharing a spirit world with the devil and waiting for men on earth to find the right sutra to move Him?

When we pray, we are bound to visualise something. One man said he thought of God *as a kind of oblong blur*. I ask sick people to turn their mind to Jesus, away from themselves and their needs, which is at least better than a vague cloud of light somewhere. But visualisation is much different. It means we should conceive vividly exactly what we want in size, shape, number, colour and so on, or visualise Jesus going or doing something we wish, even backward in time.

Psychological Salvation

This form of intensive visualisation is now a mind-science, and part of a psychological method, even of psychological salvation, as described in my chapter on demon exorcism. In Inner Healing, visualisation is not unlike hypnotic trance, and people see things happening, and even Jesus being projected to bring peace or deliverance. Can Jesus be projected?

Does Jesus actually go back into a past situation, when a person was a child? Can we put Him there by thinking it, or by it being suggested to us in a psychological trauma or 'sleep'? Can we get Him to do things in the past which He didn't do? Is there any promise in Scripture that says He will materialise in the situation if we bring Him in by our mental concentration? There is not. Jesus doesn't actually go into that childhood episode, of course.

What is this inner vision then? If Jesus does not move into the past and forgive us, as is described, what is this forgiveness? Who is it that goes and which people believe they see suddenly appearing in mental projection? That is a disquieting question.

Jesus doesn't go when we put Him there by mentally visualising Him. We can't manipulate or direct Him. If He does not go there in reality, how can a person be healed or forgiven or forgive somebody – somebody who may be dead in fact?

There are two possibilities. The first is demon impersonation. But from that a born-again blood-washed believer would be protected. The second is auto-suggestion. The process is entirely psychological. By that means the patient feels he has had power to forgive, and his mind has cleansed itself of hate or resentment or sin (if it works). It is all in the mind – psychological salvation. He must have forgiven himself, and saved himself, not Christ; self-salvation – the New Age aim. If psychosomatic healing takes place (trauma), it is a false miracle, not of God.

'Ye Shall Be As Gods'

The underlying aim of mankind is self-dependence, with no reliance upon God. This was at the heart of the sin in the Garden with Satan's suggestion 'Ye shall be as gods'. This, I believe, is why Jesus called him *a liar and the father of lies – a murder from the beginning* (John 8:44). Self, putting Self in the place of God is a self-deceit which leads to every crime, including Hitler's determination to establish a super-race.

We admire people's courage when they tackle their lives alone. God does not. Are we to admire the woman who leaves her good husband and lives a life just to show him that she can do without him? But the world has invented many theories and systems to help mankind stand equal with God and independent of Him, from the moment when Adam and Eve used fig leaves to cover their outraged sense of modesty. God did better, and gave them fur coats.

Humanism puts man in the centre of the scene, man is the worshipper of himself. His natural religiousness is dealt with by self-satisfaction. The true God is an onlooker while we break the first commandment 'Thou shalt have no other gods before me'. Communism promises perfection by means of material evolution. New Age has a religio-political slant as a form of socialism.

But we now have man-centred religions, cults and systems. It is the sin of antichrist (2 Thes, 2:4; Rev. 13:8). By means of eastern meditation and mysticism people are taught to look within themselves for the higher Self.

The West has its own good makers. Mormonism sees men as part of God and Christian Science's science of mind appears to be to the same thing, not distinguishing mind from Mind.

Bishop Berkeley (1685–1753) suggested everything was a projection of Mind and did not exist in actuality (called Subjective Idealism). There is also the Manifest Sons of God movement whose followers believe they will be Christ, as a body at least.

Unitarianism speaks of all men as potential sons of God like Jesus. The Shepherding, or submission doctrine declares that God mandates His authority over men who can themselves mandate it to others. It does not seem to have occurred to them that this is an incipient form of playing God, leaders become 'as gods' to those who must obey them as they would obey the Lord.

'*The Seduction of Christianity*' quotes Casey Treat, pastor of the Seattle Christian Faith Centre, making his congregation repeat 'I'm an exact duplicate of God'. He quotes also a number of other popular religious presenters not all known in Britain but making similar Divine claims. By theological excesses people are believing that they now have divine powers as equal beings with God.

The Whole Counsel Of God

Not every false doctrine even bothers with Scripture. Experience or results are enough. But usually the Bible is used. Selected Scriptures, few or many, may be strung together and yet be in conflict with the general tenor of the Bible. Men do not have quasi-godhood or quasi-Divine authority. Everywhere in the Bible men are shown to be dependant, suppliant, ALTOGETHER OTHER THAN GOD, unworthy, living by the grace of God.

The word-faith teaching runs counter to the whole book of Psalms for example – every Psalm, wherein God is sought, petitioned, trusted, hung on to, but never once does a verse make a man lift himself up and say 'All I need to do in my troubles is simply positively confess all is well.' The Psalmists confessed NEGATIVELY hundreds of times (see Psalm 88), and also confessed their faith in God, but never as a formula to manipulate things. Only God can help us, and He is not to be manipulated. He will do nothing except according to His

Word. This is the ultimate test of the spirits, whatever wonders they try to dazzle us with.

16   Tongues and Truth

Mark Twain said that at fourteen years old he could hardly stand his father's ignorance, but at twenty-one he was surprised how much the old chap had picked up. In my case, at fourteen my pastor seemed to have nothing else to teach me. I had no problems, and the Bible was perfectly clear.

In fact only one thing puzzled me – the sheer bulk of Scripture. Did it really need sixty-six books to talk about salvation, that, and maybe one or two other things? The second advent of Christ, being a little more complicated might be allowed the whole of Revelation. The few texts on Divine healing and the baptism in the Spirit seemed enough for those doctrines.

Long before my teens ended, however, I came to the conclusion that I knew nothing. Any single page of Scripture represented a hundred questions and the quantity of Divine thought swamped me, and was mostly beyond me. Sometimes I tell myself I am still at that stage.

God does not stand still. We will never catch up with Him. Salvation, which, as a boy, I thought I encompassed seven times every Sabbath like Israel round Jericho, began opening up, wall after wall falling to expose wealth beyond wealth. Luther grasped one simple text: 'The just shall live by faith', and a library of theology arose from it. *So what will come from discovering Acts 2 as the Holy Spirit leads us into all truth*? A new spring has broken forth and a new river formed.

What – No Theology

One of the things I once knew everything about was the baptism in the Spirit. The Bible said it, you had the experience, you spoke with tongues, and that was that. Later as the Public Relations Officer to the British Pentecostal Fellowship, I found a trifle more was needed – a whole library would have been a help to begin with.

We were often asked 'Where is your theology of the baptism in the Spirit?'. Theology? What had that to do with it? What theology was needed beyond the promise of the Father?

However, what could I say? It occurred to me that it wasn't our doctrine in the first place. It had always been plainly there in Scripture. It was Bible. *Why then hadn't the church long before us produced its own theology about the baptism in the Spirit*? Generally it meant no more than receiving the Spirit at confirmation, or an inward unfelt event at conversion, or by faith, which was certainly nothing like we read in Scriptures.

But, particularly, the baptism in the Spirit is tied up with the Ascension of Jesus *but where was the theology of the Ascension?* Ascension Day and Pentecost were church holidays, yet, when the Pentecostals arrived, teaching about Christ in glory did not relate very much to dynamic experience today. Why hadn't the Church already produced it?

It seemed scholars didn't know quite what to make of it. Modernist liberals didn't believe it, and shrugged it off with uncertain and speculative opinion. However, a *Time* article recently said that today sceptics are becoming sceptical about scepticism. Let us hope so. Meanwhile 250 million people now accept the blessings of Acts for themselves.

Many Truths Are One Truth

As a Pentecostal evangelist 'cumbered about with much serving', discoveries come to me along the way. I had room for them! A homespun conviction has emerged, and provided me with fire, and steam. The way it happened began after my first sermon as a college student, when I had put the green, blue, and black handwritten notes in an envelope grandly inscribed with date, title and where preached – Opus 1 number 1.

'Lonely as a cloud' it waited at the end of a bleak, empty four-foot shelf which I could not imagine ever filling up, the widow's mite, all I had. My entire library of books sprawled on another shelf, too few to support one another. Another sermon would be as marvellous as the multiplication of Elisha's meal.

Somehow the miracle happened, and soon there were six envelopes – my entire ministry. Desperate I turned to prayer, though I felt even God could not find another crumb in my spiritual Mother Hubbard cupboard. So, would He please have me sent to a different church every six weeks? Presently it struck me that what I was preaching was simply doctrine – bits I had picked up – no more than a collection of theological odds and ends. I needed a lot more bits. After several decades I'm still a collector. But I noticed something – *the more I picked up the more it suggested a great picture – that all truths together made one Truth, the final Truth*.

Christ's Way With Scripture

There can be no isolated truth. Every piece in the jigsaw belongs to all the other truths to complete the picture of the Man Christ Jesus who said 'I am the Truth'. What doesn't fit doesn't belong. Scripture is a symphony of interwoven themes. A few texts are not enough. 'The devil can cite Scripture for his purpose. 'An evil soul producing holy witness', as Shakespeare declared. At the Temptation, Christ reminded the devil that man must live by EVERY word of God, Jesus *'expounded unto them in ALL the Scriptures the things concerning himself'* (Luke 24:27).

Christ's method is worth noting at this point. For example, we find this in John 7, 37/38: *'Jesus stood and cried saying, If any man thirst, let him come unto me and drink. He that believeth on me, as the Scripture hath said, out of his belly shall flow rivers of living water.'* Now no text says that, though there's an echo of what He said in several places, such as in Zechariah 14:8, or Psalm 105:41. When He talked of 'the Scripture', as did others in the New Testament, it did not mean a proof text, but ALL Scripture, the authority of the entire Book, text and texture.

Well Of The Word

Jesus Himself shows here that the baptism in the Spirit is not a doctrine pirouetting on one text, but on 'Scripture'. It belongs from Genesis to Malachi. Since Pentecost belongs to all Scripture it throws light on everything a Christian believes, and opens up a whole area of new understanding. This I show for example in chapters on revival.

With the torch of Pentecostal light we can also take a good look at some of the new things on offer. There is a plethora of novel charismatic ideas. Some are offered us by prophecy, but we must 'prove all things'. One pastor recently announced that through prophecy the Lord had instructed him to make certain changes in the meetings. 'We are going to do what the Lord says,' he explained, 'but if it doesn't work we will go back to the old way.'!

Some innovations come with crusading zeal dignified with the word revival or similar, declared to eclipse the glory of the 'classical' doctrine of Pentecost. 'The new thing God is doing' must be accepted or we shall be left behind. And yet, but for the sacrifice of the older generation of Pentecostals and their faithfulness during unimaginable discouragement there would be no Pentecostal churches to preach any new thing to.

One 'new thing', is that God is waiting for new church 'structures' before doing mighty things. The parable of Jesus in Luke 5:36–38 is quoted. New wine skins are needed for new wine, new church order and new worship can bring the new blessing of God. Some pastors are willing to see their churches fall apart as 'a cleaning process', so that the new wine can come in.

This is in fact quite a curiosity of Biblical interpretation. What our Lord had in mind had nothing to do with church structures. That is read into His words quite gratuitously. His words are used for a quite different purpose. It concerned a totally different situation and Jesus addressed his parable to Jewish religionists, not classic Pentecostals!

Perhaps we could take a fresh look. *In fact was Jesus recommending the old or the new?* Putting aside traditional ideas about the new, we can then see that Jesus was recommending the OLD, not the new. The new wine was the teaching of scribes and doctors of the law, by which novelties and traditions they made the Scripture 'of none effect'. Jesus said, 'the old is better' (v.38) and *the new wine does the damage* (v.35). Mere novelty. 'New wine' in Scripture was often just heady cheap 'plonk', one year old, not to be compared with vintage wines and no fit symbol for the kingdom (Acts 2:13). The old wine had to be watered for its richness. The wine at Cana which Jesus made was quality wine, not hurried pressings. (See *Expository Times*, vol.99 no.8 p.234.)

Examining the present new forms of worship and new church structures, they turn out to be just as human and man-made as the old ones. In fact, are they new? Not that that matters. If we want to change the style of worship or where we meet or how we conduct proceedings or how we evangelise, why not? It is all one to God.

Change might be a good thing sometimes, even change for change's sake. But the Spirit of God is not that fussy. If He was it would be plainly declared in Scripture. If 'church structures' were vitally important they would be declared to be so in Scripture and the proper 'structures' plainly set forth, not hinted at in a remote parable.

The Baptism in the Holy Spirit is the best of God's wine, call it new or old. It bathes everything with glory – doctrine, worship, the creeds, people, the preacher and the listener: '*It is the Spirit which quickeneth*'. Organisation helps, but does not quicken, nor does physical posture, nor musical style. Outward observances, method, or other circumstances are a matter of indifference to the Spirit.

If anybody likes to use Old Testament allegory as a basis for truth – and that is peculiar but common today – look at the story of Elisha and the widow. *The miracle oil flowed into every kind of vessel they could get hold of*. Pentecost fills all forms and all circumstances. It is not forms, places, man-made arrangements, outward shapes: '. . . *neither in this mountain nor at Jerusalem, but . . . in spirit and in truth*', (John 4:24).

I have felt the presence of God in every kind of situation. In every kind of church, however 'structured', I have seen people converted and healed and enjoyed 'the fullness of the blessing of the Gospel of Christ'. There was power in a Hungarian church with the slowest and oldest of hymns, and in the southern rhythm of the Bible Belt, and I have been deeply moved by a classical aria such as Mendelssohn's 'If with all your hearts ye truly seek me, ye shall every truly find me'. Sitting in my own home, or walking through the city rain, the Lord has been as much present as one could bear in this world. No circumstance made any difference except the state of my own heart.

Now was there a greater thing than Pentecost for the church? a greater day after the day of Pentecost? It completed the work of Christ following His Ascension and sending forth of the Spirit to abide with us. The next act is Christ's return – typified by the High Priests' passing through the veil and then his returning, appearing meanwhile in the presence of God for us.

After the baptism of the Spirit and the giving of His gifts the apostles and disciples did not move on to any new epoch, except to know Him better by growing in grace. *Nothing eclipsed their Pentecostal day.* 'When he had by himself purged our sins, (he) sat down on the right hand of the Majesty on high, (God said), Sit on my right hand, until I make thine enemies thy footstool'. No further work is prophesied in any way in the programme of Christ except His coming again.

New light will always break forth from the Word, but any radical advance must have its related act in the programme of Christ's life and first coming. New things must be based on what Christ did. Forgiveness relates to Calvary, new life to the Resurrection, the baptism in the Spirit to the Ascension. What other act of Christ is there to which some great new thing relates? *None whatever*!

Everything else would flow from the Holy Spirit, many a refreshing shower, many a new encouragement, many mighty moments, new understandings, but all deriving from the same experience. Through the Holy Spirit, Christ will build His church and distribute gifts and convict the world of sin, righteousness and judgement. Through the Spirit He will be with us always.

When anybody speaks of a greater thing, it is obvious that the greatness of the Pentecostal baptism has not been appreciated – or even experienced. It is the beginning, and from it we move on in revival power into ever new things, which are the old also.

However when the baptism in the Spirit is claimed without tongues, which is the only evidence ever mentioned in Scripture, then I can understand why something else might be considered an advance. But anyone having received the Spirit with tongues, the old, rich wine, would never consider the new, some later innovation greater. Receiving 'gifts' alone without the baptism in the Spirit, is not to be compared either. The Holy Spirit is all.

This 'classic' truth has swept the world as no 'new thing' ever will. Within the Pentecostal-charismatic garden many new plants keep appearing. The Father has planted that garden, but weeds will appear, as Jesus warned us. He did assure us that *'Every plant which my heavenly Father hath not planted, shall be rooted up'*. If they are not, they will lead only a struggling existence, but 'classic' Pentecostal groups still flourish and burgeon. They provide by far the major strength to world-wide church growth, and are the main arm of evangelism and of all activites and service to society.

Something Else Than Tongues?

Many want to manage without tongues, for some inexplicable reason. They even use Scripture to argue there are other ways to know they have received the Spirit. Anything but tongues! Even 'receiving by faith' will do, without any experience at all! Or less than that, that the Holy Spirit was received on behalf of us all 2,000 years ago by the first Christians! Others regard the baptism and tongues as just one of various alternatives, quite marginal and optional.

However you cannot separate Pentecost and speaking with tongues without surrendering the Pentecostal position. Speaking with tongues as the initial evidence of the baptism in the Spirit is the one thing that names us as Pentecostal. It was the crux, the flash point of the new revival. Pentecostals bear battle scars for this testimony and many a hurt. Let this be quite clear – but for tongues there would be no modern Pentecostal movement.

The longer I compare developments and Biblical interpretations, the clearer it is that this gift is vital. Tongues are a hallmark of true Pentecost.

For what God's purpose is, there is no alternative. Some think we can know we receive the Spirit by the power we have, or by a spiritual gift, or by evangelistic success. But none of these was taken as evidence in Scripture. Indeed all the gifts are found in the Old Testament *when there was no baptism in the Spirit*, except for this one gift of tongues. This was reserved for the outpouring of the Spirit in the new dispensation, its unique sign and banner. *Of all Bible miracles it is different, reserved for a thousand years as the sign-gift of the outpouring of the Spirit.*

Against this, it has often been argued that tongues were a worry to Paul in Corinth. They were. Corinthians were childish and treated tongues as something to show off about. But for that matter so were other things a problem in Corinth, such as prophecy, marriage, food and even the Lord's table of communion. But abuse does not alter the profound importance of any of these things, including tongues.

However, there are some thrilling answers to some fascinating questions which I want to move on to. What is speaking with tongues and what is really happening to us when we do speak as the Spirit gives utterance?

17 Sign of the New Man

Wonder

Everybody knows that according to Scripture, speaking with tongues is a sign of the presence of the Holy Spirit. But is that all Scripture says of the experience? Far from it. We also read that '*your body is the temple of the Holy Spirit*' (1 Cor. 6:19). Further, we speak with tongues '*as the Spirit gives utterance*' (Acts 2:4).

Now, what is really going on? Attempts to explain how the Spirit gives utterance usually belittle it: 'Ecstatic speech', 'uprush from the subconscious', 'trauma', 'psychological'. Rationalise the gift and absurd suggestions are made. Nils Bloch Hoell, in *The Pentecostal Movement*, thinks that people speaking languages which they have never known, do it by telepathy! But, never in all human experience has any example of such marvellous telepathy ever been known. I believe in miracles but I am not that credulous.

Something tremendous is taking place, but not something ridiculous. *Mortal flesh is imbued with immortal Spirit*. That is a possibility which has been realised long enough. We are His temples, but what does that mean? We might point to a place of worship and say 'that is my temple', but we don't live there. We walk in and out. It does not have any effect upon the building itself.

That, however, is quite different from the way God inhabits a temple. He pervades and permeates the place, fills it. He identifies Himself with it, and He is the glory of it. We never do. If we are His Temples He does not visit us, coming in and out occasionally, but takes up residence. He infuses Himself into human nature, identifying with us, the Spirit in the flesh. Clearly this is a great wonder and Divine mystery.

When Paul first said, '*Know ye not that your body is the temple of the Holy Spirit*' he could not have startled the heathen

mind more. 'Spirit', or God, to them was untouchable by
earthly creatures. Any kind of link, they thought, could not be
immediate and direct. It needed a ladder of mediators, moving
from lower to higher by degrees from gross to refined. Flesh
was made by another and evil power, a *Demiurge* god, and
they therefore considered material things and flesh as vile and
unclean.

This was the 'wisdom of men' which Paul scorned in classical
times. Seneca called the body 'destestable', and the mystery
religions spoke of 'the tomb of the flesh' – *Soma sema*. When
Socrates was to die by drinking the fatal hemlock he reasoned
about the after-life. (Plato's *Phaedo*). His assumption was that
the body is a hindrance to understanding reality. To Bible
Christians his arguments read very strangely. Christians enjoy
a relationship with God IN THE BODY, through the Holy
Spirit. There is one Mediator. He is the ladder set up between
earth and heaven, He told Nathanael in John 1:51.

I Am A New Creation

The presence of the Spirit of God within us is however only
possible when we are brought back into something like God's
original image, cleansed from guilt. When Adam fell, only the
ground broke his fall! It was a fatal fall. The saving act of God
is to put us together again, and restore our damaged spiritual
capacities. We become 'new creatures.'

That is a work only the Creator can perform. '*We are his
workmanship created in Christ Jesus*' (Ephesians 2:10). The
specific purpose of this creation was to make it possible to
receive the Holy Spirit. That man, made new in Christ, and
filled with the Spirit, is an extraordinary person. We must say
more of this later.

Today we are familiar with the name 'charismatic' to describe
a speaker with tongues. But the word 'charismatic' is not really
good enough. It merely means gifted, and a Pentecostal person
is more than gifted. He is not somebody who speaks with
tongues or has healing gifts. He is a new creature in Christ Jesus
and full of the Holy Spirit. Tongues are a sign of something far
greater. God is Himself the 'unspeakable gift'.

That is always the case with God's gifts. The entire scheme of salvation itself is more than something God sends, or even arranges, while He sits in heaven. The hymn puts it 'He flew to my relief', Forgiveness is not just an act of the recording angel wiping our slate clean. When we are 'justified by faith' it isn't simply something that goes on in God's mind which He allowed Paul to tell us about. It is all 'in Christ'. Salvation comes in the form of the Saviour. Forgiveness comes only with the presence of the One we sinned against. Justification brings Him over the dark mountains to walk with us.

The kind of forgiveness Jesus gave was no mere verbal assurance. It affected people. IN HIS PRESENCE people felt forgiven. It is His presence, as the Saviour, and our knowing it, that gives the guilty conscience peace. All we do is come. When Jesus forgave, the lame leaped; He had forgiven them, He! If HE did not condemn, and if HE would receive them, that was all that mattered in earth or heaven.

True forgiveness meant unclean women felt pure and washed His feet with penitential tears of love. Zaccheaus was beside himself with happiness and didn't care tuppence about his swindled thousands, and generosity bursts from his redeemed heart, like Scrooge on Christmas morning. Custom men like Levi were entranced, left their offices and threw a party, feasting to celebrate HIM.

A gift, a ring on the finger, leaves a lady still what she was. It is not the sparkle of a diamond ring which makes her radiant, but her lover. The born-again Christians want more than spiritual gifts, a ring on the finger, but His indwelling presence. The gifts are temporary anyway – '*Where there are prophecies, they will cease; where there are tongues, they will be stilled*'. But the gift of the Spirit is permanent, while 'gifts' are only a love sign.

'Pneumatised' Men People

The Divine breath breathes into us. Breathing into cold clay the Lord created Adam, we read in Genesis. The breath of God is the Spirit of God. He breathes into people today to make them new in Christ Jesus. We become 'partakers of the Divine nature'. When Ezekiel saw God's breath blow across the dry bones, they lived again. Jesus said in John chapter 20 verse 22: '*Receive ye the Holy Ghost*' as He breathed upon them, and within days the breath of the winds of heaven (the Pneuma) filled them (Acts 2:4) and they became 'Pneumatised', not men of spirit, but men of THE Spirit.

When we receive Christ, who would know it as they pass us in the street? 'They cannot see the glory that is shining round my head' as one hymn-writer put it. There is more. The Spirit of God takes up residence in the castle of our personality.

Now that is what we are, so can no way be found for us to BE like that outwardly? A musician must sometimes be a musician, and play, and an artist must show it. When can we be the children of God from whose beings flow rivers of living water? Must we always remain 'normal'? Must we for ever shut up all our music within us?

The music will out . . . and that is why we speak with tongues, that is when the waters flow for all to see. Jackie Pullinger, working behind forbidden walls in Hong Kong where Chinese gangs hid, came to expect conversions and change of life with these criminal leaders when men spoke with tongues, as happened to Cornelius and his household in Acts. A real Saviour who died on a real cross gives a real power sign of the redeeming power of the Gospel.

The New Testament describing the experience of Christian believers always seems to me to grope for superlatives. A new experience needs new words. There is no parallel to the wonder of salvation. More than one new expression is coined or adapted to express it. The Bible abandons moderation of language when it describes salvation. It speaks of new birth, regeneration, becoming sons of God, being translated out of darkness into light, receiving eternal life, found when lost, quickened from death, the power of God working within us mightily, of the Spirit of resurrection indwelling us, of being made perfect in Christ, as inheritors of the saints in light, being glorified, being seated with Christ in heavenly places and much more – something extraordinarily powerful.

The incredible fact is that God has shared His own life with us. *Tongues, or something of the sort, seems to be the only way to give vent to such an experience of the transforming glory of God. The baptism in the Spirit can never be spoken of as a spiritual experience only. It is also physical.* In that case, the only satisfactory sign has to be physical also; physical but produced by the Spirit. If there could be such a sign other than speaking with tongues, I confess I have not been able to imagine what it might be. Healing would not do – we might not be sick. It would have to be a halo or some similar visible supernatural effect which God does not give for fairly obvious reasons . . . such as sitting on a bus, or talking to the boss, or wearing a crash helmet!

How then can what we are come out? Of course in behaviour and manner, goodness, love, patience. But we are more than moral beings. We are full of God. We are 'pneuma-tised'. So – how can that be evident? God has done more than improve our disposition. He has infused our entire personality with the Spirit of God, and we are 'changed from glory into glory'.

A man's true self must have some outlet, especially when full of the Spirit, as the prophets such as Jeremiah said. The tongue must express it. The tongue is our organ of self-communication to the outside world. When I speak, it is ME, coming through. WHAT A PERSON IS, only the tongue can truly communicate. We say we only know somebody when they open their mouth. We may declare we are children of God, or for that matter we can say we are space travellers from Andromeda. Saying it is nothing. What's the evidence? We can say we are witnesses that Christ is alive but anybody can say that. Looking like it is another thing. *But when we speak with tongues we are acting what we are, people filled with the Spirit.* We SHOW ourselves to be Pneuma-tised beings. WE speak with tongues ONLY as *THE SPIRIT* gives utterance.

However, there is much more than that, as we shall see.

18 Who is Speaking?

As a boy, before the baptism in the Spirit I experimented and found I was as greatly un-gifted for speaking a made-up language of my own as I was in several other directions. As young lads we used to pretend to be foreigners, inventing our own esperanto, when we heard crew members from foreign ships in our city-port. Our jabber amused our families.

Later, still a schoolboy, thinking that maybe the *glossolalia* needed a bit of priming, as some charismatics actually propose, I made more serious attempts, but only to prove again I lacked all linguistic inventiveness. However, from the day the Spirit endowed me, *trying to speak with tongues has never been necessary; effortless and spontaneous, a fluent language is released.* 'They spake with tongues as the Spirit gave them utterance', as in Acts 2.

The Hidden Instinct

Tongues did not seem unnatural to me, though it is supernatural. Nobody understands the complex nature of human personality, so it is not strange that a capacity for tongues might exist within us, and perhaps for far more than tongues. To speak with tongues does not make us freaks. It helps to make us what God intended. If there are odd Pentecostals, they would be odder still but for the Holy Spirit. From this experience benefit flows into every part of the human make up, psychologically, physically, morally. It balances, steadies, and adds ever-increasing character.

Perversion

To be Pentecostal is not at all the same thing as having a fascination for occultism. I asked the Lord for the Spirit and He did not give me a scorpion. He gave me Bread, not a stone,

Pentecost is the opposite of Spiritism. Spiritism is the counter-feit of Pentecost. The medium in the seance is invaded *from outside*. He or she becomes a passive vehicle for another alien 'thing'. A medium's own personality withdraws while another entity takes over. The medium becomes a non-person or mere thing or instrument for a power from beyond. It is an unholy prostitution of man or womanhood. Scripture calls it spiritual adultery. Why? Because we were designed to be vessels of God and of no other.

We were born with a capacity for God to dwell in us. That is our natural state. Any other power compels us to surrender our human sovereignty, which God never does. Spirit-possession is a perversion of the natural desire of a creature for the Creator. Any other occupying power is an enemy. We can open our-selves to God, OR to some dark force, BUT NEVER BOTH. The port of entry is always our will, the royal gateway for God only, and the territory of human nature is empty without Him. We are traitors to ourselves when we allow any other to enter.

The Spirit's coming is supernatural, but it is also the most natural thing in the world. We were made for Him, like seed was made for water before springing into life, though buried half a century in desert sand. When He comes we bear the fruits of the Spirit.

The Mystery

I previously said that Pentecostal truth relates to all other truth. Here is an example, Paul, in Ephesians 5. verse 32 takes up what he calls the 'mystery' of marriage. It is delicately expressed in Scripture: '*Thy desire shall be to thy husband, and he shall rule over thee. A man will leave his father and mother and be united with his wife and they will become one flesh*' (Genesis 3:16). Paul uses this as a picture of the amazing revelation of the bond between Christ and the Bride of Christ.

The instinct of attraction between male and female is one of nature's most powerful urges. In the wild, the instinct of sur-vival is largely sexual, mindless and totally irresistible, to make the species' continuation possible. No doubt the appetite is as strong in mankind, but we have the intelligence to make it serve us instead of us serving it.

Christian marriage includes vows, love, respect, thought and control, turning animalism into human dignity and intelligent joy. Immorality may be defined as animalism. Fornication is the indulgence of crude sensuality lacking any spiritual under-standing, like sheep 'which nourish a blind lifee within the brain'. People use one another like non-persons, and discard one another when done. The word 'pornography' comes from the Greek word *pornei* which relates to selling, so that a woman is a de-humanised commercial sex-object.

Eve was meant to want to be wanted. She is for Adam, and he is for her. After Eve was given to her husband, he was drawn to her in a way he was attracted by nothing else. The real joy of life is not in things, but people. Without love, people become things. Then the unique satisfaction of humans with humans evaporates. Happiness is people we love. Eden was Paradise, but without Eve Adam was lonely.

'*Now the Lord God had formed out of the ground all the beasts of the field and the fowl of the air. He brought them to the man to see what he would name them*'. But animals are not persons. Eve came to him on a unique level of desirability. Eve responded with equal desire. They come together but she is not violated, not degraded, but is ennobled.

That relationship is God-made. It is 'the way of a man with a maid' which Proverbs compares and says is as proper as a bird flying or a ship sailing, and yet it remains, says that writer, '*too wonderful for me, which I know not*'.

This is what Paul describes as the 'mystery'. There is no such 'mystery' between animals, only in humans. The biological act alone does not make creatures one flesh, or it would make two animals or insects one flesh. *It takes more than an act of the flesh to make a marriage.* Conducted without personal regard and respect the one for the other, it is depravity and animalism. The mystery of oneness has gone. It carries the odour of the brothel, or of rape, the worst thing a man can do to a woman.

True marriage cannot be just physical. It consists of the linking of personalities with a sense of committal, discovery, trust and surrender. *Only that kind of marriage of 'true hearts' is indissoluble.* When divorce or bereavement takes place it is traumatic and rupturing. Personality itself is infringed. The hurt man or woman has experiences as if their own self were leaving them, floating away out of sight. It is a pre-death death. Marriage creates a reality. 'True love never dies a natural death'.

We read of woman being created for man, and that the man is the head of the woman. *But both man and woman were made for Christ, just as Eve for Adam, and the love-bond is far greater, 'All things were created by him and for him'* (Colossians 1:16). If we understand we will add *'were created by him and for him'* to love. We are not given to Him as a doll is given to a child, nor as a tool or an instrument to a workman. We may be channels, but we are not 'channels *only*'. We may be 'vessels' but the thought of God 'using' us is hard to find in Scripture.

Even in the Old Testament, in the book of Judges where we might look for it, the expression seems to be deliberately avoided. Judges 6:34, I'm told, has been translated *'The Lord clothed himself with Gideon'*. That is the way God associates with men. It is not clear who 'used' who. It is a case of partners in action together.

God's relationship with mankind is too close to speak of Him using us. We need not be pedantic, of course, as we all commonly speak of a man being used of God, and we know what we mean. But speaking of marriage, we know that if a wife felt her husband 'used' her, it would be the end of the marriage.

As a woman is made for a man, and a man for a woman, we were made for Him. The intimacy between the Redeemer and the redeemed is such that only the marriage bond can illustrate it. The figure is familiar in Scripture. The prophets Isaiah, Jeremiah, Ezekiel, and Hosea spoke that way: *'Thy Maker is thine husband; the Lord of hosts is his name'* (Isa. 54:5). Jesus described Himself as the Bridegroom (Matt. 9:15. 25:5). John the Baptist called Him the Bridegroom and so does John in Revelation.

Ezekiel 16 is descriptive of the Divine Husband as saving Israel His wife, and Paul says Christ is 'the saviour of the body', that is, the Bride (Eph. 5:23). The act of salvation involves Christ and the believer identifying with one another. He doesn't SEND us salvation. He IS salvation, our Saviour by personal operation. He redeemed us by Himself and for Himself. He became the Ransom, the price of redemption.

It is illustrated in Exodus 21. A Hebrew servant could keep his wife – the property of the master – if he gave up his own freedom. He had to offer himself as a bond-servant not to her, but to somebody else, the employer he served. *He gave himself FOR her, so that he could give himself TO her*.

It illustrates our salvation beautifully. Christ gave Himself FOR us that He might give Himself TO us as our Bridegroom. Our oneness with Him is expressed in other terms too. We were 'raised' with Him, and are seen as 'seated together with Him' on high, and our life as 'hid with Christ in God'. Such statements run through the New Testament in bewildering description.

But spiritual unity is not all. The important thing I wish to say is this: there was fleshly unity also: 'Forasmuch then as the children are partakers of flesh and blood, he also himself likewise took part of the same. Wherefore IN ALL THINGS it behoved him to be made like unto his brethren' (Heb. 2:14–17).

Indeed when Christ became Man He was betrothed to the whole human race. Christ became 'one flesh' with the entire Adamic race: '*God sending his own Son in the likeness of sinful flesh, and for sin, condemned sin in the flesh*'. There was in fact a union, a closeness, between Christ 'the second Adam' and ourselves, which is unique, possible only to Him.

It is a relationship which no human being has with another human being. We are all related to the first Adam but the bond to Christ is closer. In Adam we die, but in the second Adam we live. It is even more real *to Christ*. He is aware of being Man in the profound depths of His being. His favourite name for Himself was 'the Son of Man'.

The marriage unity, of course, remains only a picture. The reality is new and unique, and is described by Paul as a 'mystery'. We experience but cannot explain it. *We now arrive at what I want to make very important – SPEAKING WITH TONGUES IS PART OF THAT BRIDE AND BRIDE-GROOM MYSTERY*. We cannot explain its mechanics. We don't know how the mind of man and the mind of God come together. But the experience is valid – the mystery of God in the flesh.

The glory of it! His desire for us, His love! If we have spoken about the drawing power between male and female, this is still only a two-dimensional symbol. '*God SO loved the world . . .*'. The 'so' should be emphasised as a word of measurement, but it is measuring infinity, God's love. What we know on the surface, as on a photograph, exists, as Paul puts it in 'breadth, length, depth and height' in God's four-dimensional greatness. If we dare say it, there is an irresistible attraction between heaven and earth. The full expression of it brings us to the Cross, of course.

This Is Evidence Of Much More

What then about speaking with tongues? Speaking with tongues is only possible by such a Divine-human unity. It neither takes away from our humanness, nor from the sovereign majesty of God. Tongues are a remarkable earthly evidence of a heavenly union, God and man in one, too subtle for definition.

An ocean of blessing exists in that unity, but *one point where the waters break through is speaking with tongues*. This is a sign not only of the presence of the Spirit but of His permanent residence within, God in our flesh. God was first incarnated in Christ Jesus. The marvel of the 'hypostatic union' was His alone, never to be experienced by anybody else. 'The Word made flesh', the Son of God.

We are only His creatures. But on our level, *Christ's incarnation has made possible a beautiful Divine-human fellowship*. It buds and flowers in a million ways. Speaking with tongues is an immediate mark. It is like the Divine life which caused Aaron's dead rod to bud. It is the miracle evidence of a miracle within. It is the Royal Standard fluttering at the masthead outside to show the King is in residence shedding glory within. 'We have this treasure in earthen vessels'.

Of course, *being made one with Him brings more than tongues*. God is in us, working with us. '*I labour, striving according to his working, which worketh in me mightily*' (Col. 1:29). '*I live and yet not I, but Christ liveth in me*', Paul testified. Even as we work out our own salvation it is God that works within us, we learn from Philippians 2: 12/13. Christians never question these statements, but profess to experience them – God in us. In that case who could object to tongues?

Tongues are no more than another form of all that God is doing within us. They are just an outward manifestation. What else is there? *The real miracle is that God is with believers at all.* It would be an odd thing if it could not be seen in some way. It is surely not so astonishing for God Himself to reveal His inward presence with an outward sign? Speaking within tongues seems ideal.

God will do nothing without us, and we can do nothing without Him. We can learn that from speaking with tongues. *Pentecostals have never thought of such a thing as utterances in tongues without the Holy Spirit. Neither is any other Christian activity possible without Him.*

The only thing is, we can do things on our own – preach, for example, but that is just as unDivine and fruitless as speaking with tongues without Him. *It is not what we do, but what He does through us that matters.* 'Without me ye can do nothing'; and without US He won't. If our effort is fruitless, then it is only OUR effort, not His. But the *glossolalia* has even greater implications.

Tongues And Incarnation

Let us look again at 'God in the flesh' – there are always new wonders there. God the Son became Jesus born of Mary, but it is very hard to think of that as a far-off event all on its own, like a super-nova a million light years away. *God does nothing without it affecting us.* Otherwise, the Cross would be ineffective. He affects us, for '*He is the One with whom we have to do*'. Furthermore, *we affect Him*, unphilosophic as it may be. '*Inasmuch as ye did it ye did it unto me.*'

Jesus came to show us how things really are. He made them. *What He was helps us to appreciate what everything is.* If He COULD be Man and God, that was because the possibility is woven into creation, Christ, Man and God, was not an impossible aberration. Everything was made for it. Jesus was never a foreigner. He was no misfit, no freak of nature. *'He came unto His own'*. He is at home in creation. He made it, He likes it, and it doesn't clash with what He is. (See the following chapter.)

It was surely an incredible act of condescension when the Son of God to took upon Himself our likeness. But that was not because our nature was alien to Him. The Greeks of His time would have said it was unthinkable. They thought that flesh was evil, and that God and human flesh could never come together. But *'God saw all that He had made and behold it was good'*. Nothing is evil that God makes.

Nature bore the Divine stamp from the beginning, including our personality. *'God said, Let us make man in our image, after our likeness'*. What He made He made from Himself. The life of man was what He gave. When He became Man, He simply conjoined Himself with what had already come from Him. Even the heathen 'live and move and have their being in Him' (Acts 17:28).

The Nature Of Nature

All the universe is built on spiritual foundations. Science is already struggling with crude ideas along that line, investigating (and thereby spreading) the 'New Age' philosophy. But they are off centre. Behind what we see lies the creative forces of God. He constantly upholds existence. *Everything is an on-going miracle*. That's how the Old Testament people saw it, and they were right. The visible things and the invisible are inseparable. The invisible made the visible. So the whole universe rests on spiritual pillars. Once we realise this, then Christians have an answer long sought by science, theology, and philosophy. This is the new 'cosmology', the truth about all existence, earthly and cosmic. Without the invisible there would be nothing visible. 'He made all things.'

Now this is supposed to be a materialistic and unbelieving age. But I am becoming less sure about that. In fact it is TOO believing. *'I perceive that you are too religious'* as Paul told the Athenians. It seems we will believe anything. Around the entire globe superstition prevails. Reading horoscopes is one small example. It is popular and probably most people think 'there is something in it' and it has even been argued for on metaphysical grounds. Mr Tom Regan stated in 1988 that major world issues were dated for discussion by President Reagan as and when suggested by an astrologer, consulted by the President's wife Mrs Nancy Reagan.

Beneath the veneer of the space age lies man's primitive fear. He reaches towards the stars because he is afraid of them – as if they were gods weaving human fate. Millions believe that our lives are determined by unseen forces generated in the constellations. It is part of the New Age idea. It is staggering that as the earth moves into the age of Aquarius, according to astrological showing, business itself talks about it.

Has the universe a Divinity of its own, and can it be subject to spiritual forces? Is everything God? That is the theory accepted by millions. 'Inner Consciousness', 'Higher Consciousness', 'Positive Thinking' and similar mystic teachings, 'Global reality' 'cosmic forces' and the world-soul, such things are the superstitions of the age of Aquarius – the New Age, and that is what it means. This is the most powerful and sinister spiritual heresy today. New Age teaching speaks of God as 'immanent in all things'.

Scripture is vastly superior to this superstition. It presents a startling concept. God is immanent, but not part of the rocks and flowers. He is not them, and they are not Him. But He is in His creation and more than that – He is also transcendent, outside and beyond creation. He is the 'wholly Other', and yet *'He upholds all things by the word of His power'*. *'The heaven of heavens cannot contain Him'*, yet *'He is not far from any one of us'*.

All that is to be clearly said first, *but there is another factor at work*. In the world is discord and alienation. There is that mysterious thing called sin: *'Your iniquities have separated between you and your God, and your sins have hid his face from you, that he will not hear'* (Isa. 59:2). Cut off from God. How could that be rectified?

There was only one way. In wonderful graciousness and mercy God joined Himself with humanity. That drastic act equalled the work of creation itself. God and Man became one in Christ, an atonement. Christ entered into nature, and at the Cross entered into nature polluted by sin, and bore sin in His own body. What a reconciliation!

Something else had to be dealt with also. That was the heart of man, that rejects God and goodness. There was the problem factor. There had to be a kind of forgiveness which went to that core. The essence of justice as God Himself knows it had to be satisfied. The theology of the Cross is there. Another day I would like to write about it. Meanwhile there we must leave it.

Now all that I have been speaking about has a lovely sign – speaking with tongues. Because the world is as I have said, and because Christ has made an atonement, and because He has come into the world, speaking with tongues is part of it all. Behind every material thing is the spiritual, and the spiritual breaks forth from behind the physical in tongues uttered as God gives the utterance. He is there after all!

Science will discover more and more about the universe. I know scientists are far from walking examples of lives lived by keen logic. They have every human failing. They like to win fame, by hook or by crook if only by sensational theories which put their names in the headlines. They could mishandle the truth, and be blinded by their own prejudices. It is time for them to recognise the spiritual nature of Nature. If not knowledge will advance backwards.

The Pentecostal group that first met in the year 1901 were anything but scientific. But they touched God. They knew the truth. Through them came *a sign and confirmation of the true nature of Nature. They spoke with tongues*. It was indeed a sign. It signified that 'Things which are seen were not made of things which do appear' (Heb. 11:3). Nothing will get beyond that. The Pentecostal is a living attestation of the nature of things.

That merely opens up a thousand exciting thoughts, especially about the things we believe. But what I might say now I will continue in a further chapter.

19   Tongues and the Incarnation

In our home, before we were converted, taking up spiritual interests was as remote from our minds as climbing Everest. Now religion was bad enough but one day a visitor mentioned tongues. Tongues! I was very young, but even I felt sympathy with the way older folk reacted. My parents and grandparents with whom we lived, received the intimation as if the Amazon jungle had reached the front door and denizens with bones through their noses were about to leap into the parlour.

Scorn seemed natural. Grandpa-number-two was expected back from sea to get drunk on Saturday and family reading for Sunday would be the News of the Underworld. What superiority ignorance breeds!

Things eventually changed and Christ came into our home. In due course I myself spoke with tongues. But everybody will realise that with a background like ours we were all reticent to mention such a dark secret. We had no inclination to attract the derision we ourselves had once poured upon these Pentecostals. In fact the entire church felt the same. We Pentecostals were practising something of which other churches thoroughly disapproved. They considered tongues dangerous to mental health. We felt uncomfortable associating with other believers.

Tongues speakers had a jaundiced repute for about sixty years after Anglican vicar Alexander Boddy first asked Thomas Barratt to introduce Pentecost in England at Sunderland. In fact, at that very moment, in the same area, one of the most godly evangelical leaders was proving it possessed seven marks of Satan! Even in 1988 a Southern Baptist seminary (USA) has made it a condition for students and faculty that they do not speak with tongues; and that college is not alone still.

There is something about this phenomena which arouses a feeling of 'I'll have none of that' and if anybody has experienced it they shouldn't. To be fair to such critics we could hardly expect that 'tongues people' would be immediately welcomed like a rich uncle from Australia, especially after all the far-fetched stories about us. Showing that it was in the Bible made it worse. On the celebrated Day of Pentecost the venerated disciples had spoken with tongues, true, but who did Pentecostals think they were? Tongues! Could tongues (of all things) really be in keeping with majesty of God? Miracles yes, but would God slot such an eccentric possibility into His common sense and natural world? Well, has everything God does got to be the essence of majesty and dignity? What about ducks, kittens, children? Talking of spiritual gifts and the body of Christ, Paul pointed out that some parts of the body are 'less honourable'.

However as I speak with tongues in the Spirit I find it to be a majestic and elevating experience. Whatever it appears to onlookers, my mind soars into sublimity with this manifestation. Nobody has ever yet felt they were being odd, or lacking in dignity while speaking with tongues.

'Fleshly'?

Some Christians are anxious to avoid what is 'of the flesh'. Tongues are at first sight carnal, excessive emotion. The phenomenon is admittedly 'of the flesh', a physical happening. But in Scripture 'fleshly' does not always mean unspiritual carnality. Sometimes it does indicate the nature of man which is fallen and evil, but sometimes it merely refers to physical things. We read of the *'works of the flesh'* in Galatians 5: 19, but also that *'Jesus Christ our Lord was made of the seed of David according to the flesh'* (Rom. 1:3). (See William Barclay's *'Flesh and Spirit*.)

So this has tremendous import. *Speaking with tongues is a confirmation that what is physical and full of feeling may still be full of God*. It is in line with the whole teaching of the Bible. Unfortunately the evangelical doctrine of Creation is not very well developed. Because of that many seem to think God exists far above His created world, and has little to do with it except spiritually.

Israel would not have had the slightest difficulty about 'tongues'. They saw God at work in everything around them. The

Spirit of God came upon men like Samson, and Saul, and all the worthies of Israel, and could make even a dumb ass to speak.

Unfortunately the orthodox tradition of the faith has never quite shaken off a feeling that our body is a suspect part of our nature. Sex was regarded as unclean, during many centuries, despite Paul's efforts to set our minds at rest on this score. The flesh and its feelings are not always to be quelled.

Note this – the sins of the spirit are called the works of the flesh, such as hatred, jealousy, envy, and anger mentioned in Galatians 5:19, Paul uses the term 'flesh' there in his own technical sense distinguishing them from the fruits of Spirit.

The Holy Spirit comes and INDWELLS US BODILY, lifting our spirit. With such a glorious Third Person abiding with us, what is so remarkable is His joy and makes us shout, clap and dance? Or that He 'gives us utterance'. That is a form of 'fleshly' experience – gratification if you like – not to be avoided. He is in it.

Some say tongues 'pander to the flesh'. But why 'pander'? That is the catch. Who made man's body? And is God's pleasure to be forbidden it? God 'pandered' to the flesh when He gave us such a vast wealth of physical enjoyments. If we think they are wrong, then let us be consistent and live like the hermits lived, in caves, on bread and water. He gave the human body the ability to see, taste, hear, smell and feel, together with the sense of beauty and wonder.

Condemning all 'fleshliness' – even using the word, has turned too many good things into bad. If you enjoy it is it wrong? For some, even music in church is questionable. Is God more pleased with us fasting, not eating, than when we do eat? After He spread the table before us? Does He always approve when we deny ourselves. Is God a God of 'don'ts?'

On the contrary. The satisfaction of speaking with tongues lines up with what the Word says: '*God giveth us richly all things to enjoy*' (1 Tim. 6:17) and that is not an isolated verse. The entire Old Testament rings with the pleasures of God's good world: '*Israel may enjoy every man the inheritance of his fathers*' (Numbers 36:8). Asceticism is a heathen not a Biblical idea, part of 'religion' as man conceives it. It pleases me to think of the Spirit enjoying with me my own physical experience. That is exactly what happens when I speak with tongues as He gives utterance, He and I pouring out praise for all God's mighty works.

In Israel the most religious occasions were feasts in which joyfulness was not only commanded, but had to be celebrated with food and wine: '*Worship before the Lord thy God: And rejoice in every good thing which the Lord thy God hath given thee, and unto thine house, thou, and the Levite, and the stranger that is among you. Offer peace offerings, and eat there, and rejoice before the Lord thy God*' (Deut. 26:11, 27:7). This kind of thing is reiterated over and over in the Deuteronomy legislation for the State of Israel.

Suppose these Mosaic laws were imposed upon a modern state. Suppose the British Parliament ordered everybody to enjoy themselves, rejoice and be happy for a week, as in Deut. 12: 13–16! It would throw a lot of people into complete gloom and dismay. Some people's job is to find things to complain about, not be happy about.

Present day politics hardly provide grounds for praise and thankfulness on a universal scale. It would be interesting to see how some people would cope with a problem they have not yet tackled – rejoicing! *Unless of course they were Christians who practise joyfulness at least every Sunday*.

Incidentally the feast in Deuteronomy 16 is called a 'solemn' feast, so it seems God's idea of being solemn is rather different from ours! That is how God planned it for Israel. Solemnity is interpreted in an inverse direction to Scripture in some strict Christian circles. I said that some churches are doubtful about music, and any singing is always unaccompanied by instruments. Well they are then safe in not pleasing the flesh! At least mine! If God is pleased when we do not please the flesh He must be very pleased in some hard-seated mission halls. And that after God has filled the universe with incredible beauty!

Acts done in the flesh can be 'spiritual'. *The body is just as much able to receive from God as the spirit or soul of man, and of being holy*. Does God only do 'spiritual' things? Cannot our senses be Divinely blessed when God comes to us? He made them! The blessing we receive from God and the service we render Him would mainly be impossible without our bodies.

God comes to us not as spirits but as humans. Speaking with tongues points to the real truth. Human nature, body, soul and spirit is one whole. Tongue speaking is the entire personality functioning together. It represents a *spiritual* act (Paul says 'my spirit prayeth'), with a *physical function*, by which our *soul* addresses itself to God. We are indeed 'made whole' at that moment at least.

We are not 'tripartite' as Schofield Bible notes said, that is three separate or corresponding parts. We are a trinity of parts, not three separate 'things' tied up in one bundle. Man is not a soul in a body, with an attached spirit.

We have an extended consciousness at death while waiting for the Resurrection of the body, the final stage of redemption. Human beings are flesh, but flesh constructed upon a spiritual foundation. Thus in the Resurrection we shall 'have a body like His glorious body'. Jesus had flesh and bones after His resurrection.

So, for instance, why can't a musician play while communion is being served? He could play 'in the Spirit'. If God could teach David's fingers to war, which rather puzzles some of us, He can bless fingers on a keyboard. As one young man prayed: '*Lord bless our brother's guitar playing. We know Lord you can bless anything*'.

If we are commanded to sing in the Spirit why not play in the Spirit? If bread and wine can be a means of blessing, why not music? In my personal efforts God has been pleased to bring saving grace to bear upon very many lives as I have used both artistry and music. God made me, and did not give me flesh as an obstruction, but rather a vehicle, and indeed a 'dwelling place' for the Holy Spirit. The experience of speaking with tongues according to the Scriptures is proof and confirmation.

The Revolution

In almost all the classical revivals of the past one of the noted features has been physical. Prostrations, trances, paralysis, were common, even if some effects were excessive, and should have been stopped. There were also miracle cures of the sick, and Wesley reports all these things.

For all that, revival theology has never accounted for these physical effects. They occur whether we like it or not. I recall laying my hands upon a young Asian woman who had never been in a Christian church in her life. She was first in line and I had not said a word about physical effects, but she immediately fell to the floor.

When the truth of Divine healing began to be recognised, some inkling began to dawn that Christianity was for body as well as for soul. It has been almost forgotten although mentioned by early church fathers. Irenaeus, disciple of Polycarp who knew John the Apostle, declared, '*The body is capable of salvation*', and Justin Martyr, martyred c. AD 165 maintained that God called man, body and soul, to salvation.

The church later swung far away from its original body-soul-spirit Gospel to a purely spiritual hope, believing that the age of miracles was needed no more! Many devout people get along with that kind of outlook even now.

This-worldly and other-worldly aspects must be kept in balance. For the liberal Gospel spiritual values are judged by their political benefit and come over as current political slogans, particularly left wing, as a Christianised socialist manifesto, the Gospel de-gutted. The essential dynamic of the Holy Spirit at work in redemption is lost.

Professor J. C. O'Neill, of Edinburgh University, spoke at his Inaugural Lecture in 1985 of 'the power of Christianity' but added 'I confess myself sceptical about this alleged power . . . My sketch map of the New Testament . . . finds so little trace of the powerful inward religion that allegedly produced the modern world'. Or to put it into the language of Paul in 2 Timothy 3:5, '*Having a form of godliness but denying the power thereof*'.

On the 250th anniversary of John Wesley's conversion, a Methodist leader on the BBC described what happened in Aldersgate Street in 1738. He thought Wesley wasn't really 'converted', but became enlightened about the fact that the poor were being forgotten by the Church. It was not so much that his heart was warmed by the assurance of sins forgiven but that he became taken up with social work.

It seemed to me that this modern Methodist wanted history re-written. The Founder of Methodism apparently didn't really understand what had happened to him. He would have to ask today's Methodists. Maybe we ought to correct Wesley's Journal for him?

In fact, everything Wesley wrote about, and what he preached until his death in 1791 arose from a true, Holy Spirit, evangelical conversion, based on the objective reality of Christ's death for sinners. That experience became the driving force that fuelled him for over fifty years of itinerant ministry and organisation. It certainly proved more socially effective than the social emphasis has in this century.

The Pentecostal revival brings into focus that the Holy Spirit has not come merely to inspire support for left or right wing ethics. The Gospel does not save us by ethics but by Holy Ghost dynamics. The Church should go to the world with one power and one only, the blessing of the Spirit for both soul and body.

There are not two Gospels, one a cult message for the spirit and the other a practical message for human material need. There is one Gospel, and it doesn't even have two halves to choose between. It is one Gospel with many effects, all resting on one central proclamation of Jesus Christ and Him crucified.

Tongues And The Gospel

Now speaking with tongues happens to be a clear sign of all this. In fact how could there have been any speaking with tongues, EVEN ON THE DAY OF PENTECOST if Christ's Gospel did not bring together flesh and Spirit? If the faith is purely spiritual, there could be no tongues; if it is purely social there would be no power.

At fourteen years of age the winds of heaven suddenly swept down upon me and I spoke with tongues. If it wasn't God, what was it? I wasn't in a trance. My mind was not traumatised. I had full consciousness and control, and as I spoke the blessed Spirit of God directed my speech. If anybody argues that I had given up my control to another power, let them say so. But I know I had not. I had restrained any outburst with a handkerchief in my mouth, but I could have walked away from it there and then. I did not feel it was wrong to allow God in and speak through me. Surely we belong to God and 'we are not our own'? It has been said that God gives a sound mind, as if we were not of a sound mind to speak with tongues. Well, what about the apostles? Didn't they have a sound mind when they spoke with tongues? They were mortals like us.

Tongues have proved to be a pretty tough proposition for religious doubters. Only the prejudiced or the gullible would accept psychological and other explanations. It is sensible enough to believe what Acts 2:4 says, that 'the Spirit gave them utterance'. What is difficult about believing the Almighty can achieve a small effect like that if we believe in God at all?

Truths And All Truth

Now if the Gospel is indeed for the whole man, what Christian truth is not affected? No doctrine can be treated as *purely* spiritual, heavenly, or other-worldly. When we know all truth, it has to embrace heaven and earth, body and soul, things visible and invisible. Taken so, new splendours must lie before us as Christian belief is explored. Even the doctrine of God must take into account that 'the Word became flesh'. The physico-spiritual nature of Christianity is quite evident. *If that is true then physical miracles will not be exceptional. They will be normal.*

The Great Sign

In fact, there is a far greater evidence of this than speaking with tongues. The Great Sign was Christ Himself, God in the flesh. When God became Man the shepherds were told of it. Then they were given a sign, and that sign was '*Ye shall find the babe wrapped in swaddling clothes, lying in a manger*' (Luke 2:13).

The Incarnation had this sign: the Babe in a manger wrapped in clothes and accessible to such poor men as they were. God our Saviour was helplessly vulnerable, within reach. God, not found at the end of a maze of intricate routines, ritual, and religiousness, only in the Temple, with its preliminary washings and sacrifices, through the first and second veil with blood and burning incense, and that only by proxy of a High Priest, but God in a manger. The sign was He could be found like any other person. They could walk to Him just across the fields, accessible just when they chose.

Nor was God any longer known only by mystics, or even just 'by faith'. As a sign of a Saviour He was 'wrapped in swaddling clothes'. Anything like that had never been dreamed of in the world's history. No longer need humans feel themselves members of a sub-creation, unworthy of Divine intimacy. He had made Himself available to the outsiders, not just by esoteric processes of meditation, and not even just invisibly near, but visible within His own creation, and *part of it*. '*The Word was made flesh and dwelt among us. He was in the world and the world was made by him*' (John 1:10).

It is hard to realise. We still want to confine Him to the spiritual moment or the consecrated place. We want Him to wait until we adopt the right pose and clothes, like getting ready to see the vicar in the vestry. Is God found only in the dim-religious light shrouded in the smoke of incense, where we must even close our eyes to pray? Should we talk about church as His dwelling place, as if we had to re-create His natural habitat there because He would otherwise not survive the rigours of our unsanctified world? He is not a foreigner, nor a different species. God is Man, '*He came unto His own*'.

In fact He is One of us. He always was. Even before He manifested Himself on earth He 'walked' with Israel and had a tent like they did by which He showed His oneness with them. '*In all their affliction He was afflicted*'. His coming was not God INVADING the planet Earth. I don't invade my own house. The Earth is the Lord's. Christ could not invade His own territory. He did not breach our privacy, intrude into human affairs, as a Divine Interloper. His birth was a Nativity, a coming to His own. He is our Brother, and if I understand it right, always was, for Hebrews 2:17 says '*He was made like unto His brethren*'. The only question is, what does that mean to us NOW? Nothing?

More Than A Sign

Tongues may be a sign of the Divine-human composition, but Christ is THE Sign. Even that needs qualifying. Signs point to something, but Christ points to nothing except Himself. He is the Sign AND what is signified. All signs point to one thing, Jesus, and so does the manifestation of tongues.

What Christ is, that is the truth about everything. He is what everything is all about. Reality and its nature are summed up in Him. He is the Explanation, the Answer to the riddle of the universe and the mystery of existence. Behind all that exists, behind the atom is Christ, maintaining existence, and from Him everything takes its character. There is no correct cosmology without Christ. All centres on what He is.

There is mystery here. The Person of Christ is beyond us, but not beyond God. In Christ He perfected Man. His own presence did not alter human-ness because man was made for God from the start. All the attempts to define what He was, seem to me to assume that there was something about Him unnatural, anomalous. The only thing strange about Him is His perfection. By nature we are clay. By His nature He is Spirit, but the two are brought together in Christ in perfection.

Christ's coming into the world was not only fore-ordained, but was part of the creative plan of God. He did not come *because* we sinned. The bare suggestion that He wouldn't have come if we had never sinned just won't do. It puts a premium upon sin. It turns Christ's coming into an award for wickedness. Jesus loved us not BECAUSE we sinned, but *although we sinned*. He knew our foul ways beforehand and was '*the Lamb slain from the foundation of the world, a lamb without blemish foreordained before the foundation of the world*' (Revelation 13:8, 1 Peter 1:19/20). *He would have come into His own world anyway* – God so loved the world. He made it for Himself (Rev. 4:11). It was conceived in His heart, came out of his own Being, and He had the closest affinity with it.

In Christ we see where God stands in relation to our world. He is in it. There is no part with which He has nothing to do. He is not a Spirit that can only contact spirit by mystic relationship. He is not shut outside the citadel of human nature, finding no way in. He is Jesus Christ, Son of Man, Son of God, healing the sick, feeding the hungry, making men's bodies the temples of the Spirit.

'*The world was made flesh and dwelt among us*'. That statement covers all future physical manifestation in our material order, and that without limit. What ever God does affects us all. What He is we cannot ignore. What God did in Bethlehem reveals what He is, what our world is, what we are, and shapes human destiny.

But Tongues Say It

The nature of the Gospel is two-fold, for body and spirit. It will break through in mortal experience, and tongues are a notable moment when that happens. However, onlookers only see the physical element, a man speaking. They can't see the Spirit of God behind it. So they will put it down to something else, as they did on the day of Pentecost, saying the disciples were full of new wine. It will look physical – only. But here is a new cause – God.

If anyone demands to see the other element, the inspiring Spirit, we can only ask how they think that is possible? How can an onlooker perceive it? How can we prove what we know, that the Spirit of God is within us? We couldn't. It is ridiculous for anybody to argue that it is only a man speaking. How does he know that? He can't see God anyway, so a critic cannot argue God is there or not there. If He is, there's no way a critic would know.

Seeing God is impossible when anyone doesn't want to, One of the greatest proofs of our sinfulness is that we may be near God and not know it. Jacob at Bethel is an example and the Jerusalem deputation of leaders in the house where '*the power of God was present to heal them*' (Luke 5:17), but none of them was healed. They didn't want to know.

People look for God, but sometimes where they hope they won't find Him. They may be afraid to find Him. The old saying that some don't go to church because they don't find God there isn't true. The majority don't go because they think they MIGHT meet God there! Our Spiritual faculty has been affected. Divine realities, like our radio waves, come to us unperceived because our receiving equipment is faulty.

But, whether an onlooker sees it or not, WE know why we are speaking with tongues; God is in residence. '*The spiritual man judgeth all things*'. It is beyond our comprehension but not beyond our knowledge. We enjoy what we can't explain. We are like Peter, whose knowledge of theology was elementary but He knew that Jesus was the Christ the Son of God, and Jesus said that flesh and blood (brains) had not revealed this to him, but His Father.

We know. We taste the powers of an age to come, and enjoy the Spirit from heaven in this world. That is our Pentecostal witness.

20 Discipleship

Being an evangelist, I suppose I ought to take it to heart when informed that 'Jesus said make disciples not decisions'. I would oblige if I could, though evangelists don't 'make decisions' – except about what to have for lunch, and things of that sort. But what can we do about 'making disciples'?

Although there are only two verses in Scripture about 'making disciples', one of these is specially important as it comes in the Great Commission of Jesus in Matthew 28:19. The Authorised Version reads: *'Go ye therefore, and teach all nations'*. 'Teach' here is literally *'disciple all nations'*. The other is Acts 14:21: *'they preached the Gospel to that city and taught many'*. Literal translation from the Greek is *'having made many disciples'*.

One rather important point. Matthew does NOT tell us to 'make disciples IN all our nations'. The Greek is nothing like that. Literally it means 'disciple all nations', but that is impossible if we interpret it 'make nations disciples', because a nation cannot be a disciple. But a 'disciple' means a 'learner'; the Authorised Version correctly translates it 'teach all nations'. It can't be anything else.

What Is A Disciple?

First let us be sure that we know what was meant in Scripture by a disciple. Words change their content especially in English, and as it happens the word 'disciple' certainly has. So what is the equivalent term now? In fact there are two words to consider, 'disciple' and sometimes 'following' Jesus, though they were never actually named 'followers'. The first word, 'disciple' comes from the Greek *mathetes* (from *manthano*, to learn), that is someone who MADE THE EFFORT to learn. This word *mathetes* 'learner' comes 264 times, but only in five books, – the four Gospels and Acts. Jesus used it in His famous invitation in Matthew 11: 28 – 30: *'Take my yolk upon you, and learn (mathete) of me'*.

The other description, 'follow' (Greek, *akoloutheo*), appears seventy-seven times but is an ordinary word for follow and does not always refer to disciples. The crowds also 'followed' Jesus. Like 'disciple', the word is confined mainly to the Gospels.

Further, there is a strange fact – the word 'following' is deliberately not used any more in the New Testament. It also avoids even expressions derived from it, or any even similar words. We find it just once in Revelation 14:4: *'These are they that follow the Lamb whithersoever he goeth'*.

There are other words which might have been applied. Words like 'accompany', 'companion', or 'company'. But they never are applied to those travelling with Jesus. The reason is BECAUSE THE PURPOSE OF THE NEW TESTAMENT WAS TO REVEAL A NEW RELATIONSHIP.

So we can confine our attention to these two words 'disciple' and 'follow', as they are used almost exclusively for them alone.

1   They convey the idea of people wanting to learn, *mathetes*
2   They also relate to following or associating with Jesus. *akoloutheo*

Now we cannot take these two words at their dictionary value. Jesus added so much to their meaning, and made them Christian words. He did this because He warned people that merely following Him with mental knowledge wasn't good enough, they had to take His yolk also.

Incidentally, discipleship doesn't come into the Old Testament at all. The principle there is trust and obedience, not 'following' God or imitating God as a model. The conception ancient Israel had of God's majestic transcendence and 'Otherness' could never have inspired any idea of being like Him. Not even Moses, who spoke with God face to face, ever talked about being like God, nor hinted at such a possibility in all his writings. It is one of the wonderful things about Christianity that God came down as Man, somebody we want to be like. This made a personal walk and transforming friendship with Him possible. God was expressed in human terms for us humans to follow.

Wonder Possibility

Here is something very important. *His discipleship was unique because He came to set up a new relationship between God and Man, in Himself.* This relationship He had with followers was in itself the main part of the revelation He came to impart. *The great thing about His discipleship was just being with Him.* Indeed that is everything – God with us, and discipleship or anything else can go no higher. All other blessings and effects come from it.

Paul the apostle brought this fact forward in a remarkable expression in Ephesians 3:20 – 21, about those who had *'learned Christ (mathete) . . . as the truth in Jesus'* (Eph. 3: 20 – 21). Just as we might learn music, or art, similarly *He becomes what we learn.* Jesus invited people to *'learn of me'* (Matthew 11:29), and to do so they had to take His yoke upon them. *That is discipleship.* You cannot learn Christ without being yoked. I will return to this later in this chapter.

Among the Jews, the Rabbis had disciples (*talmids*) who 'sat at their feet' as Paul said he did, to learn. They did not necessarily gain from their master's way of life, except obedience. They were in fact servile, and subordinate. Christ's discipleship was in complete contrast. He made no demands of servanthood or submission of that kind whatever upon anybody. Those who teach submission to a pastor's orders are imposing upon them a state which Jesus did not impose upon His own disciples. His disciples were free agents, and not accepted on terms and obligations.

The only thing Jesus did, even when people volunteered, was to show them what kind of conditions could arise in following Him. It could mean deprivation. But they were not asked to swear to die if the circumstances arose, nor make any other commitment. There was no official role with rules of admission. They were free to follow if they chose, and Jesus kept reminding them about counting the cost: *'Whosoever doth not bear his cross . . . cannot be my disciple'* (Luke 14:27). That is, *in heart*. He would never turn them away, but they would lack the spirit of a true follower. Following meant catching the entire *ethos* of His life, and if they didn't learn from His life and be like Him there was no point in following.

He chose twelve, and invited others to follow Him too. *Nevertheless it is doubtful if a single one of them understood discipleship or really had this attitude*, which is why He told them to count the cost (Luke 14: 28 – 35). Even the Twelve took a long time to grasp what they could be letting themselves in for, although He made it clear enough. In fact, James and John thought it would lead to them sitting on thrones with Christ, not suffering. So far were they from understanding, that Peter rebuked Jesus for even suggesting He might die at Jerusalem saying *'this be far from Thee Lord'*, After His death and Resurrection they still had hopes and ambitions of kingdom glory. The notion of a disciple embracing hardship just did not penetrate until they had received the Holy Spirit. Then the glory and truth burst upon them (Acts 1:6).

So a disciple was ONLY a learner, and had much to learn. They were not specimen Christians by any means at that stage, but raw recruits. In those days they certainly did not suffer very much. They did not go hungry, and did enjoy much popularity. True, they protested that they had left all and followed Jesus (Matt. 19:27), but they also asked what they would get for it! Peter was exaggerating their sacrifice quite a lot too, for they had not foresworn their families nor their work to that extent – nothing like modern missionaries. They were often back home, and in fact adopted a way of life which many young people today enjoy.

Their readiness to die wasn't too noticeable either! They were not of the martyr-mould at first. They fumed with indignation to think anybody should oppose them. That wasn't what they bargained for. On one occasion they wanted to burn down a whole village in vengeance! So if evangelists are to 'make disciples', their converts need not be examples of full surrender to claim the title.

The Teaching

Jesus taught His disciples, but He did not teach them to be disciples. They already were. He taught them to be Christians. The idea of a disciple is to learn of Christ. A 'discipleship class' is absurd. At least if it is to teach people TO BE disciples. Disciples are learners. You must be a disciple first, then you learn, and you don't learn to be a disciple. If disciples are learners – have they to be taught to be learners? Jesus taught His disciples, but not TO BE disciples, for they already were, as we said, but they learned about Jesus himself. *Discipleship consisted of a growing relationship with Him.* The kind of teaching He gave them was what all Christian teaching should be, LEARNING CHRIST, not just discipleship. Disciples are not a product of classes, but of the grace of God. They learn afterwards.

But if we are thinking about being disciples, then we must get it clear WHY – what is discipleship for? It is to learn Christ. It is not to become part of the battalion of the elite, to experience discipline and acquire a kind of degree in spirituality. *The object is to know the Lord.* Indeed, all such efforts, called discipleship or anything else – sanctification, holiness, or growth in grace, have the same end, to bring us the experience of the knowledge of Christ.

What we call 'discipleship' today, is another word for walking with God, or living the Christian life. The real principles of discipleship are summed up in what Paul said: (Phil. 3: 7,10): *'What things were gain to me, those I counted loss for Christ, that I might know Him, and the power of His resurrection, and the fellowship of his sufferings, being made comfortable unto his death'.*

Discipleship for every Christian, is, and always must be, walking and learning of Jesus, WHETHER WE CALL IT THAT OR NOT. That may seem obvious enough, but we must say that now, because that is not by any means the last thing that ought to be said on this issue.

The next thing to think about is the strange fact that the New Testament drops the word 'disciple' after the Gospels and Acts. In twenty-two New Testament books it is never found. This is obviously significant and important. Even Peter mentions the old familiar word only once, speaking in Acts. The narrator of Acts (Luke), did sometimes call Christians 'disciples' but just as often 'them that believe'. Any other name for Christians had not then become usual. In the beginning 'disciples' was a general description of Christ's people so of course the name clung to them for a while after He had gone. But 'disciples' was never the way Christians were addressed by the epistle writers Paul, Peter, James, John, and Jude. They had other terms. The explanation is obvious, that *a disciple was a person who followed Jesus only during His earthly ministry.* In fact that is the basic sense of disciple (*mathetes*) a physical follower. Afterwards there was a change. A very big one in fact as we shall see.

Why a change? There was indeed a very good reason. *History had undergone the greatest convulsion since the world began.* A new dispensation had come through the mighty acts of Christ's death and Resurrection. It dawned upon the disciples what those last great moments of His life had effected. The Holy Spirit brought revelation upon revelation to them.

The Great Light

All the time they were with Him, they never grasped what was then developing. They were 'disciples' because THEY WERE THE PEOPLE LEARNING TO TELL THE REST OF THE WORLD ABOUT CHRIST. *They learned for us and brought knowledge to us.* That is what made them Apostles. Now we know what nobody then knew, and we had it from these chosen learners. The world hasn't to have a discipleship stage again and come into the truth afresh. The Church has come. Here is 'the pillar and ground of the truth', through which the truth is proclaimed everywhere.

After Christ died, rose again, ascended to glory and sent the Holy Spirit of truth upon them, they were transformed men. *They rose above the former discipleship level.* Knowing what

Christ had done, they began to realise He had done it for them
and the whole world. THEY DISCOVERED WHO THEY
WERE IN CHRIST, far more than disciples. *They saw they
were the Redeemed, the Church, new creatures, princes in the
kingdom, SONS OF GOD, partakers of the Divine nature, the
temples of the Spirit, and much, much more!*

Their apprenticeship was over, they had *'learned Christ'*. To
'learn Christ' is the purpose and object of discipleship, and
once we have learned, we know who He is and what He has
done for us. Christ – what a subject! And they themselves –
'in Christ', members of Christ! Now a new title has to be found.
A new affinity arises, a richer fellowship. Discipleship was a
past stage. *'Now are we the sons of God'.*

So Paul addresses believers now as 'saints', the sanctified,
but never disciples. The word was not used even when it might
have been. For example, in sermons recorded in the Acts of
the Apostles, Peter, Paul, and Stephen said nothing about their
hearers 'being made disciples'. They preached pretty much the
same sort of thing as evangelists would today (allowing for the
differences of background).

*Apostolic evangelism did not set out to 'make disciples', but
children of God.* The message of Christ's cross and His redeeming love dominated their transformed outlook. Any reader of
the New Testament after the first three Gospels will see the
unfolding of a progressive revelation. Discipleship is changed
for redemption, the kingdom for the Cross. They preached
forgiveness, the resurrection, the coming King and the promise
of the Holy Spirit. Far more than that THEY WERE NOW
ENJOYING THINGS WHICH AS DISCIPLES THEY FIRST
BEGAN TO HEAR ABOUT. Maturity had come and they
were 'made perfect' in Christ. They had moved into the dimension of power and fullness – the true hallmark of Pentecost.

Indeed if the exclusive emphasis laid upon discipleship today
in some circles is correct, then the apostles seem to have
become somewhat negligent, for they failed to refer to it and
we never find them urging it upon their hearers as some do
today.

Disciplined Disciples?

Were disciples so named because they were disciplined? The
answer is a very definite 'No'. This confusion has arisen because
we translate *mathetes* with our word 'disciple', which relates to
discipline, subjection, or implicit obedience as in an army.
Originally the English word did mean the same as the Greek
word, just a learner. English still retains this rare usage in fact
but today 'disciple' commonly conveys the idea of being under
strict surveillance, under orders. That is not what the Bible
word means at all. We speak of somebody being 'disciplined',
and so it has been wrongly assumed that Christian disciples
should be under pastoral 'discipline'.

It is very important to realise that discipline and the Bible
word for disciple are quite different. In Greek there are several
words for discipline, but none is linked with 'disciple'. You
never find Jesus 'disciplining' anybody. He never reprimanded
them, much less imposed any penalty or penance. His only
rebuke was for their unbelief and ignorance.

*We should take particular notice that He never made Himself
a Lord over their everyday activity.* He was their Master, but
not a master ordering His servants or workers. If they followed
Him, He imposed no duties or obligations. He accepted them
as willing people who wanted His presence but were free to
come and go as they wished. He respected their freedom and
choice, and would even support them in it, expecting them to
display the spirit of freedom. He appointed twelve 'to be with
Him', but they were not bound, nor subject to any sanctions.
What they did, or did not do was 'unto Him', but there was
neither praise nor rebuke. Any directions He gave them were
moral and spiritual.

Discipleship And Evangelism

*We were sent to preach Christ, not discipleship, and to lift Him
up, then all men will be drawn to Him. Christ's bonds are love.*
One can study the records for ever without finding any hint
that the apostles 'made disciples' in the sense of bringing them
under the rule of discipline. When men associated with Jesus

they had no rule book to sign, no list of required conditions. He never put them on the carpet for neglecting duties, for they were given none.

His expectations of obedience did not extend to practical matters, do this, do that, go there, come here, but only to spiritual. He insisted that His yoke was easy, His burden light, because He had one law – love – and nothing is more joyous than to love. Loving is the essence of joy.

Through the long ages of church history this principle has been forgotten. The Church has tried to keep Christians up to scratch by rules. This kind of effort to attain true Christian faith by promise and commitment produced the various monastic orders and their forms of 'Rule', the Rule of Benedict, for instance. But keeping rules always fails, even under strict supervision and discipline. One order of monks whipped one another every Friday, encouraged by Cardinal Peter Damiani. Happy days! But corruption always set in and another new order would be created with another more strict 'Rule'.

Admitted, any church organisation will have its rules, particularly for those it employs. Ordinary members will have to observe the arrangements for running things, such as for voting, and activities. Members can only expect to remain members if they keep to the arrangements. But beyond organisational procedures what should arrangements and rules be? Should they be there at all? Do they comply with Christ's rules? Do they discriminate between Christian and Christian by standards we choose?

Churches should not impose rules which are likely to exclude those who are already members of Christ, born-again. Christ accepts us not because we attain a certain level of discipleship or spirituality, but on the grounds of repentance and faith, only. That should be the only admission condition for all churches.

Rules are an anomaly when they touch Christian life. They contradict what the Church is all about, and is supposed to represent. It represents the rule of love, not law. If a church only manages to pursue its course by putting its members under rules and obligations, it is no church. What sort of membership is that? People should serve from the heart. But if they do serve from the heart, why make rules? Why make obligatory

what is voluntary? *Obligatory church faithfulness is worthless.*
It is certainly not what Christianity means and such a congregation doesn't represent that whole-hearted loyalty and love it
is supposed to represent. It is mere legalism, the opposite to
everything the Church stands for.

*The Christian doesn't need rules to make him loyal, faithful,
sincere. If he does he is no Christian anyway and shouldn't be
a member.* I keep meeting this argument that 'even if you join
a club you have to sign to keep the rules'. But has the Church
of the First-born to take its example from a club? Surely we
should say 'ONLY clubs ask you to sign membership rules'.
Clubs need rules. Clubs exist for purposes which have nothing
to do with virtue and spirituality. Laws are for sinners! What
kind of church is it that thinks they are necessary?

A Christian Church is the ecclesia of the redeemed. It is called
to be a witness to the power of God to keep, to create unity,
to create spontaneous love and loyalty, generosity and goodness. That is its nature. That is why anybody wants to be a
member. Rules say that members cannot be trusted to do what
they joined to do. Spontaneous love is the chief characteristic
of a church – so what have rules got to do with it?

When we believe on Christ, and are born again, we become
members of the body of Christ. *'For by one Spirit are we all
baptised into one body . . . and have been all made to drink
into one Spirit'* (1 Cor. 12:13). If this is so, then that should be
the grounds of acceptance in every church if it is His church.
Jesus said, 'He that receiveth you, receiveth me. He that despiseth you despiseth me.' (Matt. 10:40. Luke 10:17). And it won't
do to say, 'but he wouldn't sign the membership covenant or
attend the discipleship class!'

More Than Disciples

I said that 'disciple' and 'follower' are words dropped after the
Gospels, and other words were used. One of them is *mime-
omai*, 'to imitate', but it is used only four times, in a special
sense. The idea of imitating Christ is quite admissible of course,
as Peter says *'Christ left us an example that we should follow
in his footsteps'*. But merely imitating is a very weak represen-

tation of the dynamic principles given us in the New Testament. *It is not that we have to make ourselves like Christ, but it is His work and promise that He will do the making. 'We are His workmanship created in Christ Jesus unto good works'. 'It is God that worketh in you both to will and to do of His good pleasure'* (Eph. 2:10, Phil. 2:13). His responsibility is to make us like Himself. A self-made man is usually an example of shoddy workmanship. And evangelists shouldn't attempt the job either – Christ is the maker of men.

John's Gospel is particularly emphatic about the nature of discipleship. He defines it in Christ's words. First: *Henceforth I call you not servants: but I have called you friends'.* The word friend here has a greater force than just 'pal' or 'chum'. It means someone who shares secrets. That relationship far exceeds discipleship. A Christian is a personal representative of Christ, an ambassador of a kingdom of freedom and love, personally possessing the life of Christ

Second: *'If ye continue in my word, then are ye my disciples indeed'.* Who is a disciple? One who loves Christ's words. Third: *'Herein is my Father glorified, that ye bear much fruit: so (in that way) shall ye be my disciples'.* A fruitful life identifies the true disciple, not a life submitting to dictatorship.

Fourth: *'By this shall all men know that ye are my disciples, if ye love one another'.* This was the great 'Rule' of the Order of Christ – love, always love, only love. Discipleship without love? Impossible, not with all the prayers, obedience and religiousness in the world. Love is the world's meaning (John 15:16, 8:31, 15:8 and 13:35).

Those four conditions make up true discipleship – without somebody imposing discipline, which was never intended by Christ. A disciple is a 'Christ-ised' person, not merely disciplined. He is loved by Christ and so learns to love. That kind of learning cannot be gained as a follower of Christ from books or classes, but only by living with Jesus.

Why Be A Disciple?

What is discipleship for? The disciples of Greeks and Jews took up disciplined training and study SO THEY COULD ALSO

BECOME MASTERS. Are we aiming to merely move up the
tree, or up the pyramid of delegated power from the pro-
bationer member to senior minister? The aim of Christ's disciples should be completely different. In His Kingdom there is
only one Lord, and no quasi-lords. He does not share His
sovereignty. HE – He alone – is Lord. *'My glory I will not give
to another'*. He surrenders or delegates Lordship and authority
over men to nobody. He is a kingdom without a hierarchy,
without a pyramid of power, privilege of rank.

The very purpose of the Kingdom is to eliminate all competition to Christ and *'put down all rule and authority'*. Disciples
did not have disciples, and say 'go here, do this, obey me'. Nor
did any New Testament prophet or pastor command obedience.
It is taught that we should ALL submit to one another. What
is ours to give or to do is not somebody else's to command. It
is presumption to demand what is offered willingly. Jesus said,
*'Neither be ye called masters: for one is your master, even
Christ'*. He indeed was Lord, and had every right to order His
servants. *But he didn't do it!* (John 13, 13/14). Who am I to
usurp an authority He never exercised? 'The servant is not
above His Lord' (John 13: 13/14). Pastors are not church Czars.
Jesus was no disciplinarian, dictator or autocrat. He taught
them service not generalship, humility, not rank. His lesson
was love.

*One writer has put it that 'everybody in the kingdom must do
the will of the King'* Yes . . . well, we'll try. But I listened to
one writer, speaking in London introducing what he called
'discipleship', with astonishment. In his view doing the will of
the King meant doing the will of the pastor. As if the pastor
was God's vice-regent on earth, and sole interpreter of the
Divine purpose.

God doesn't run things that way, retailing His orders through
another party. The Bible makes that perfectly clear. He has no
need. In this dispensation each man knows God, and *'there is
only one mediator between God and man, the Man Christ Jesus'*.
*'They shall not teach every man his neighbour saying "know the
Lord": for all shall know me from the least to the greatest'*.

*Even Christ positively refused to exercise His Lordship in
areas where God had already made men and women responsible.*

God made us in His own image. He has given us the power of judgement, and wisdom, and freedom of will over our personal affairs, where to live or with whom, what we eat, what our jobs are, how we run our homes He wants us to accept responsibility for. That applied to His disciples. He said, *'Who made me a ruler or a divider over you?'* (Luke 12:14).

Similarly when Martha wanted Jesus to use His authority to tell Mary to help with the domestic preparations, He declined. He also pointedly avoided saying what should be done in other spheres, such as in politics and business (Matt. 22:19).

Peter followed the same rule. When believers were raising money for the 'all things common' scheme in Jerusalem, he said, *'While it remained, was it not thine own? and after it was sold, was it not in thine own power?'* He knew no prescriptive right to control other people's finances. Individuals are personally responsible for their decisions despite any prophet or leader. What they tell us to do cannot exonerate us when we do what is wrong, therefore we must be left to use our own judgment (Matthew 25, 15–28). Jesus respected people's personal preferences and never put them under any duress. He honoured their right to exercise their own will.

Paul called himself a 'slave of Jesus Christ'. But this did not endow others with the power to order him around, and the number of instances when Christ directed him this way or that is very limited and special. No Christian is a spiritual serf owing fealty to any thane or lordling. They should never surrender their freedom but *'stand fast in the liberty werewith Christ hath made us free'*.

Deitreich Bonhoeffer

Before ending this matter I feel it is important to make a comment on Deitreich Bonhoeffer's famous work *The Cost of Discipleship*. It seems obvious that it is this book which has deeply influenced those who preach a strong discipleship and submission doctrine, directly or indirectly. I recently read and re-read his disturbing challenge, made notes all the way through, and pondered it.

This German 'confessor' pastor was a tremendous personality, ready to obey whatever seemed to him to be God's will to the end, 'dying daily', to self. He lived as if he was born to be a martyr. He lived out his faith, and was hanged by Hitler. Strangely he was executed for taking part in a plot to assassinate the Fuehrer although he had renounced violence as unChrist-like.

Bonhoeffer's mind worked in paradoxes, and the whole book is a strange example of it. One of his tensions of thought seemed to me basic, but impossible to reconcile. It was this. He gives a brilliant exposition of Christ's substitutionary work. It is almost fundamentalist. Yet, he stresses the absolute NEED of discipleship, and, if I read him correctly, suggests we cannot be saved without it. Only disciples are Christians.

If discipleship, absolute obedience to Christ's Lordship is the way of salvation, who then can be saved? What becomes of the substitutionary work of Christ? Bonhoeffer suggests that unless we are prepared to die for Christ, then Christ did not die for us. His work doesn't work unless we work. He saves those who save themselves, it seems. He speaks of churches as being full of people who are not Christians because they are not disciples.

We must not confuse discipleship with the new birth, or with justification by faith. Evangelists are not to preach discipleship, for it does not save anybody. The Gospel saves. Discipleship may follow, but I would rather say that Christian maturity follows. We are not saved by discipline. We are saved by grace. We are forgiven people, not achieving people. We need not submit to any church authority or shepherd for our salvation, except the Great Shepherd.

The road to glory is not paved by works of righteousness which we have done. It is not our giving our lives which brings us redemption, but He giving His life. Jesus is no oppressor making heavy demands. He gives us no yoke, but only says, 'Take my yoke. My yoke is easy and my burden is light'. We share His, but as Spurgeon said in the last words he ever preached 'He takes the heavy end of the yoke'.

21   High Calling

One More Test

After months of concentration to establish what standards should apply to Pentecost, there is one entire virgin field to explore. I can only point to it. There is no way to articulate its importance.

We might measure up to such things as I have brought forward, and be satisfied – too satisfied. We can be biblical – and soulless. Orthodoxy in doctrine, soundness in practice, rectitude in walk, but there are other things. What about motive, disposition, sacrifice, generosity, largeness of mind and heart, and all those revelations of perfection we keep on suddenly seeing *in the life of our Lord?*

Pentecostal hallmarks must be Christian hallmarks. A Pentecostal should measure up not merely to the rules, or be charismatic, but should be like Jesus. We might be wrong in many things in church, but the ultimate test of Pentecost is the quality of a Pentecostal personally. Is He Christ-like? That is what it is all about.

Jesus was somebody people could live with. Some great men are impossible. So are some little men. Greatness goes to some people's heads. One reads of devoted, self-sacrificing Christians, investing long lives in lands where they never know comfort or pleasure, but they add to their own deprivation because nobody can suffer them, rugged individuals, too rugged for comfort. Jesus was peerless, with a distinction only God can carry, yet He was one of us, a companion to the wisest and heard gladly by the common people. They'd go days and weary miles to be with Him.

There can be that kind of exclusive concern for the Lord's work that keeps everybody at arms' length – we can be such very busy people we have little time for people, but people are what God leaves us here FOR.

Maybe some don't quarrel, they are uninterested, uncongenial, poor company. Jesus was good to be with. One of the truly great men of the last century was Sir William Wilberforce, once a fop and playboy, but coming into an evangelical experience he became the champion of the Empire's slaves, winning an immortal name. Yet he was described as 'delightful company.' So was Jesus.

Glimpses

The half-brothers of our Lord, James and Jude, must have had nothing but wonderment in the end about Him. Soon after He had ascended they wrote about Him, and, orthodox Jews as they were, called Him Lord and Saviour. And that despite the fact that Jesus had said no prophet is honoured by his family. What did it?

Whatever it was, there was nothing that put them off. They never said, 'He may be all right when he's doing His work, and He's good then and preaches marvellous sermons, but we've lived with Him'. Jesus didn't turn the charm on in public. No religious smile, never artificial, never self-conscious pose. What people saw was Him, purely Him, the changeless Christ. I wonder often how He could say the straight things He did say and in the circumstances He did. But it was the way He said it. How do we say it? We never read anything about His expression, His manner, His tone of voice. Why? It could only be known by those who knew Him on earth. Nobody except those who meet Jesus can have a glimmer as to what it is like. Only Christians can understand Christians, and why they are so wrapped up in Jesus.

Can we preach Hell – with unction? Did He? We are good at telling off. Was He? Was He helpful, thoughtful? Did He listen to people full of their own troubles, or had the Son of God more important things on His mind than His mother's and the family's prattle? When He had not a moment to spare how did He always spare people a moment?

Why are we not told? *The reason is that He was Himself and we have to be ourselves. That's first. And next we can't be like Him by imitation, but only by His Spirit. 'I live, yet not I, but*

Christ liveth in me'. The word 'imitate' hardly occurs in the
Bible. He is not set before as an example, except maybe a
couple of times. Why? *Because we don't know enough about
Him in the everyday*. Frankly I don't know what Jesus would
do in most situations of my life. I'm married, for instance, and
He was not. We haven't been told much. But that is not the
way, anyway.

There was something deeper than an ideal model, something
that spoke of where He had come from – the bosom of God.
The Spirit of God was upon Him, and that adds something that
absolute moral purity and correct behaviour can never express.

We get a glimpse of family life when He went to Cana of
Galilee. It seems He was a guest and His mother had something
to do with arrangements. Things went badly wrong. A shortage
of wine at a wedding was inexcusable, and might even have
family or even legal repercussions. A calamity. Now Cana is
spoken of as His first miracle. He was not invited to the wedding with any idea that He was a wonder worker. When His
mother told Him they had no wine, why did she? What did she
think He could do about it? It is obvious that she did expect
Him to do something, because of the way He answered her:
'Woman, what have I to do with you?' It was a remark she
didn't misunderstand – we read of other people saying it without offence, but we have lost the idiom of it now. Whatever it
was, it didn't put Mary off, because she immediately instructed
the servants to do whatever He said.

So, that is what she hoped – that He would sort it out with
the servants and find some solution. *But never for a moment
did she expect a miracle* – she had no knowledge of miracles,
and must have wondered about His remark that 'My hour has
not yet come'. What hour?

It amounts to this, that out of everybody else there – half
the village no doubt, nobody knew what to do. But Mary had
the idea – ask Jesus. If that doesn't tell us something it ought.
Evidently she knew how He could sort things out and get
over a crisis. He had never worked a miracle in His home,
but Mary had a Son who always handled things that looked
impossible and they seemed to work out well.

He did it without miracles, and incidentally often still does,

but of course we usually want Him to do it the miracle way.
He does not always need to do anything so dramatic. So that
was how He was. That's my idea of a Pentecostal, son, guest
or anything else.

Many a touch, unintentional or not, marks the Gospels with
the finger print of Christ. For example, in John (1:39) we are
told what time it was when Andrew and John first met Jesus –
the tenth hour (7 p.m.). They never forgot that. Meeting Christ
was unforgettable – once they had met Him. It always is of
course. Most of us can remember what time we received Him,
and the very day, and where. But then for us that would be
so, for we know Who He is. But for them He was unknown,
and yet that first contact made an unforgettable impact upon
them and every detail registered upon their minds, even the
time: 'Whom having seen they loved'.

Meeting US – what is it like? I remember sitting in the garden
of Gordon's Tomb of the Garden, Jerusalem, waiting – and, I
suppose the fact he had been there was the common thought
among us. Then a sense of utter relief wafted through and
melted many to tears. Meeting Him is an experience. Meeting
Pentecostals? Well?

The effect He had upon people without saying a word, was
astonishing. We all have experiences when we go into shops or
offices and stand there ignored, annoyed at the arrogance
behind the counter. I remember being in the railway station at
Zagreb in Yugoslavia. Two counter clerks were playing about,
throwing paper balls at one another. They didn't know I was
watching them. Then somebody walked in for attention, and
the two of them were instantly preoccupied and kept him waiting until they had time to bother with him. I think it could
have been like that when Jesus went to the receipt of customs,
and spoke to Levi. That inland revenue man would be quite
used to keeping people waiting. Maybe He did the same to
Christ. What happened?

Jesus stood waiting – if 'waiting' is a word you can ever use
about Somebody so alive. Levi knew, and enjoyed his little
authority. Then after scratching with his pen a while, without
looking up, Levi said, 'Yes?' Jesus did not answer. Levi asked
again, 'Yes? What is it?', and looked up with his usual official

and important glare. When he did, he looked straight into the eyes of Jesus, still silent. Levi looked, and those eyes became oceans – heaven entered his soul. Jesus simply said, 'Follow me!' From that moment Levi was captivated, and followed Him for ever.

There were plenty of others. The sinner woman to whom Jesus said nothing, who came in to the party, infamous, a man-eater. Amid the chatter, the busy servants, the eating, her eye alighted on this new figure, Jesus. Men were her meat. But not this One. She stared. And a vast longing for a new love as high as heaven engulfed her. She sank, brimming with silent tears, as close as she dared, but only to His feet. Her tears dripped between his toes She had no towel, but let down her luxurious hair to dry his feet. As she did, a wave of relief went through her soul – her touch on Him cleansed the past like a hurricane through a valley of murk. She felt clean, too clean ever to sully her soul again.

There were the Temple police – as tough and unsentimental a lot as was needed in those turbulent and murderous days. 'Arrest that man!' they were ordered. They came back without Him saying, 'Never man spake like this man.' The thief on the Cross, distracted with his own cruel pain, saw the battered and bleeding Jesus, never so stripped of dignity, never so unappealing in physical presence, suddenly blaze with glory in his mind's eye. Jesus drew, and created TRUST! 'Lord, remember me . . .'

A thousand times it happened. Then He was gone, and the Church took His place – the first Pentecostals. And *'they took note of them that they had been with Jesus'*. Somehow, despite its wretched failures, the Church still reflects Him. But oh, so dimly. Is that what Pentecost means – to relight the lamp in the eyes of the Church to resemble Him in Whose eyes were 'lamps of fire'?

In fact, is the true hallmark of Pentecost just there, in the eye, of me, of you, of us all? Beverley Nichols, that writer of irresistible charm, tells how he went to church and heard preachers talking about satisfaction in Christ, and the joy of serving Him. But he said it didn't show in the preachers' eyes. They had all the words, . . . but not the music.

So long as it is just the supernatural we want, or prosperity, or healings, or gifts, or wonders, or good preaching, or something to do, or a successful church, we are missing it all. HE is all, and brings all. 'Thou O Christ art all I want. More than all in Thee I find.' Somehow those Wesleys got it right every time. No wonder we go on singing their sentiments and our hearts ache with the glory of another world.

> O love of God, how sweet thou art!
> When shall I find my willing heart
> All taken up by thee?
> For love I sigh, for love I pine,
> This only portion Lord be mine,
> Be mine this better part.

'Love's Invisible Soul'

We have discovered in Christ, especially the Christ of Pentecost, a well of hope and a wealth of goodness. It is a practical down-to-earth Jesus we read about in the Gospels, and Whom we experience in our lives. I have stressed the power of the Gospel for this world.

But it needs a counterbalance. God has not sent Jesus into the world merely to raise our standard of living and effect a general share-out of money. Some charismatic-Pentecostal meetings seem entirely about problems in life, psychological hang-ups, complexes, fears and failures, met by techniques and counsel. It is not a good meeting unless there is a sensation, a gift, a wonder. But is that all there is? To hear the voice of God deep in one's soul and be elevated to a new plane of existence, that is the most urgent of all needs.

Jesus knew our needs. But He said *'Seek ye first the Kingdom of God and His righteousness and all these things shall be added unto you'*, i.e. clothing, food and drink. They were the incidentals. There is a Kingdom to find. It is not charisma but Pneuma, not things but the Eternal.

How simply Jesus takes hold of the mundane and makes us see the heavenly! He is the immanent Christ, present to give us bread, to give us healing, to come down to the littleness of life and share it with us, in a dirty first-century village. But He is at the same time the transcendent Christ, lifting us to glory.

'Tis mystery all, immense and free.' We take the cup, an inch of wine, look into it, and it shows forth His glory, depth upon depth, into God Himself. That crumb – a particle of bread such as one might toss to the birds, and it takes on a form that satisfies all souls for all eternities, 'This is my Body, broken for you'. A door opens in heaven.

Pentecost began when men spoke of glories beyond their knowledge in languages beyond their knowledge, *'the wonderful works of God'*. It began in transcendent fashion, angels coming to earth at the birth of Christ. 'All the light of sacred glory gathers round His head sublime.' *Transcendence is, must be, the Pentecostal hallmark*. Man cannot live on an earth which has no heaven – why bother? His life is otherwise an endless crawl through tunnels with only a memory of light.

In the last few years the Pentecostal-charismatic worship has recognised the need for something more lofty than prosperity theology. Its answer has lately been to balance the psycho-physical focus of power-preaching with songs about majesty, high-domed glory, beauty and infinity. But only sometimes does it succeed a little. The trouble is with the medium. We sing about the sublime in unsublime terms. The genre of today's coarsened culture, the new popular style with lyrics without beauty or poetry, consisting of a mere collection of words about majesty in some far off dimension, misses the splendour. It fails to catch the spirit of things Beyond, starts up no anticipation of heaven. It is like a railway poster of sunny Bournemouth in a dreary winter station.

The odd thing is that it is not singing about transcendent greatness which gives us transcendent exaltation of spirit. The illiterates of two hundred years ago had songs which made earth seem part of heaven, but they sang of Redeeming love.

> Here it is I find my heaven,
> While upon the Lamb I gaze.
> Love I much? I'm much forgiven
> I'm a miracle of grace.

There are theologies which I have spoken of in the preceding chapters which fall short of that. The Success-Prosperity teaching is a faith only equal to the promise of communistic-socialism's coming golden age, the same thing by different means. When we ARE prosperous and successful – what then? Is Prosperity theology essentially any different to the Latin church's Liberation Theology? At least one can understand the latter when priests meet mothers letting their babes suck blood at their breasts because, not having eaten for days, there is no milk for them.

Paul knew how to be hungry, but declared 'The Kingdom of God is not meat and drink but righteousness, peace and joy in the Holy Ghost'. A preacher – much publicised, sent me free a tape of one of his sermons. I don't know why, for I often hear far better sermons. But I took time off to listen to it all. Sermon? It sounded to me like a manipulation of his congregation.

He quoted Jesus to back up his ideas. 'I am come that ye might have life and have it more abundantly'. He commented that means more money, more good things, plenty of food, a good job, a good family. What an idea! Actually that text means nothing of the sort. There is more than one word for 'life' in Greek, and they have distinct uses in the New Testament. In this text it is *zoe*, not used for animal life, but always for God's life. Jesus promised something beyond bread. He declared 'A man's life consisteth not of the abundance of things which he possesses.' The bread that does not perish.

It is strange, but in the humblest mission hall, with the most familiar old hymns, heaven opens. In Christ immanence and transcendence coalesce, talk of Him as poorly as you will. All things cry glory. Augustine said it best, and describes the love of Jesus as '. . . *a brilliance that space cannot contain, a sound that time cannot carry away, a perfume that no breeze disperses, a taste undiminished by eating, a clinging together that no sateity will sunder.*'

It cannot be transferred into speech. It is music. A colleague listening to Mozart on his car stereo told me it echoed the inexpressible majesty of God, and he burst into praise singing in tongues to the cadences of the most exquisite music perhaps ever to be written. In moments like that what does prosperity matter?

But, Augustine, Mozart, or any other does not say it like the Word of God in Hebrews 12:18ff

> For ye are not come unto the mount that might be touched, and that burned with fire, and the voice of words; But ye are come unto mount Sion, and unto the city of the living God, the heavenly Jerusalem and to an innumerable company of angels, to the general assembly and church of the firstborn, which are written in heaven, and to God the Judge of all, and to the spirits of just men made perfect, and to Jesus the mediator of the new covenant, and to the blood of sprinkling that speaketh better things than the blood of Abel. Wherefore we receiving a kingdom which cannot be moved let us have grace. For our God is a consuming fire.

. . . the hallmark of Pentecost.

THE CROSS AND THE SWITCHBLADE

David Wilkerson

One of the best sellers of Christian paperbacks! An amazing
and breathtaking description of one man's adventure in faith
into New York gangland. If Christianity can work here it will
work anywhere.

No Christian should miss this modern Acts of the Apostles.
£1.95

JONI

Joni Eareckson Tada

In this international bestseller, Joni, the victim of an accident that left her totally paralysed from the neck down, reveals the struggle to accept and adjust to her handicap.

Joni's story has been made into a full length feature film. £1.95

THE TORN VEIL

Gulshan Esther, with Thelma Sangster

Gulshan Fatima, the youngest daughter of a Muslim Sayed family, lived a quietly secluded life at home in the Punjab. A trip to England began a spiritual awakening that led ultimately to her conversion to Christianity. She has since preached to thousands of Muslims and many not only have found faith but have, like her, found physical healing. £1.95